Mastering Rust

Mastering Rust helps the reader master the powerful Rust programming language for creating stable and versatile applications and projects.

Rust is a dependable and robust programming language that was created with today's needs in mind, which is something that several other scripting languages lack.

Rust was developed to provide high functions comparable to those of C and C++, and with a focus on code integrity, which is, arguably, lacking in languages such as C. Rust is a dynamically typed language that emphasizes performance and reliability, particularly in parallelism and storage organization. Rust allows you to store data on the tower or the shedload, and it recognizes the importance of performance optimization. It permits even more effective memory usage as well as faster memory management than most other programming languages in its league.

Make no mistake about it – Rust is a programming language with a strong learning curve, and is considered complicated by even the most experienced of developers. The rewards for learning Rust are aplenty, but the learning process itself requires a good deal of determination and hard work.

Nonetheless, Rust aims to provide a secure, concurrent, and practical systems language in ways that other programming languages do not, and this is primarily why Rust is often the preferred choice for building complex and highly stable apps. Rust boasts of advantages over many other programming languages in terms of expressiveness, speed, sound design, and memory storage. Though the language is new and constantly changing with time, there is an excellent opportunity in this field for future employment. That said, to learn the reliable language that is Rust, you need to have an equally reliable companion guide in your hands, and this is where *Mastering Rust* comes in.

With *Mastering Rust*, learning Rust programming language becomes a charm, and will undoubtedly help readers advance their careers.

The *Mastering Computer Science* series is edited by Sufyan bin Uzayr, a writer and educator with more than a decade of experience in the computing field.

Mastering Computer Science

Series Editor: Sufyan bin Uzayr

Mastering Rust: A Beginner's Guide
Divya Sachdeva, Faruq KC, and Aruqqa Khateib

Mastering Visual Studio Code: A Beginner's Guide
Jaskiran Kaur, D Nikitenko, and Mathew Rooney

Mastering Django: A Beginner's Guide
Jaskiran Kaur, NT Ozman, and Reza Nafim

Mastering Ubuntu: A Beginner's Guide
Jaskiran Kaur, Rubina Salafey, and Shahryar Raz

Mastering KDE: A Beginner's Guide
Jaskiran Kaur, Mathew Rooney, and Shahryar Raz

Mastering Kotlin: A Beginner's Guide
Divya Sachdeva, Faruq KC, and Aruqqa Khateib

For more information about this series, please visit: https://www.rout-ledge.com/Mastering-Computer-Science/book-series/MCS

The "Mastering Computer Science" series of books are authored by the Zeba Academy team members, led by Sufyan bin Uzayr.

Zeba Academy is an EdTech venture that develops courses and content for learners primarily in STEM fields, and offers education consulting to Universities and Institutions worldwide. For more info, please visit https://zeba.academy

Mastering Rust

A Beginner's Guide

Edited by Sufyan bin Uzayr

CRC Press

Taylor & Francis Group
Boca Raton London New York

CRC Press is an imprint of the
Taylor & Francis Group, an **Informa** business

First edition published 2023
by CRC Press
6000 Broken Sound Parkway NW, Suite 300, Boca Raton, FL 33487-2742

and by CRC Press
4 Park Square, Milton Park, Abingdon, Oxon, OX14 4RN

CRC Press is an imprint of Taylor & Francis Group, LLC

Library of Congress Cataloging–in–Publication Data

Names: Bin Uzayr, Sufyan, editor.
Title: Mastering Rust : a beginner's guide / edited by Sufyan bin Uzayr.
Description: First edition. | Boca Raton : CRC Press, 2022. | Includes
    bibliographical references and index.
Identifiers: LCCN 2022020964 (print) | LCCN 2022020965 (ebook) | ISBN
    9781032319049 (hbk) | ISBN 9781032319018 (pbk) | ISBN 9781003311966
    (ebk)
Subjects: LCSH: Rust (Computer program language) | Computer programming.
Classification: LCC QA76.73.R87 M355 2022 (print) | LCC QA76.73.R87
    (ebook) | DDC 005.13/3--dc23/eng/20220805
LC record available at https://lccn.loc.gov/2022020964
LC ebook record available at https://lccn.loc.gov/2022020965

ISBN: 9781032319049 (hbk)
ISBN: 9781032319018 (pbk)
ISBN: 9781003311966 (ebk)

DOI: 10.1201/9781003311966

Typeset in Minion
by Deanta Global Publishing Services, Chennai, India

Contents

Mastering Computer Science Series Preface

THE *MASTERING COMPUTER SCIENCE* covers a wide range of topics, spanning programming languages as well as modern-day technologies and frameworks. The series has a special focus on beginner-level content, and is presented in an easy-to-understand manner, comprising:

- Crystal-clear text, spanning various topics sorted by relevance

- A special focus on practical exercises, with numerous code samples and programs

- A guided approach to programming, with step-by-step tutorials for the absolute beginners

- Keen emphasis on real-world utility of skills, thereby cutting the redundant and seldom-used concepts and focusing instead on industry-prevalent coding paradigm

- A wide range of references and resources to help both beginner and intermediate-level developers gain the most out of the books

The *Mastering Computer Science* series of books starts from the core concepts, and then quickly moves on to industry-standard coding practices, to help learners gain efficient and crucial skills in as little time as possible. The books assume no prior knowledge of coding, so even absolute newbie coders can benefit from this series.

The *Mastering Computer Science* series is edited by Sufyan bin Uzayr, a writer and educator with more than a decade of experience in the computing field.

About the Editor

SUFYAN BIN UZAYR IS a writer, coder, and entrepreneur with more than a decade of experience in the industry. He has authored several books in the past, pertaining to a diverse range of topics, ranging from History to Computers/IT.

Sufyan is the Director of Parakozm, a multinational IT company specializing in EdTech solutions. He also runs Zeba Academy, an online learning and teaching vertical with a focus on STEM fields.

Sufyan specializes in a wide variety of technologies, such as JavaScript, Dart, WordPress, Drupal, Linux, and Python. He holds multiple degrees, including ones in Management, IT, Literature, and Political Science.

Sufyan is a digital nomad, dividing his time between four countries. He has lived and taught in universities and educational institutions around the globe. Sufyan takes a keen interest in technology, politics, literature, history, and sports, and in his spare time, he enjoys teaching coding and English to young students.

Learn more at sufyanism.com.

About the Editor

CHAPTER 1

Getting Started with Rust

IN THIS CHAPTER

➤ Getting started

➤ Installation

➤ Basic program

The Rust programming language is demonstrated for both beginners and experts. The Rust programming language is intended to improve memory safety; however, it is still developing.

WHAT EXACTLY IS RUST?

Rust is a system programming language created in 2006 by a Mozilla engineer named Graydon Hoare. He called it a "safe, concurrent, and practical language" that supports the functional and imperative paradigms.

Rust's syntax is comparable to that of the C++ programming language.

Rust is free and open-source software, which means that anybody may use it for free, and the source code is openly provided so that anyone can enhance the product's design.

In 2016, 2017, and 2018, the Stack Overflow Developer Survey named Rust as one of the "most liked programming languages."

There is no such thing as direct memory management, such as calloc or malloc. Rust manages memory internally.

DOI: 10.1201/9781003311966-1

1

Rust was developed to deliver excellent performance comparable to C and C++ while prioritizing code safety, which is the Achilles' heel of the other two languages. The Rust programming language is presently employed by well-known software giants such as Firefox, Dropbox, and Cloudflare. From startups to huge enterprises, many firms are adopting this technology in production.

Who Rust Is for

The Rust programming language is excellent for many people for various reasons.

Let's have a look:

- **Teams of developers:** Rust has shown to be quite effective for the "team of developers." Low-level programming code has defects that testers must thoroughly test. However, in the case of Rust, the compiler refuses to compile the code if it includes flaws. By working in parallel with the compiler, the developer may concentrate on the logic of the program rather than on the flaws.

- **Students:** Many people can learn to construct an operating system using Rust. The Rust team is working to make system principles more approachable to the general public, particularly those new to programming.

- **Companies:** Rust is used by both large and small businesses to complete various activities. Command-line tools, web services, DevOps tooling, embedded devices, audio and video analyses and transcoding, cryptocurrency, bioinformatics, search engines, Internet of Things applications, machine learning, and even large portions of the Firefox web browser are among these activities.

- **Developers of open-source software:** Rust is an open-source language; the source code is available to the public. As a result, they may utilize the source code to enhance Rust's design.

Rust's Increasing Popularity

Rust is the most popular programming language, according to the Stack Overflow Developer Survey 2020, which polled approximately 65,000 developers. It also won the championship for the sixth year in a row.

In addition, Linux kernel engineers recommended creating new Linux kernel code in Rust in 2020. To be clear, they did not wish to redo the entire kernel, which was built in C initially, but rather to add new code in Rust that would function with the current infrastructure. Linus Thorvalds, the founder of the open-source operating system Linux, supported the idea and is eager to see the project's achievements.

Facebook has further extended its ties with Rust by joining the Rust Foundation, a group created in 2021 to promote Rust development and make it "a mainstream language of choice for systems programming and beyond." Rust is used by Facebook, Amazon Web Services, Google, Huawei, Microsoft, and Mozilla.

What Makes the Rust Programming Language Unique?

Rust is a strongly typed programming language that prioritizes speed and safety and extraordinarily safe concurrency and memory management. Its syntax is comparable to C++. It is an open-source project that began at Mozilla Research. The Rust Foundation has taken up the torch and is leading the language's development in 2021.

Rust tackles two long-standing concerns for C/C++ developers: memory errors and concurrent programming. This is regarded as its primary advantage.

Of course, one might argue that contemporary C++ focuses more on memory safety (for example, by implementing smart pointers), but many issues remain unsolved.

One of these is a "use after free error," which occurs when a program continues to utilize a pointer after being freed, for example, by running the lambda function after releasing its reference-captured objects.

In Rust, on the other hand, the borrow checker, the compiler component that guarantees that references do not outlive the data they refer, is present. This feature aids in the elimination of memory violation bugs. Such issues are recognized during the compilation process; therefore, trash collection is not required.

Furthermore, in Rust, each reference has a lifespan, which specifies the scope for which that reference is valid. This innovation overcomes the problem of invalid references while also distinguishing Rust from C and C++.

When we consider that over the last 12 years memory safety concerns have accounted for over 70% of all security flaws in Microsoft products, the necessity of proper memory management becomes instantly clear. A similar figure has been reported for Google Chrome.

There are two ways to write code in Rust: Safe Rust and Unsafe Rust. Safe Rust imposes additional constraints on the programmer (for example, object ownership management), guaranteeing that the code functions properly. Unsafe Rust allows the programmer more freedom (for example, it may work on raw C-like pointers), but the code may fail.

The risky Rust mode gives you more possibilities, but we must exercise extreme caution to guarantee our code is secure. To do this, we can encase it in higher-level abstractions that ensure that all abstraction applications are safe. As with other programming languages, employing unsafe code should be treated with caution to prevent undefined behavior and reduce the danger of segfaults and vulnerabilities caused by memory insecurity.

One of the most significant advantages of Rust is its dual-mode concept. In C++, on the other hand, we never realize we've written dangerous code until our product collapses or a security breach occurs.

Concurrent Programming Has Been Simplified

Rust simplifies concurrent programming by preventing data conflicts at build time. When at least two independent instructions from different threads attempt to access the same memory location simultaneously, at least one of them attempts to write anything, and there is no synchronization to create any precise order among the various accesses, a data race occurs. Memory access without synchronization is undefined.

Data races are detected in Rust. Suppose given object access does not allow several threads (i.e., it is not designated with an appropriate trait). In that case, it must be synchronized by a mutex, which locks access to this specific object for other threads.

Only one thread gets access to an object to guarantee that its operations do not damage it.

Operations on this object are atomic from the perspective of other threads, which implies that an observed state of the object is always valid. We cannot witness any intermediate state arising from another thread's action on this object. The Rust programming language can detect and report improper actions on such objects at build time.

Other languages have synchronization techniques, but they are unrelated to the objects to which they refer. The developer's responsibility is to ensure that the object is locked before using it.

Some Challenges to Overcome while Programming in Rust

Of course, not everything is perfect. Because Rust is a new technology, specific desirable libraries may not yet be available. Nonetheless, the Rust package library crates.io has been rapidly expanding since 2016, and the strong community of Rust developers is a promising indication for future growth.

Also, for developers who aren't used to working with a language where problems in the code are identified at compile time, seeing a slew of error messages might be aggravating. As a result, creating code takes longer than in more popular languages such as Python. Rust's developers, on the other hand, are working hard to make these error messages as helpful and actionable as possible.

Even if seeing so many error warnings when coding might be annoying, keep your eye on the broader picture. Memory safety imposed at build time avoids defects and security vulnerabilities from occurring after our software has been released. Correcting problems will undoubtedly cost us both our nerves and our money during this stage.

Last but not least, creating Rust code takes extra work due to the relatively high entrance threshold. We must devote some time to learning the language. It is also necessary to have a solid understanding of C++ or another object-oriented programming language. The learning curve is far from flat.

But if we can overcome all of these challenges, the advantages of utilizing Rust will be the ultimate reward for our work.

What Is the Purpose of Rust?

Rust is an established technology that is already in use in the industry. It helps us control low-level details as a systems programming language. We can store data on the stack (used for static memory allocation) or on the heap (used for dynamic memory allocation). RAII (Resource Acquisition Is Initialization) is an essential programming idiom mostly associated with C++ but is also present in Rust: once an object exits scope, its destructor is called, and its owned resources are released. We don't have to perform it by hand, and we're safe against resource leakage problems.

As a result, memory may be used more efficiently. Tilde employed Rust in their Skylight product to rebuild several Java HTTP endpoints. They were able to cut their memory use from 5GiB to 50MiB due to this.

Because Rust does not have an active garbage collector, other programming languages may utilize its projects as libraries via foreign-function interfaces. This is a good case for existing projects where high performance while preserving memory safety is crucial. In such cases, Rust code may replace select areas of software where speed is critical without rebuilding the entire product.

Rust is a low-level programming language that provides direct access to hardware and memory, making it an excellent choice for embedded and bare-metal development. Rust may be used to create operating systems and microcontroller applications. In reality, several operating systems written in Rust exist, including Redox, intermezzOS, QuiltOS, Rux, and Tock. As I said earlier, there are plans to create additional Linux kernel enhancements in Rust. Mozilla uses it in their browser engines, where the language was created.

Rust's high performance and safety are the attributes that drew scientists to it and led to it being used for big data analysis. Rust is lightning fast, making it an excellent choice for computational biology and machine learning, where enormous volumes of data must process quickly.

At CodiLime, we're also testing whether Rust can replace C in network contexts requiring high data speed. In our proof-of-concept, we created an application in Rust that used DPDK libraries (written in C) to assure speed while simultaneously ensuring memory safety.

Why Should We Use Rust?

To summarize, the significant advantages of including Rust in our next software project are as follows:

- Memory safety is ensured while maintaining high performance.

- Concurrent programming is supported.

- The crates.io repository has an increasing number of Rust packages.

- A vibrant community is driving the language's evolution.

- Backward compatibility and stability are both guaranteed.

Features of Rust

Rust is a programming language for systems. Rust has the following capabilities:

- Zero cost abstraction

- Error messages

- Rust features

- Minimal time

- Threads without data races
- Pattern matching
- Move semantics
- Guaranteed memory safety
- Safe memory space allocation
- Efficient C bindings (Figure 1.1)

  1. **Zero cost abstraction:** We can introduce abstractions without compromising the code's runtime performance. It increases code quality and readability without sacrificing runtime efficiency.

  2. **Error messages:** Compared to GCC, C++ programming has significantly improved error messages. In terms of clarity, Rust goes one step farther. In our application, error messages are presented with formatting and colors and also propose misspellings.

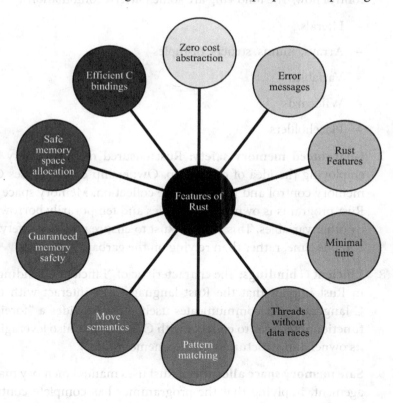

FIGURE 1.1   Features of Rust.

3. **Type inference:** Rust has a Type inference feature that automatically detects the type of an expression.

4. **Move semantics:** A copy action may be replaced with a move operation when a source object is a temporary object.

5. **Threads without the data races:** When two or more threads simultaneously access the same memory address, this is referred to as a data race. Because of the ownership mechanism, Rust supports threads without data races. Only the owners of separate objects are sent to various threads via the ownership mechanism, and two threads can never possess the same variable with write access.

6. **Pattern matching:** Rust has a pattern matching capability. Pattern matching in Rust uses patterns in conjunction with "match" expressions to provide additional control over the program's control flow. The following are some pattern combinations:

   - Literals

   - Arrays, enums, structs, or tuples

   - Variables

   - Wildcards

   - Placeholders

7. **Guaranteed memory safety:** Rust ensured memory safety by employing the idea of ownership. Ownership compromises C's memory control and Java's garbage collection. Memory space in Rust programs is owned by variables and temporarily borrowed by other variables. This enables Rust to ensure memory safety at compile time, rather than relying on the garbage collector.

8. **Efficient C bindings:** The characteristic of "Efficient C bindings" in Rust implies that the Rust language may interact with the C language as it communicates itself. Rust provides a "foreign function interface" to connect with C APIs while also leveraging its ownership structure to ensure memory safety.

9. **Safe memory space allocation:** Rust uses manual memory management, implying that the programmer has complete control over where and when memory is created and deallocated. In C,

we use the malloc function to allocate memory and subsequently initialize it, whereas Rust rejects these two actions with a single '~' operator. This operation converts the smart pointer into an int. A smart pointer is a type of value that regulates when an item is released. Smart pointers are called "smart" because they not only monitor the location of an object but also know how to clear it up.

INSTALLING RUST

The first step is to install Rust. To begin, download Rust using rustup, a command-line application for managing all Rust versions and associated tools.

Rust in Windows Installation

- On Windows, navigate to https://www.rust-lang.org/install.html and follow the installation instructions. After completing all of the instructions, Rust will install, and the screen will appear.

- Rust's PATH variable is automatically added to your system PATH after installation.

- The command prompt is opened, and the following command is executed:

$ rustc --version

- After running this command, we should see the version number, commit hash, and commit date.

- If we do, it signifies Rust was successfully installed. Congratulations.

Installing Rust on Linux or macOS

- If we are using Linux or macOS, open a terminal and enter the following command:

  $ curl https://sh.rustup.rs -sSf|sh

- The program above downloads a script and begins the installation of the rustup utility. This will install the recent version of Rust. If the installation is successful, the following message will be displayed:

  Rust is now installed.

- After your next login, this installation will automatically add Rust to your system path. If you wish to execute Rust without restarting the terminal, run the following command in your shell to add the path to our system PATH manually:

  $ source $HOME/.cargo/env

A linker is required after installation. When you attempt to start our Rust program, we will receive an error stating that a linker could not be executed. It indicates that the linker is not present in our system. C compilers always produce the right compiler. Set up a C compiler. Furthermore, some Rust packages rely on C code and require a C compiler.

Updating and Uninstalling Rust

Update: After installing Rust with "rustup," update to the newest version. To upgrade to the most recent version, use the following command:

```
$ rustup update
```

Remove: To uninstall Rust, use the following command from the shell:

```
$ rustup self uninstall
```

RUST FIRST PROGRAM

Let's write a basic program in the Rust programming language. Open the notepad file and type the following code:

```
fn main()
    println!("Hello, World");
```

- **main():** It is always the first line of code in any Rust executable. Curly brackets {} surround the main() function. The main() method doesn't take any arguments and does not return any value.

- **println!:** It's a macro in Rust. It does not contain "!" if it calls the method.

- **"Hello, World":** It is a string passed as an argument to println! and is printed to the console.

Procedure for Creating, Compiling, and Running the Program

1. Open the notepad file and write the code in it.

2. Save the file with the extension.rs.

3. Launch the command prompt.

4. Enter the directory's path. Assume the project is on the D drive.

5. Run the rustc command to compile the preceding program.

6. Finally, execute the application using the command filename.exe.

REASONS WHY RUST IS THE WAY OF THE FUTURE

Rust was named the most popular programming language in the Stack Overflow 2020 survey, with 86% of engineers saying they will continue to use it. For language designers, this is nothing new: Rust has won the study every year since 2016. On Tiobe Index, Rust is also gaining popularity, ranking #18 among the most popular languages in September. It also scored well in our sentiment-based ranking of functional programming languages, taking first place in the most favorable sentiment class.

Rust, which was created in 2006 as an alternative to C++ by former Mozilla engineer Graydon Hoare, is steadily creating a name in the developer community. It is presently used to construct online applications, embedded computers, distributed services, and command-line interfaces. A good example of this popularity is Microsoft's gradual shift away from C++ (due to a growing number of security problems) and toward Rust.

Why is Rust so popular among programmers when there are so many different languages to choose from? One of the key reasons is that Rust addressed several obvious difficulties in other languages to the point where some developers claim that the architects of Rust must have known all of the possible problems visible in C++ in mind.

Rust vs. Other Languages

Rust offers benefits over several other languages that are currently popular among developers. Let us go through a few of them.

Advantages of Rust vs. C++

When compared to C++, Rust is safer. Rust protects both its abstractions and the abstractions created by developers, whereas C++ does not. Specific errors in C++ might result in arbitrary behavior, but Rust assists you in focusing on what is truly essential. And, while C/C++ remains one of the most popular programming languages, it frequently causes issues. Rust is just easier to learn; the learning curve is not as steep, there is no technical debt in Rust as there is in C++, it supports more concurrency, and its speed is comparable. Rust allows us to write unsafe code, but it always defaults to safe code.

Advantages of Rust vs. Java

When it comes to Java, it turns out that it is significantly slower than Rust, especially when compared to C in several sectors. On top of that, we should consider speedier startup times and a reduced memory footprint. Java employs Garbage Collection for memory management, which reduces speed (but it is worth noting that it simplifies code).

Advantages of Rust vs. Python

Rust is well-thought-out. Rust allows us to wrap statements in lambda, and everything is an expression, making it easy to compose specific portions of the language. Python does not do this. Rust lacks classes; therefore, object orientation is not as developed as in Python. Python also encounters the need to write additional tests and production outages or runtime problems. Rust reduces the cost of identifying and fixing potential issues.

Advantages of Rust vs. Go

Go's expressiveness is lacking. Rust is a versatile and expressive architecture that enables the creation of new container types capable of holding various components, generics, traits, and algebraic data types. We have less control over both resources and memory while using Go.

What Makes Rust the Future?

Rust Increased the Safety of Memory

Memory management difficulties are one of the most serious problems that developers face. In other languages, it is quite simple to overlook a coding issue, resulting in the dreaded error code and the effort required to discover and solve it. A far more significant problem arises when a code error leads to security breaches in today's environment, this is too risky. Data security breaches in major and popular websites or applications occur far more frequently than we want. What's the reason? Application flaws or misconfigurations are often to blame.

Rust is thought to be memory-safe. Rust programming is not permitted by dragging pointers, buffer overflows, and other memory-related mistakes. It allows you to describe how memory should handle and how values should be put out in it while also taking care of the control and safety lines without sacrificing performance, making it a valuable asset to Rust.

Improving memory safety was one of the key aims of Rust's creators and one of the language's main selling factors. Their code compiler is quite stringent, and each variable or memory location that is utilized is examined automatically.

Suppose any syntax problems, null values, dangling modifiers, or memory safety concerns are detected. In that case, Rust will not compile the code and warn about unsafe code, allowing for speedy identification and correction of the underlying issue. How does it accomplish this?

Every value in Rust has an "ownership." When a value is passed or returned, ownership is transferred to a new scope one at a time. If the "owner" of the value moves out of the scope, the value is discarded. Rust maintains track of memory and automatically frees it in this manner, preventing all flaws from entering the main code. That implies there will be no surprises during runtime.

This system will examine memory management at build time, making it easier to find and repair issues and eliminating the need for trash collection.

However, there is more to memory than that. Building sophisticated systems is frequently associated with significantly computation-bound activity and generating *a lot* of temporary memory. Such an offload can significantly impact the performance of any Java Virtual Machine, and many programming languages, including Scala, are incapable of dealing with it.

However, Rust can. It allows for the creation of memory-efficient code without the need for memory management or the use of modern conveniences such as closures, and it runs with little to no runtime overhead, making it suitable for real-time or embedded projects and easily integrating with other languages or projects.

Rust's Community Is Expanding

Of course, the Rust community and quantity of libraries are nowhere near as large as, say, C++. However, as the Rust programming language grows in popularity, so does the number of developers and enthusiasts who join. The number of community-created frameworks, libraries, and development tools (known as "crates") is now close to 57,000, and more are being uploaded daily.

Rust has an active and inviting community in addition to a growing collection of tools and frameworks. There are various places to go if we need assistance with a problem or to learn more about using Rust. In addition to the community chat and user forum, Rust features an active subreddit section.

Rust Is Quick and Adaptable

Rust is regarded as a moderately fast language. It can run far quicker than Scala when employing generic code, especially in performance-critical jobs. There is a good chance that it will be three times quicker than Scala or Java in some places. It is simple to pick up and utilize other packages, and Rust's cargo build tool simplifies code.

Rust is Extremely Fast Due to a Few Factors

- Because it is statically typed and compiled, the compiler may optimize the code for speed.

- It provides static trait dispatch, similar to C++ templates but cleaner.

- It explicitly monitors variable ownership. Rust does not presume that every variable with an address can change at any moment, allowing for optimizations without negatively impacting the code.

- It assumes that variables are immutable by default (so optimization is easier).

- It provides algebraic data types, which are also useful for optimization.

- It does not have any overheads, no runtime, and no unexpected delays owing to a lack of trash collection.

- It provides no-cost abstraction.

Rust may alternatively be thought of as a programming language comparable to C++, but it is easier to optimize and has fewer unpleasant advanced programming capabilities.

Rust Has a Wide Range of Applications

If a project requires a secure and reliable execution environment, away from the necessity of performance and low-level optimizations (but high-level Rust functional programming approaches), Rust should pass the test.

Rust is recognized as a low-level language that is best suited for best systems, embedded programming, and other performance-critical applications. It also used in 3D video games.

Rust Is Used by Several Large Companies

Despite being a relatively new language, developers have already recognized Rust as a step in the right direction to boost programming security and convenience of use. However, not only coders are interested in Rust; corporations, particularly large ones, have already migrated or intend to switch to Rust. Ryan Levick (Microsoft cloud developer evangelist) stated at the AllThingsOpen virtual conference in May 2020 that Rust as a language is "the industry's greatest hope for addressing multiple issues head-on." While Microsoft does not intend to abandon C++ anytime soon, many of its infrastructures gradually transition to Rust.

And Microsoft isn't the only firm that has seen the potential benefits of moving to the Rust programming language; Dropbox, Sentry, Amazon, and Mozilla are among the organizations that employ the Rust programming language.

In this chapter, we covered the concept of Rust, as well as its history, characteristics, purpose, and applications. Furthermore, we learned about Rust installation, the first Rust program, and the reasons why Rust is the way of the future.

CHAPTER 2

Common Programming Concepts

IN THIS CHAPTER

➤ Variables and mutability

➤ Data types

➤ Functions

➤ Tuples

➤ Array

➤ Comments

➤ Control flow

The previous chapter covered Rust's definition, and its history, benefits, and uses. We also learned about Rust's installation and basic programs.

This chapter discusses concepts in practically every programming language and how Rust operates. At their heart, many programming languages have a lot in common. None of the concepts described in this chapter are unique to Rust, but we'll explore them in the context of Rust and explain how to use them.

DOI: 10.1201/9781003311966-2

Variables, fundamental types, functions, comments, and control flow will be covered in detail. These fundamentals will be covered in any Rust program, and knowing them early will provide us with a solid platform to build on.

VARIABLES IN RUST

A variable is a sort of named storage that programs may access. Simply put, a variable is a type of data structure that allows programs to store values. In Rust, variables are linked with a specific data type. The data type dictates the variable's memory size and layout, the range of values stored inside that memory, and the set of operations on the variable.

Variable Naming Rules

This section will go through the various rules for naming variables:

- A variable's name can be letters, numbers, and the underscore character.

- It starts with a letter or an underscore.

- Because Rust is case-sensitive, upper- and lowercase letters are separate.

Syntax

When declaring a variable in Rust, the data type is optional. The value assigned to the variable determines the data type.

The syntax for defining variables is as follows:

let variable_name = value; // no type-specified

let variable_name:dataType = value; //type-specified

Example:

```
fn main() {
    let fees = 35_000;
    let salary:f64 = 45_000.00;
    println!("fees {} and salary is {}",fees,salary);
}
```

IMMUTABLE

By default, variables are immutable in Rust. In other words, the value of the variable cannot change once a value is bound to a variable name.

Let us understand this with an example:

```
fn main() {
    let fees=25_000;
    println!("fees is {} ",fees);
    fees=35_000;
    println!("fees changed is {}",fees);
}
```

The source of the mistake is indicated in this error message; we cannot set values to the immutable variable fees twice. This is just one of the numerous ways Rust allows programmers to write code while benefiting from the safety and ease of concurrency.

MUTABLE

By default, variables are immutable. To make a variable changeable, prefix it with the term mutable. A mutable variable's value can alter.

The syntax for defining a mutable variable is seen below:

let mut variable_name = value;

let mut variable_name:dataType = value;

Example:

```
fn main() {
    let mut fees:i32=35_000;
    println!("fees is {} ",fees);
    fees=45_000;
    println!("fees changed {}",fees);
}
```

Variables and Constants: What Are the Differences?

The inability to modify the value of a variable reminds us of another programming notion seen in most other languages: constants. Like immutable variables, constants are values attached to a name and cannot be changed, but there are a few distinctions between constants and variables.

To begin with, we are not permitted to use mut with constants. Constants are not just immutable by default; they are also immutable at all times.

Constants are declared with the const keyword rather than the let keyword, and the value type must annotate. Don't worry about the technicalities for now; we'll go into types and type annotations in the "Data Types in Rust" section. Just remember always to annotate the type.

Constants can declare in any scope, including the global scope, making them helpful for variables that need to be known by several code areas.

The last distinction is that constants may only be set to a constant expression, not to the result of a value that can only be computed at runtime.

Here's an example of a constant declaration with the name THREE_HOURS_IN_SECONDS and the value set to the result of multiplying 60 (number of seconds in a minute) times 60 (number of minutes in an hour) by 3 (number of hours we want to count in this program):

```
const THREE_HOURS_IN_SECONDS: u32 = 60 * 60 * 3;
```

Rust's constant name convention is all capital with underscores between words. Because the compiler can only evaluate a restricted number of operations at build time, we can opt to write out this value in a more understandable and verifiable manner rather than assigning this constant to the value 10,800. More information on what operations can be performed when declaring constants can be found in the "Bibliography" section on constant evaluation.

Constants are valid for the duration of a program's execution within the scope in which they were declared. Constants are important for numbers in your application domain that numerous portions of the program may need to know about, such as the maximal amount of points every game participant is permitted to gain or the speed of light.

Naming hardcoded values used throughout your software as constants helps future code maintainers understand what those values represent. It's also useful to have only one location in our code that needs to be changed if the hardcoded value needs to be modified in the future.

DATA TYPES IN RUST

The Type System represents the language's many different types of values. The Type System checks the provided values before the software stores or manipulates them. This ensures that the code functions correctly. Greater code hinting and automatic documentation are also possible with the Type System.

Rust is a statically typed programming language. In Rust, each value has its own data type. Based on the value provided to the variable, the compiler may automatically determine its data type.

Variable Declaration

To declare a variable, use the let keyword.

```
fn main() {
    let company_string = "RustPoint";   // string type
    let rating_float = 3.5;              // float type
    let is_growing_boolean = true;       // boolean type
    let icon_char = '♥';                //unicode character type
    println!("company name:{}",company_string);
    println!("company rating on 5:{}",rating_float);
    println!("company is growing :{}",
             is_growing_boolean);
    println!("company icon:{}",icon_char);
}
```

The data type of the variables in the preceding example will deduce from the values assigned to them. Rust, for instance, will assign the string data type to the variable company string, the float data type to rating float, and so on.

The println! macro accepts two parameters:

1. A unique syntax {}, which acts as a placeholder

2. The name of a variable or a constant

The variable's value will be used to replace the placeholder.

Scalar Types

A scalar type is a value that has just one value. For instance, 10,3.14,'c'. Rust has four distinct scalar types.

1. Integer

2. Floating point

3. Booleans

4. Characters

Integer

A number with no fractional component is called an integer. To put it simply, the integer data type is used to represent entire integers.

Integers are further subdivided into signed and unsigned. Negative and positive values can store in signed integers. Positive values can only store in unsigned integers. Below is a complete discussion of integer types.

Sr. No.	Size	Signed	Unsigned
1	8 bit	i8	u8
2	16 bit	i16	u16
3	32 bit	i32	u32
4	64 bit	i64	u64
5	128 bit	i128	u128
6	Arch	isize	usize

An integer's size can be arch. This indicates that the machine's architecture will determine the size of the data type. An integer of size arch is 32 bits on an x86 machine and 64 bits on an x64 system. An arch integer is often used to index some type of collection.

Illustration

```
fn main() {
    let result = 20;        // i32 by default
    let age:u32 = 30;
    let sum:i32 = 5 - 25;
    let mark:isize = 20;
    let count:usize = 40;
    println!("result value is {}", result);
    println!("sum {} and age {}", sum, age);
    println!("mark {} and count {}", mark, count);
}
```

Integer Range

Each signed variation may hold integers ranging from $-(2^{(n-1)})$ to $2^{(n-1)}$ -1, where n is the amount of bits used. For example, i8 may hold values ranging from $-(2^7)$ to 2^7 -1; in this case, we replaced n with 8.

Each unsigned variation may hold numbers ranging from 0 to(2^n)-1. For example, u8 can hold integers ranging from 0 to (2^8)-1, or 0 to 255.

Integer Overflow

An integer overflow happens when the value assigned to an integer variable exceeds the data type's Rust-specified range. Let me illustrate this with an example:

```
fn main() {
    let age:u8 = 255;
    // 0 to 255 only allowed for u8
    let weight:u8 = 256;        //the overflow value is 0
    let height:u8 = 257;        //the overflow value is 1
    let score:u8 = 258;         //the overflow value is 2
    println!("age {} ",age);
    println!("weight {}",weight);
    println!("height {}",height);
    println!("score {}",score);
}
```

The unsigned u8 variable has a permitted range of 0–255. The variables in the above example have values larger than 255 (upper limit for an integer variable in the Rust). When the preceding code is executed, it will produce a warning literal out of range for u8 for the weight, height, and score variables. After 255, the overflow values will begin with 0, 1, 2, and so on.

Float

In Rust, float data types are categorized as f32 and f64. The f32 type is a single-precision float, whereas the f64 type is a double-precision float. The type that is used by default is f64. Consider the following example to have a better understanding of the float data type:

```
fn main() {
    let result = 20.00;
    let interest:f32 = 8.35;
    let cost:f64 = 16000.600;    //the double precision
    println!("result value {}",result);
    println!("interest {}",interest);
    println!("cost {}",cost);
}
```

Automatic-type Casting

In Rust, automatic-type casting is not permitted. Take a look at the following code. The float variable interest is given an integer value.

```
fn main() {
    let interest:f32 = 9;
                        // integer assigned to float variable
    println!("interest {}",interest);
}
```

Number Separator

To make huge numbers easier to read, we may add a visual separator underscore to separate digits. This is 60,000, which can be written as 60_000. This is demonstrated in the following example:

```
fn main() {
    let float_with_separator = 11_000.545_001;
    println!("float value {}",float_with_separator);
    let int_with_separator = 60_000;
    println!("int value {}",int_with_separator);
}
```

Boolean

The true or false are the only two possible values for Boolean types. To declare a Boolean variable, use the bool keyword.

Example:

```
fn main() {
    let isfun:bool = true;
    println!("Rust Programming Fun ? {}",isfun);
}
```

Character

Rust's character data type accepts integers, alphabets, Unicode, and special characters. To declare a variable of the character data type, use the char keyword. The char type in Rust represents a Unicode Scalar Value, which implies it may represent much more than simply ASCII. The Unicode Scalar Values span from U+0000 to U+D7FF and from U+E000 to U+10FFFF.

Let's look at an example to learn more about the Character data type:

```
fn main() {
    let special_character = '@'; //default
    let alphabet:char = 'D';
    let emoji:char = '😃';
    println!("special character {}",special_character);
    println!("alphabet {}",alphabet);
    println!("emoji {}",emoji);
}
```

Compound Types
Compound types can combine multiple values into a single type. Tuples and arrays are the two primitive compound types in Rust.

Tuple Type
A tuple is a generic means of combining several items of various kinds into one compound type. Tuples have a set length: they cannot be increased or decreased in size once stated.

A tuple is formed by putting a comma-separated list of values within parentheses. Each place in the tuple has a type, and the types of the tuple's distinct values do not have to be the same. In this example, we've included optional-type annotations:

Filename: src/themain.rs

```
fn main() {
    let tup: (i32, f64, u8) = (600, 7.4, 2);
}
```

Because a tuple is considered as a single compound element, the variable tup binds to the entire tuple. To extract individual values from a tuple, we may use pattern matching to destructure a tuple value, as seen below:

Filename: src/themain.rs

```
fn main() {
    let tup = (600, 7.4, 2);
    let (a, b, c) = tup;

    println!("The value of b is: {}", b);
}
```

This program begins by creating a tuple and assigning it to the variable tup. It then employs a pattern to divide tup into three distinct variables: a, b, and c. This is referred to as destructuring since it divides one tuple into three pieces. Finally, the program outputs b's value, which is 7.4.

In addition to pattern matching, we can use a period (.) followed by the index of the value we want to retrieve to directly access a tuple element. Consider the following scenario:

Filename: src/themain.rs

```
fn main() {
    let x: (i32, f64, u8) = (600, 7.4, 1);
    let six_hundred = x.0;
    let seven_point_four = x.1;
    let one = x.2;
}
```

This program generates a tuple, x, and then creates new variables for each element based on their indices. The initial index of a tuple is 0, as it is in most computer languages.

The tuple with no values, (), is a peculiar type with just one value, which is alternatively represented as (). The type is known as the unit type, while the value is known as the unit value. If an expression does not return any other value, it returns the unit value implicitly.

Array Type

An array is another approach to creating a collection of multiple values. An array, unlike a tuple, must have the same type for all of its elements. Arrays in Rust differ from arrays in other languages in that they have a fixed length, similar to tuples.

In Rust, array values are represented as a comma-separated list within square brackets:

Filename: src/main.rs

```
fn main() {
    let a = [11, 22, 33, 44, 55];
}
```

Arrays are handy when we want our data to be allocated on the stack rather than the heap or to ensure that we always have a set number of elements. However, an array is not as adaptable as a vector. A vector is a similar collection type given by the standard library that may be expanded or contracted in size. If we're not sure whether to use an array or a vector, go with the vector.

We might want to use an array rather than a vector in a program that needs to know the names of the months of the year. Because such a program is unlikely to need to add or subtract months, we may use an array because we know it will always have 12 elements:

    let month = ["Jan", "Feb", "Mar", "April", "May", "June", "July",

        "Aug", "Sep", "Oct", "Nov", "Dec"];

We would write the type of an array in square brackets, followed by the type of each element, a semicolon, and then the number of items in the array, as follows:

    let a: [i32; 5] = [11, 22, 33, 44, 55];

Each element is of type i32 in this case. The number 5 after the semicolon indicates that the array has five elements.

This syntax for writing an array's type seems similar to the syntax for initializing an array: if we want to construct an array with the same value for each member, we specify the initial value, followed by a semicolon, and then the length of the array in square brackets, as demonstrated here:

    let a = [33; 55];

The array named a will contains five elements that will initially be set to the value 33. This is same as writing let a = [33, 33, 33, 33, 33], but more concisely.

Accessing the Array Elements

An array is a single fixed-size block of memory that may be allocated on the stack. Indexing may be used to access items in an array, as seen below:

Filename: src/themain.rs

```
fn main() {
    let x = [11, 22, 33, 44, 55];
```

```
    let first = x[0];
    let second = x[1];
}
```

Because the value at position [0] in the array is 1, the first variable will receive 1. The variable second will receive the value 2 from the array's index [1].

Invalid Array Element Access

What happens if try to access an array element that is past the array's end? Consider the following example:

Filename: src/themain.rs

```
use std::io;
fn main() {
    let x = [11, 22, 33, 44, 55];
    println!("Enter array index.");
    let mut index = String::new();
    io::stdin()
        .read_line(&mut index)
        .expect("Failed to read the line");
    let index: usize = index
        .trim()
        .parse()
        .expect("Index entered was not number");
    let element = x[index];
    println!(
        "Value of the element at index {} is: {}",
        index, element
    );
}
```

This code has been successfully compiled. If we run this code with cargo run and input 0, 1, 2, 3, or 4, the program will output the value at that index in the array. If we instead input a number past the end of the array, such as 15, we will get an error.

The program generated a runtime error when it used an incorrect value in the indexing procedure. The program terminated with an error message, however the last println! instruction was not executed. Rust checks to see if the index we've specified is less than the array length when using indexing to access an element. Rust will panic if the index is larger than or equal to the length. This check must occur at runtime, especially in this scenario, because the compiler does not know what value a user would provide when they execute the code.

This is one of Rust's memory safety ideas in action. This type of check is not performed in many low-level languages, and if an erroneous index is provided, invalid memory can access. Rust protects us from this type of mistake by leaving immediately rather than allowing the memory access and continuing.

CONSTANT IN RUST

Constants are values that cannot alter. When we declare a constant, its value cannot change. The term const denotes constants. Constants must be typed explicitly. The syntax for declaring a constant is as follows:

    const VARIABLE_NAME:dataType = value;

Constant Naming Convention in Rust

The naming convention for constants is identical to that of variables. In a continuous name, all characters usually are in the capital. When declaring a constant, the let keyword is not utilized, as it is when declaring variables.

In the following example, we utilized constants in Rust:

```
fn main() {
    const USER_LIMIT:i32=110; // Declare integer constant
    const PI:f32=3.14;        //Declare float constant
    println!("user limit {}",USER_LIMIT);
                              //Display value of constant
    println!("pi value {}",PI);
                              //Display value of constant
}
```

Constants vs. Variables

This section will look at the differences between constants and variables.

- The const keyword is used to declare constants, while the let keyword is used to declare variables.

- A variable declaration may or may not include a data type, but a constant declaration must have a data type. As a result, using const USER LIMIT=110 will result in an error.

- A variable declared with let keyword is immutable by default. You may, however, change it by using the mut keyword. Constants are unchangeable.

- Constants may only set to a constant expression, not the result of a function call or any other value computed at runtime.

- Constants can declare in any scope, including the global scope, making them handy for variables that need to be known by several portions of the code.

Variable and Constant Shadowing

In Rust, programmers can specify variables with the same name. In this scenario, the new variable takes precedence over the prior variable.

```
fn main() {
    let salary=110.00;
    let salary=2.50;
    // reads the first salary
    println!("Value of salary :{}",salary);
}
```

The code above declares two variables called salary. The first declaration is given a value of 110.00, whereas the second declaration is given a value of 2.50. While displaying output, the second variable shadows or hides the first variable.

While shadowing, Rust supports variables of various data types.

Consider the following scenario:

The code uses the term uname to declare two variables. The first declaration is given a string value, whereas the second is given an integer value. The len function determines how many characters are in a string value.

```
fn main() {
    let uname = "Mohtash";
    let uname =uname.len();
```

```
    println!("name changed to the integer : {}",uname);
}
```

Constants, unlike variables, cannot be shadowed. Compiler will produce an error if the variables in the above program are replaced with constants.

```
fn main() {
    const NAME:&str = "Mohtash";
    const NAME:usize = NAME.len();
    //Error: `NAME` already defined
    println!("name changed to the integer : {}",NAME);
}
```

STRING IN RUST

In Rust, the string data type is divided into the following categories:

- String Literal(&str)

- String Object(String)

String Literal

When value of a string is known at build time, string literals (&str) are utilized. String literals are a collection of characters that have been hard-coded into a variable. Assume company="Rust Point" is an example. String literals can be find in the std::str package. String literals are also referred to as string slices.

The string literals firm and location are declared in the following example:

```
fn main() {
    let company:&str="RustPoint";
    let location:&str = "Ludhiana";
    println!("company : {} location :{}",
            company,location);
}
```

String literals are by default static. This ensures that string literals are guaranteed to be valid throughout the program. We may also specify the variable directly as static, as seen below:

```
fn main() {
    let company:&'static str="RustPoint";
    let location:&'static str="Ludhiana";
    println!("company : {} location :{}",
            company,location);
}
```

String Object

The String object type is available in the Standard Library. Unlike the string literal, the String object type is not part of the core language. The standard library pub struct String defines it as a public structure. The string is a collection that can expand. It is a mutable type with UTF-8 encoding. The String object type can use to represent string values that are sent to the program at runtime. The heap is used to allocate a String object.

Syntax

We may use any of the following syntax to build a String object:

String::new()

The preceding syntax generates an empty string.

String::from()

This generates a string containing a default value passed as a parameter to the from() function.

The example shows how to utilize a String object.

```
fn main(){
    let empty_string=String::new();
    println!("length {}",empty_string.len());
    let content_string=String::from("RustPoint");
    println!("length {}",content_string.len());
}
```

The above example uses the new method to generate an empty String object and the from method to build a String object from a string literal.

String Object – Common Methods

Sr. No.	Method	Signature	Description
1	new()	pub const fn new() → String	This function generates a new empty string
2	to_string()	fn to_string(&self) → String	The provided value is converted to string
3	replace()	pub fn replace<'a, P>(&'a self, from: P, to: &str) → String	All pattern matches are replaced with another string
4	as_str()	pub fn as_str(&self) → &str	The entire string is extracted as a string slice
5	push()	pub fn push(&mut self, ch: char)	This string is added with the provided character
6	push_str()	pub fn push_str(&mut self, string:&str)	This method appends a specified string slice to the end of this string
7	len()	pub fn len(&self) → usize	This function returns the length of this string in bytes
8	trim()	pub fn trim(&self) → &str	Removes preceding and trailing whitespace from a string slice
9	split_whitespace()	pub fn split_whitespace(&self) → SplitWhitespace	Returns an iterator after splitting a string slice by whitespace
10	split()	pub fn split<'a, C>(&'a self, pat: C) → Split<'a, C>, where C is pattern can be &str, char, or closure that determines the split	Iterates through substrings of this string slice that are split by characters matched by a pattern
11	chars()	pub fn chars(&self) → Chars	Iterates through the characters of a string slice

Illustration: new()

The new() function constructs an empty String object with the value hello.

Example:

```
fn main() {
    let mut a = String::new();
    a.push_str("helloo");
    println!("{}", a);
}
```

Illustration: to_string()
To access all String object methods, use the to_string() function to convert a string literal to object type.

Example:

```
fn main(){
    let names = "Hello RustPoint,
    Hello!".to_string();
    println!("{}",names);
}
```

Illustration: replace()
The replace() method accepts two parameters: the first is a string pattern to search for, and the second is the new value to be replaced. Hello appears twice in the names1 string in the preceding example.

The replace function replaces all the instances of the string Hello with the string Rowdy.

Example:

```
fn main(){
    let names1 = "Hello RustPoint,
    Hello!".to_string();   //the String object
    let names2 = names1.replace("Hello","Rowdy");
                                   //find and replace
    println!("{}",names2);
}
```

Illustration: as_str()
The str() method returns a string slice that includes the entire string.

Example:

```
fn main() {
    let example_string1 = String::from("example_string");
    print_literal(example_string1.as_str());
}
fn print_literal(data:&str){
    println!("displaying the string literal {}",data);
}
```

Illustration: push()

The push() method adds the specified character to the end of this string.

Example:

```
fn main(){
    let mut company1="Rust".to_string();
    company1.push('s');
    println!("{}",company1);
}
```

Illustration: push_str()

Push str() appends a specified string slice to the end of a string.

Example:

```
fn main(){
    let mut company1="Rust".to_string();
    company1.push_str(" Point");
    println!("{}",company1);
}
```

Illustration: len()

The total number of characters in a string is returned by the len() function (including spaces).

Example:

```
fn main() {
    let fullnames=" Rust Point";
    println!("length {}",fullnames.len());
}
```

Illustration: trim()

The trim() eliminates leading and trailing spaces from a string. Please keep in mind that this function will not remove inline spaces.

Example:

```
fn main() {
    let fullname=" Rust Point \r\n";
    println!("Before-trim ");
```

```
    println!("length {}",fullname.len());
    println!();
    println!("After-trim ");
    println!("length {}",fullname.trim().len());
}
```

Illustration: split_whitespace()

The split whitespace() function divides the input string into several strings. As seen below, it returns an iterator, so we loop through the tokens.

Example:

```
fn main(){
    let msg="Rust Point has good tutorials".to_string();
    let mut x=1;
    for token in msg.split_whitespace(){
        println!("token {} {}",x,token);
        x+=1;
    }
}
```

Illustration: split() string

The split() returns an iterator that iterates across substrings of a string slice divided by characters that match a pattern. The split() function has the constraint that the result cannot be stored for later use. The collect method may save the split() result as a vector.

Example:

```
fn main() {
    let fullname="Canan,Rudhasharan,Rustpoint";
    for token in fullname.split(","){
        println!("token is {}",token);
    }
    //the store in a Vector
    println!("\n");
    let tokens:Vec<&str>=fullname.split(",").collect();
    println!("firstName {}",tokens[0]);
    println!("lastname {}",tokens[1]);
    println!("company {}",tokens[2]);
}
```

Illustration: chars()

Example:

The chars method can be used to retrieve individual characters in a string. To further comprehend this, consider the following scenario.

```
fn main() {
    let nm1 = "Rust".to_string();
    for nm in nm1.chars() {
        println!("{}",nm);
    }
}
```

Concatenation of the Strings with + Operator

Appending a string value to another string is possible. This is referred to as concatenation or interpolation. String concatenation produces a new string object. Internally, the + operator employs an add method. The add function's syntax accepts two parameters. The first parameter is self, which is a String object itself, and the second is a reference to the second string object. This is depicted below:

```
//add the function
add(self,&str)->String {
    // returns String object
}
```

Illustration: String Concatenation

Example:

```
fn main() {
    let nm1 = "Rust".to_string();
    let nm2 = "Points".to_string();
    let nm3 = nm1 + &nm2; // n2 reference is passed
    println!("{}",nm3);
}
```

Illustration: Type Casting

Example:

```
fn main() {
    let number = 2022;
    let number_as_string = number.to_string();
    // convert the number to string
    println!("{}",number_as_string);
    println!("{}",number_as_string=="2022");
}
```

Illustration: Format! Macro

A macro function called format can also be used to combine String objects together. The following is an example of how Format! may be used.

Example:

```
fn main(){
    let nm1 = "Rust".to_string();
    let nm2 = "Points".to_string();
    let nm3 = format!("{} {}",nm1,nm2);
    println!("{}",nm3);
}
```

OPERATORS IN RUST

An operator specifies a function that will apply to the data. The data on which operators operate is referred to as operands. Consider the following expression:

$$6 + 4 = 10$$

In this case, the operands are 6, 4, and 10, whereas the operators are + and =.

Rust's major operators are characterized as follows:

- Arithmetic

- Bitwise

- Comparison

- Logical

- Conditional

Arithmetic Operators

Assume that variables x and y have 11 and 4, respectively.

Sr. No	Operator	Description	Example
1	+	Returns the sum of operands	x + y is 12
2	−	Returns the difference of values	x−y is 3
3	*	Returns the product of values	x*y is 40
4	/	Performs division operation and returns the quotient	x / y is 3
5	%	Performs division operation and returns the remainder	x % y is 0

Relational Operators

Relational operators are used to test or specify the type of relationship that exists between two items. When comparing two or more values, relational operators are utilized. Relational operators yield either true or false as a Boolean value.

Assume X equals 15 and Y equals 25.

Sr. No	Operator	Description	Example
1	>	Greater than	(X > Y) is false
2	<	Lesser than	(X < Y) is true
3	>=	Greater than or equal to	(X >= Y) is false
4	<=	Lesser than or equal to	(X <= Y) is true
5	==	Equality	(X == Y) is false
6	!=	Not equal	(X != Y) is true

Logical Operators

Logical operators are used for joining two or more conditions together. Logical operators, like all other operators, yield a Boolean value. Assume variable X has a value of 15 and variable Y has a value of 25.

Sr. No	Operator	Description	Example
1	&&	The operator returns true only if all expressions specified return true	(X > 15 && Y > 15) is false
2	||	Operator returns true if one of the expressions specified return true	(X > 15 || Y > 15) is true
3	!	Operator returns inverse of the expression's result. For e.g. !(>5) returns false	!(X > 15) is true

Bitwise Operators

Assume variable X = 3 and variable Y = 4.

Sr. No	Operator	Description	Example
1	& (Bitwise AND)	Each bit of its integer parameters is processed to a Boolean AND operation	(X & Y) is 3
2	| (BitWise OR)	Each bit of its integer parameters is applied to a Boolean OR operation	(X | Y) is 4
3	^ (Bitwise XOR)	On each bit of its integer parameters, it performs a Boolean exclusive OR operation. Exclusive OR denotes that either operand one or operand two must be true, but neither must be true	(X ^ Y) is 1

4	! (Bitwise Not)	It is unary operator that reverses all of the operand's bits	(!Y) is 5
5	<< (Left Shift)	It shifts all of the bits in its first operand to the left by the number of places in its second operand. Zeros are used to fill new bits. Shifting a value left by one place is comparable to multiplying it by two, shifting it to two positions is equivalent to multiplying it by four, and so on	(X << 1) is 4
6	>> (Right Shift Binary Operator)	The value of the left operand is shifted right by the number of bits given by the right operand	(X >> 1) is 1
7	>>> (Right shift with Zero)	This operator works same way as the >> operator, except that the bits moved to the left are always zero	(X >>> 1) is 1

DECISION-MAKING IN RUST

The programmer must define one or more conditions to be evaluated or tested by the program, a statement or statements to be performed if the condition is judged to be true, and optionally, other statements to be run if the condition is decided to be false.

Sr. No	Statement and Description
1	**If statement** A Boolean expression is followed by one or more assertions in an if statement.
2	**If...else statement** When Boolean expression is false, the if...else statement follows the statement.
3	**Else...if and nested if statement** The if or else if statement can be used inside another if or else if statement.
4	**Match statement** A match statement checks a variable against a set of values.

If Statement

Before executing a piece of code, the if...else construct evaluates a condition.

Syntax

```
if boolean_expression {
    // statement will execute if boolean expression is
                    true
}
```

If Boolean expression returns true, the code within the if statement is performed. If the Boolean expression returns false, the first code set after the conclusion of the if statement (after the closing curly brace) is performed.

Example:

```
fn main(){
    let num:i32=9;
    if num>0 {
        println!("number positive");
    }
}
```

As long as the condition stated by the if block is true, the above example will output a positive number.

If else statement

The if...else statement can follow the statement. If the Boolean expression checked by the if statement returns false, the else block will be executed.

Syntax

```
if boolean_expression {
    // statement will execute if boolean expression is
                true
} else {
    // statement will execute if boolean expression is
                false
}
```

Flowchart

The if statement protects the conditional phrase. If the Boolean expression evaluates to true, the block associated with the if statement is performed (Figure 2.1).

The if an else statement optionally follows the statement. If the expression evaluates to false, the instruction block associated with the else block is performed.

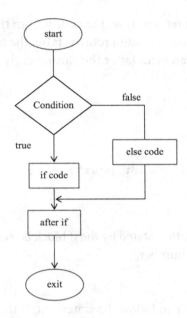

FIGURE 2.1 Statement of if…else.

Example:

```
fn main() {
    let num=15;
    if num % 2==0 {
        println!("Evennum");
    } else {
        println!("Oddnum");
    }
}
```

Nested If

The else…if ladder is good for testing many circumstances. The syntax is presented below.

Syntax

```
if boolean_expression1 {
    //statement if expression1 evaluates to true
} else if boolean_expression2 {
    //statement if expression2 evaluates to true
} else {
    //statement if both the expression1 and expression2
            result to false
}
```

There are a few things to remember while utilizing if...else...if and else statements.

- An if can have a value of zero or one, and it must come after anything else...if.

- If there are zero or more else...if in an if, they come first.

- If an else...if succeeds, none of the remaining else...if or else will be tried.

Example:

```
fn main() {
    let numb=4;
    if numb>0 {
        println!("{} positive",numb);
    } else if numb<0 {
        println!("{} negative",numb);
    } else {
        println!("{} neither positive nor negative",numb);
    }
}
```

Match Statement

The match statement checks whether a current value matches one from a list of values; it is similar to the switch statement in C. First and foremost, the expression after the match keyword does not need to be enclosed in parentheses.

Syntax

```
let expressionResult=match variable_expression {
    constant_expr1=>{
        //statement;
    },
    constant_expr2=>{
        //statement;
    },
    _=>{
        //default
    }
};
```

In the following example, state code is compared to a set of values MH, KL, KA, and GA; a string value is returned to the variable state if a match is found. The default case matches returns the value Unknown if no match is found.

Example:

```
fn main(){
    let state_code = "IN";
    let state = match state_code {
        "DL" => {println!("Found match "); "Delhi"},
        "IN" => "India",
        "KL" => "Kolkatta",
        "AB" => "Ahmdabad",
        _ => "Unknown"
    };
    println!("State name:{}",state);
}
```

Using an "if" statement within a "let" statement

The "if" expression is used on the right side of the let statement, and the value of "if" expression is assigned to "let" statement.

Syntax

```
Let vari_name = if condition{
//blocks of code
}
else{
//code
}
```

If the condition is true, the value of the "if" expression is assigned to the variable; if the condition is false, the value of "else" is allocated to the variable.

Example 1:

```
fn main()
  let x=if true
      {
```

2

```
        }
        else
        {
            4
        };
    println!("value of x is: {}", x);
```

Example 2:

```
fn main()
    let x=if false
        {
            10
        }
        else
        {
            "Rustpoint"
        };
    println!("value of x is: {}", x);
```

In this example, the "if" block evaluates to an integer value, whereas the "else" section evaluates to a string value. As a result, this program generates an error since both blocks contain values of different types.

LOOPS IN RUST

If we want to run the block of statements more than once, we may use the idea of the loop. A loop performs the code within the loop body to the end and then restarts from the beginning.

Rust is made up of three types of loops:

1. loops

2. for loop

3. while loop

Loop

It is not a conditional loop. It is a term that tells Rust to execute the block of code again and over until you explicitly halt the loop.

Syntax

```
loop{
  // statements block
}
```

Block statements in the preceding syntax are run indefinitely.

Example:

```
fn main()
 loop
 {
      println!("Hello everyone");
}
```

In this example, "Hello everyone" is displayed repeatedly until we manually stop the loop. In most cases, the "ctrl+c" command is used to exit the loop.

Exit from Loops

To exit a loop, use the "break" keyword. If the "break" keyword is not provided, the loop will run indefinitely.

Example:

```
  fn main()
let mut x=1;
 loop
 {
      println!("Hello everyone");
      if x==7
      {
         break;
      }
 x+=1;
 }}
```

While Loop

A "while loop" is a type of conditional loop. The conditional loop is used when a program needs to evaluate a condition. The loop is invoked if the condition is true; otherwise, the loop is terminated.

Syntax

while condition

// statements block;

The while loop in the preceding syntax evaluates the condition. If the condition is true, block statements are performed; else, the loop is terminated. This built-in construct in Rust can be used in conjunction with a "loop," "if," "else," or "break" declaration.

Flowchart

The general process of loop runtime can be summarized as in Figure 2.2.

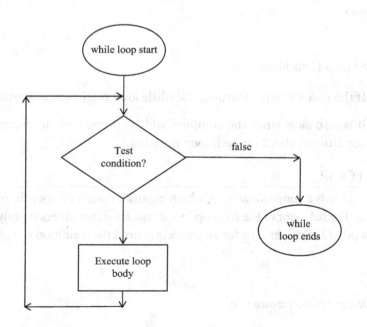

FIGURE 2.2 Statement of while loop.

Example 1:

```rust
fn main()
{
   let mut x=1;
   while x<=10
{
   print!("{}", x);
   print!(" ");
   x=x+1;
}
}
```

Example 2:

```rust
fn main()
{
 let array=[20,30,35,42,60,90];
 let mut x=0;
 while x<60
 {
   print!("{}",array[x]);
   print!(" ");
   x=x+1;
 }
}
```

While Loop Disadvantages

- If the index length is wrong, the while loop might cause a problem.

- It is also slow since the compiler adds runtime code to execute the conditional check on each loop iteration.

FOR LOOP

The for loop is a conditional loop, which means it runs for a specific amount of time. The behavior of the for loop in the rust language differs slightly from that of other languages. The for loop executes until the condition is met.

Syntax

```rust
for var in expression
{
    //statements
}
```

An expression in the preceding syntax can turn into an iterator that iterates across the elements of a data structure. An iterator is used to retrieve the value of each iteration. The loop ends when there are no more values to be fetched.

Example 1:

```
fn main()
{
 for x in 1..12
 {
    print!("{} ",x);
 }
}
```

Example 2:

```
fn main()
{
let mut result;
for x in 1..12
{
result=2*x;
println!("2*{}={}",x,result);
}
}
```

Example 3:

```
fn main()
let fruits=["apple","orange","mango","banana",
            "watermelon"];
 for s in fruits.iter()
{
   print!("{} ",s);
}
```

In the above example, the iter() function is used to retrieve each entry of the fruits variable. The loop ends when it reaches the last element of an array.

Distinctions between the While Loop and For Loop

If index length of an array is raised at runtime, the while loop exhibits the problem, but this does not occur in the case of the for loop. As a result, we can argue that the for loop enhances the safety of the code and eliminates the possibility of problems.

FUNCTIONS IN RUST

Functions are the building blocks of understandable, manageable, and reusable code. A function is a collection of statements used to carry out a specified activity. Functions structure the program into logical pieces of code. Functions can invoke access code after they have been defined. As a result, the code is reusable. Furthermore, functions make the program's code easier to comprehend and maintain.

The name, return type, and function parameters are all specified in a function declaration. A function definition defines the body of the function.

Sr. No	Function and Description
1	**Defining a function** The specification of a TA function explains what and how a given job would complete.
2	**Calling or invoking a function** To run a function, it must be invoked.
3	**Returning functions** Functions may also return value as well as control to the caller.
4	**Parameterized function** Parameters are a way for values to be sent to functions.

Function Defining

A function definition describes what and how a given activity would carry out. A function must specify before it may use it. The function body includes the code that the function should run. The guidelines for naming a function are the same as those for naming variables. The fn keyword is used to define functions. The following is the syntax for defining a standard function.

Syntax

```
fn function_name(param1,param2..paramN)
{
    //body of function
}
```

A function declaration may or may not include parameters/arguments. Functions employ parameters to transmit values to them.

Example:

```
//Defining function
fn fn_hello(){
    println!("hello fn_hello ");
}
```

Function Invoking

To run a function, it must be invoked. This is known as function invocation. When calling a function, arguments' values should pass. The function that calls another function is referred to as the caller function.

Syntax

```
function_name(val1,val2,valN)
```

Example:

```
fn main(){
    // function calling
    fn_hello();
}
```

Illustration

The function fn_hello() is defined in the following example. A message is printed to the console using this function. The fn_hello() function is called by the main() function:

```
fn main(){
    //calling function
    fn_hello();
}
//Defining function
fn fn_hello(){
    println!("hello fn_hello ");
}
```

Returning Value from a Function

The functions can also return a value to the caller along with control. Such functions are referred to as returning functions.

Syntax

To define a function with a return type, use any of the following syntax.

With the Return Statement

```
// Syntax-1
fn function_name() ->return_type {
   //statement
   return value;
}
```

Shorthand Syntax without the Return Statement

```
//Syntax-2
fn function_name() ->return_type {
   value //no-semicolon means this value is returned
}
```

Example:

```
fn main(){
   println!("pi value {}",get_pi());
}
fn get_pi()->f64 {
   22.0/7.0
}
```

Function with the Parameters

Parameters are a way for values to be sent to functions. The function's signature includes parameters. During the function's call, the argument values are supplied to it. Unless otherwise indicated, the number of values provided to a function must equal the number of arguments defined.

One of the following methods can be used to send parameters to a function.

Pass by Value

A new storage location for each value argument is generated when a method is called. The real parameter values are transferred into them. As a result, changes to the parameter within the called method do not affect the argument.

The example below declares a variable no, which is initially set to 7. The variable is passed as a parameter (by value) to the method mutate_no_to_zero(), which transforms the value to zero. When control returns to the main method after the function call, the value will be the same.

```
fn main(){
    let no:i32 = 7;
    mutate_no_to_zero(no);
    println!("Value of no:{}",no);
}
fn mutate_no_to_zero(mut param_no: i32) {
    param_no = param_no*0;
    println!("param_no value:{}",param_no);
}
```

Pass by Reference

In contrast to value parameters, when we send parameters by reference, no new storage place is generated for these parameters. The reference parameters are stored in the same memory location as the method's real arguments. By prefixing the variable name with an &, parameter values can be passed by reference.

In the following example, we have a variable no initially set to 7. The mutate_no_to_zero() method is given a reference to the variable no. The function is applied to the original variable. When control returns to the main method after the function call, the original variable's value will be zero.

```
fn main() {
    let mut no:i32 = 7;
    mutate_no_to_zero(&mut no);
    println!("Value of no:{}",no);
}
fn mutate_no_to_zero(param_no:&mut i32){
    *param_no = 0; //de reference
}
```

The * operator is used to access values stored in the memory address as the variable param no. This is sometimes referred to as dereferencing.

Passing String to a Function
The display() method receives a String object from the main() function.

```
fn main(){
    let name:String=String::from("RustPoint");
    display(name);
    //cannot access the name after display
}
fn display(param_name:String){
    println!("param_name value:{}",param_name);
}
```

COMMENTS IN RUST

Every programmer strives to make their code understandable, but there are instances when more explanation is required. In certain circumstances, programmers provide annotations, or comments, in their source code that the compiler ignores but that individuals viewing the code may find beneficial.

Here's a basic comment:

```
// hello, everyone
```

The idiomatic comment style in Rust begins a comment with two slashes and continues until the end of the line. For comments that go beyond a single line, use // on each line, as seen here:

```
// doing something complicated here
// multiple lines of comments to do it. Hopefully, the
            comment will
// explain what is going on.
```

The comments can also be added to the end of code lines:

Filename: src/themain.rs

```
fn main() {
    let lucky_numb=13; //feeling lucky today
}
```

However, we'll see them more often in this style, with the comment on a separate line above the code it is annotating:

Filename: src/themain.rs

```
fn main() {
    //feeling lucky today
    let lucky_numb = 13;
}
```

TUPLE IN RUST

A tuple is a form of compound data. A scalar type can only store one type of data. An i32 variable, for example, may only store a single integer value. In compound types, we can store multiple values at once, and they can be of various types.

Tuples have a set length; once stated, they cannot be increased or decreased in size. The tuple index begins at 0.

//Syntax-1

let tuple_names:(data_type1,data_type2,data_type3) = (value1,value2,value3);

//Syntax-2

let tuple_names = (value1,value2,value3);

Example:

```
fn main() {
    let tuples:(i32,f64,u8) = (-326,4.8,23);
    println!("{:?}",tuples);
}
```

The println!("{}",tuple) syntax cannot be used to show tuple values. This is because a tuple is a compound type. To print values in a tuple, use the println!("{:?}", tuple name) syntax.

Example:
The example below prints each value in a tuple.

```
fn main() {
    let tuple:(i32,f64,u8) = (-326,4.8,23);
    println!("integer :{:?}",tuple.0);
```

```
    println!("float :{:?}",tuple.1);
    println!("unsigned integer :{:?}",tuple.2);
}
```

Example:

The following example calls a function using a tuple as an argument. Tuples are provided to functions by value.

```
fn main(){
    let a:(i32,bool,f64) = (120,true,11.9);
    print(a);
}
//pass tuple as a parameter
fn print(y:(i32,bool,f64)){
    println!("print method inside");
    println!("{:?}",y);
}
```

Destructing

Destructing assignment is a Rust feature that allows us to unpack the values of a tuple. This is accomplished by allocating a tuple to each variable.

```
fn main(){
    let a:(i32,bool,f64) = (32,true,7.8);
    print(a);
}
fn print(y:(i32,bool,f64)){
    println!("print method inside");
    let (age,is_male,cgpa)=y; //assigns tuple to
    different variables
    println!("Age {}, isMale? {},cgpa is
    {}",age,is_male,cgpa);
}
```

The variable y is a tuple assigned to the let statement. Each variable – age, is male, and cgpa – will have a tuple with the corresponding values.

ARRAY IN RUST

We'll learn about arrays and the various features that come with them. Before we go into arrays, let's look at how an array differs from a variable.

Variables have the following constraints:

Variables have a scalar nature. To put it another way, a variable declaration can only have one value at a time. This indicates that n variable declarations will be required to store n values in a program. As a result, the usage of variables is not viable for storing a larger collection of values.

Variables in a program are assigned memory in a random sequence, making it impossible to retrieve/read the values in the order they were declared.

A collection of values that are all the same is referred to as an array. An array is a collection of elements of the same data type.

Array Characteristics

An array has the following characteristics:

- An array declaration allocates memory blocks in sequential order.

- Arrays are not dynamic. This means that it cannot resize after an array has been initialized.

- Each memory block corresponds to a single array element.

- Array elements are identified by a unique number known as the element's subscript/index.

- Array initialization is the process of populating the array elements.

- The values of array elements can be edited or modified but not erased.

Array Declaration and Initialization

In Rust, use the following syntax to define and initialize an array.

Syntax

```
//Syntax-1

let variable_names = [value1,value2,value3];

//Syntax-2

let variable_names:[dataType;size] = [value1,value2,value3];

//Syntax-3

let variable_names:[dataType;size] = [default_value_for_elements,size];
```

The type of the array is inferred in the first syntax from the data type of the array's first element during initialization.

Illustration: Simple Array

The array's size and data type are explicitly specified in the following example. The println!() function's {:?} syntax is used to print all values in the array. The array's size is determined by the len() method.

```
fn main(){
    let arra:[i32;4] = [20,30,80,50];
    println!("array {:?}",arra);
    println!("array size :{}",arra.len());
}
```

Illustration: Array without Data Type

The following program declares a four-element array. The datatype is not stated explicitly during variable declaration. The array will be of type integer in this situation. The array's size is determined by the len() method.

```
fn main(){
    let arrs = [20,30,80,50];
    println!("array {:?}",arra);
    println!("array size :{}",arra.len());
}
```

Illustration: Default Values

The following example builds an array and assigns a value of -1 to all of its elements.

```
fn main() {
    let arra:[i32;4] = [-1;4];
    println!("array {:?}",arra);
    println!("array size :{}",arra.len());
}
```

Illustration: Array with for Loop

The following example iterates over an array, printing the indices and values as it passes. The loop retrieves values from 0 to 4 indexes (index of the last array element).

```
fn main(){
    let arra:[i32;4] = [20,30,80,50];
    println!("array {:?}",arra);
    println!("array size :{}",arra.len());
    for index in 0..4 {
        println!("index is: {} & value :
{}",index,arra[index]);
    }
}
```

Illustration: Using the iter() Function
The iter() method returns the values of all array items.

```
fn main(){
let arra:[i32;4] = [20,30,80,50];
    println!("array {:?}",arr);
    println!("array size :{}",arra.len());
    for vals in arra.iter(){
        println!("value :{}",vals);
    }
}
```

Illustration: Mutable Array
A mutable array may be declared using the mut keyword. The example below declares a mutable array and alters the value of the second array element.

```
fn main(){
    let mut arra:[i32;4] = [20,30,80,50];
    arra[1] = 0;
    println!("{:?}",arra);
}
```

Passing Arrays as Parameters to the Functions
An array can be passed to functions as a value or as a reference.

Illustration: Pass by Value

```
fn main() {
    let arra = [20,40,80];
    update(arra);
```

```
    print!("Inside-main {:?}",arra);
}
fn update(mut arra:[i32;3]){
    for i in 0..3 {
        arra[i]=0;
    }
    println!("Inside-update {:?}",arra);
}
```

Illustration: Pass by Reference

```
fn main() {
    let mut arra=[20,40,90];
    update(&mut arra);
    print!("Inside-main {:?}",arra);
}
fn update(arra:&mut [i32;3]){
    for i in 0..3 {
        arra[i]=0;
    }
    println!("Inside-update {:?}",arra);
}
```

The Array Declaration and Constants

Consider the following example to better understand array declaration and constants:

```
fn main() {
    let N: usize=30;
    let arra=[0; N]; //Error: non-constant used with
                            the constant
    print!("{}",arra[20])
}
```

The compiler will throw an exception. Because the length of an array must be known at build time, this is the case. The value of the variable "N" will decide at runtime in this case. Variables, in other words, cannot be used to specify the size of an array.

The following program, on the other hand, is valid.

```
fn main() {
    const N: usize=30;
    // pointer sized
```

```
    let arra = [0; N];
    print!("{}",arra[20])
}
```

The value of a const-prefixed identifier is determined at build time and cannot be changed during runtime. usize is pointer-sized; therefore, its real size is specified on the architecture for which we are developing our program.

This chapter covered variables and mutability, data types, and functions. Moreover, we learned comments, tuples, array, and control flow with appropriate syntax and examples.

CHAPTER 3

Understanding Ownership

IN THIS CHAPTER

- ➤ What is ownership?
- ➤ References and borrowing
- ➤ The slice type

The previous chapter covered variables, functions, and data types. Furthermore, we also covered comments and control statements. This chapter will cover ownership, references, and borrowing and slice type.

WHAT EXACTLY IS OWNERSHIP?

The primary aspect of Rust is ownership. Although the characteristic is simple to describe, it has deep implications for the rest of the language.

All programs must manage how they use memory while running on a computer. Some languages offer garbage collection, which searches for no longer utilized memory while the program runs; in others, the programmer must actively allocate and delete memory. Rust has a third approach: memory is controlled using an ownership system with rules that the compiler validates at compile time. While our software is running, none of the ownership aspects will slow it down.

We discussed what ownership, references, and borrowing are in this chapter. Slice Type was also discussed. The good news is that as we gain

DOI: 10.1201/9781003311966-3

expertise with Rust and the rules of the ownership system, we will be able to write secure and efficient code intuitively.

When we grasp ownership, we'll have a solid basis for comprehending the characteristics that distinguish Rust. This chapter will learn about ownership by working through several examples that focus on a fairly popular data structure: strings.

The Stack and the Heap

Many programming languages don't need us to think about the stack or the heap very much. However, in a systems programming language like Rust, whether an item is on the stack or the heap has a greater impact on how the language acts and why certain decisions must be made. Parts of ownership in connection to the stack and heap will be discussed later in this chapter, so here's a quick primer.

The stack and heap are two alternative memory structures that our programs may utilize at runtime. The stack saves items in the order in which they are received and removes values in the opposite order. This is known as last in, first out. Consider a stack of plates: as we add additional plates, we stack them on top, and when we need a plate, we remove one from the top. Adding or deleting plates from the middle or bottom would be ineffective. Adding data is referred to as pushing onto the stack, while removing data is popping off the stack.

The size of all data placed on the stack must be known and fixed. Data having an uncertain size or a size that may vary at compile time must be put on the heap instead. We require a specific amount of space when we put data on the heap. The memory allocator selects an empty space in the heap that is large enough, marks it as in use, and returns a reference to that location's address. This is known as allocating on the heap, and it is commonly abbreviated as just allocating. Allocating does not include pushing values into the stack.

Because the pointer has a known, constant size, it may store on the stack, but we must follow the pointer to access the real data.

Consider being seated in a restaurant. When we go in, we tell the staff how many people are in our company, and they find an empty table that accommodates everyone and guides us there. If a member of our party arrives late, they might enquire where we've been seated to locate us.

Pushing to the stack is faster than heap allocating because the allocator never has to look for a new area to store new data because the top of the stack is always available.

On the other hand, allocating heap space necessitates more effort since the allocator must first find a large enough place to contain the data and then do accounting to prepare for the next allocation.

Accessing data in a heap takes slower than accessing data on the stack because we have to follow a pointer to get there. Modern CPUs are speedier when they move about in memory less. Imagine a waitress in a restaurant taking orders from many tables to continue the analogy. It's best to complete all of the orders at one table before going on to the next.

Taking one order from table A, then another from table B, then another from A, and then another from B would be a significantly slower procedure. Similarly, a processor can perform better if it works on data close to other data (as it is on the stack) rather than further away data (as it can be on the heap). Allocating a big quantity of heap space might also take some time.

When code calls a function, the values given into the function (including possibly heap-based pointers) and the function's local variables are put into the stack. When the function is finished, the values are removed from the stack.

Ownership addresses difficulties such as keeping track of which portions of code use which data on the heap, minimizing the amount of duplicate data on the heap, and cleaning away unnecessary data on the heap so we don't run out of space. After we grasp ownership, we won't need to think about the stack or the heap as much, but understanding that managing heap data is why ownership exists may help explain why it works the way it does.

Important Ownership Concepts

- The "owner" can modify the ownership value of a variable based on its mutability.

- The ownership of a variable can transfer to another variable.

- In Rust, ownership is just a matter of semantics.

- In addition, the ownership concept ensures safety.

Rules of Ownership

- In Rust, each value has a variable called its owner.

- At any one moment, there can only be one owner.

- When the owner exits the scope, the value is destroyed.

Variable Scope

We previously went through an example of a Rust program. We won't include all of the fn main() code in examples now that we've moved past the basic syntax; so if we're following along, we'll have to place the following examples within the main function manually. As a result, examples will be a little shorter, allowing us to concentrate on the important aspects rather than boilerplate code.

We'll look at the scope of several variables as a first illustration of ownership. A scope is the range of items that are valid within a program. Assume we have a variable that looks something like this:

```
let st = "hello";
```

The variable s refers to a literal string, the value of which is hardcoded into the program's text. The variable is valid from the time it is declared until the current scope expires. Listing includes comments that indicate when the variable st is valid.

```
{                        // st is not valid here, it's
                         not yet declared
    let st = "hello";    // st is valid from this point
                         forward
    // do stuff with s
}                        // this scope is now over, and
                         st is no longer valid
```

In other words, there are two critical time points here:

1. It is valid when s enters the scope.

2. It is still valid until it is going out of scope.

The connection between the scope and when variables are valid is comparable to that of other programming languages at this stage. We'll now add to this understanding by introducing the String type.

String Type

To demonstrate the laws of ownership, we need a data type that is more sophisticated than the ones taught in the "Data Types in Rust" section. All of the previously mentioned types have a known size, can be stored on the stack and popped off when their scope is complete, and can be quickly and simply cloned to create a new, independent instance if another piece of code needs to use the same value in a different scope. But we'd want to look at data kept on the heap and see how Rust understands when to clear it up.

We'll take String as an example and focus on the sections of String that are related to ownership. These considerations also apply to other complicated data types, whether offered by the standard library or developed by us.

We've already encountered string literals, which are instances in which a string value is hardcoded into our software. String literals are useful, but they aren't appropriate for every circumstance where we utilize text. One reason is that they are unchangeable. Another issue is that not every string value can be known when creating code: what if we want to collect user input and store it? The String is a second string type in Rust that is useful in these scenarios. This type maintains heap data and may thus hold a large quantity of text unknown to us at build time. Using from function, we can produce a String from a string literal, as seen below:

```
let st = String::from("helloo");
```

The double colon (::) is an operator that allows us to namespace this particular from function as String rather than using a name like string.

This type of string can be changed:

```
let mut st = String::from("helloo");
    st.push_str(", everyone"); // push_str() appends
                                literal to a String
    println!("{}", st); // This will print `hello,
                          everyone`
```

So, what's the distinction here? Why can a String be changed but not a literal? The distinction is in how these two types deal with memory.

Memory and Allocation

Because we know the contents of a string literal at compilation time, the text is hardcoded directly into the final executable. Because of this, string literals are quick and efficient. However, these features are derived entirely from the string literal's immutability. Unfortunately, we can't include a blob of memory in the binary for each piece of text whose size is unknown at build time and may vary while the application is executing.

To enable changeable, growable text with the String type, we must allocate an amount of memory on the heap that is unknown at compilation time to contain the contents. That is to admit:

- At runtime, memory must request from the memory allocator.
- When we're finished processing our String, we need the means to return this memory to the allocator.

We handle the first part: when we call String::from, its implementation requests its memory. This is rather common in programming languages.

On the other hand, the second component is unique. In languages with a garbage collector, the GC maintains track of and cleans up memory that is no longer in use, so we don't have to bother about it. Without a GC, we must recognize when memory is no longer being utilized and call code to explicitly return it, as we did to request it. Historically, doing this right has been a challenging programming task. We will waste memory if we forget. We'll have an invalid variable if do it too soon. It's also a bug if we do it twice. We must match precisely one allocate to exactly one free.

Rust has a different approach: when the variable that owns the memory exits scope, the memory is immediately returned. Here's a variant of our Listing scope example that uses a String instead of a string literal:

```
{
    let st = String::from("helloo"); // st is valid from
                                this point forward
    // do stuff with st
}                   // this scope is now over, and st is no
                    // longer valid
```

When st passes out of scope, we may naturally return the memory our String requires to the allocator. When a variable is no longer in scope, Rust invokes a specific function for us. Drop is the name of this method, and it is where the author of String may write the code to return the memory. Rust calls are dropped automatically at the final curly bracket.

This pattern has a significant influence on how Rust code is written. It may appear easy today, but code behavior might be unexpected in more complex cases where we want several variables to consume the data we've placed on the heap. Let's look at some of those scenarios now.

Ways of Variables and Data Interact: Move

In Rust, several variables can interact with the same data in various ways. In Listing, we'll look at an example with an integer.

```
let a = 8;
let b = x;
```

"Bind the value 8 to a; then make a copy of the value in x and bind it to b," we may probably estimate. We now have two variables, a and b, equal to 8. This is correct because integers are simple values with a known, defined size, and these two 8 values are placed into the stack.

Let's have a look at the String version:

```
let st1 = String::from("hello");
 let st2 = st1;
```

This code appears to be quite similar to the preceding code, so we can conclude that the function is the same: the second line would duplicate the value in st1 and bind it to st2. However, this is not the case.

The length specifies how much memory (in bytes) the String's contents presently occupy. The capacity is the entire amount of memory that the allocator gives the String in bytes. The distinction between length and capacity is essential, but not in this context, so ignore the capacity for the time being (Figure 3.1).

When we assign st1 to st2, the String data is duplicated, which means we copy the stack's pointer, length, and capacity. We do not replicate the

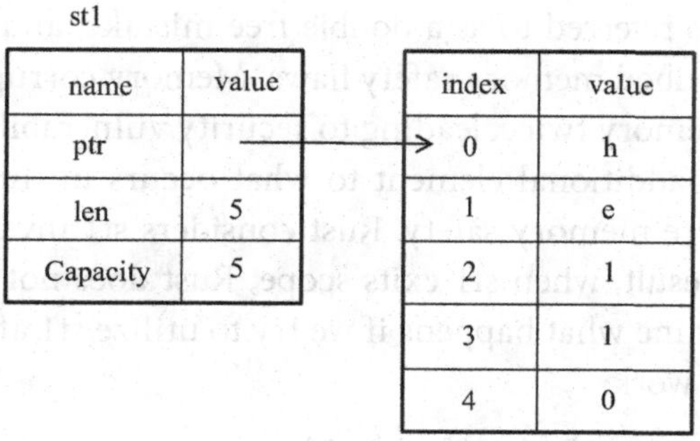

st1

name	value		index	value
ptr		→	0	h
len	5		1	e
Capacity	5		2	l
			3	l
			4	o

FIGURE 3.1 Memory representation of a String with the value "hello" linked to st1.

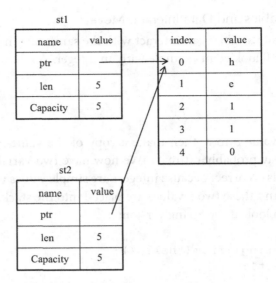

FIGURE 3.2   Variable st2's memory representation, which contains a duplicate of st1's pointer, length, and capacity.

data on the heap to which the pointer points. To put it another way, the data representation in memory (Figure 3.2).

The representation does not like the image below, which depicts what memory would look like if Rust replicated the heap data. If Rust implemented this, the st2 = st1 transaction might be highly costly in runtime performance if the data on the heap was large (Figure 3.3).

Rust automatically executes the drop function when a variable exits scope and cleans away the heap memory for that variable. However, in Figure 3.3, both data pointers point to the same place. This is an issue because when st2 and st1 exit scope, they will attempt to free the same memory. This is referred to as a double free mistake, and it is one of the previously described memory safety flaws. Memory corruption can result from freeing memory twice, leading to security vulnerabilities.

There is one additional element to what occurs in this circumstance in Rust to ensure memory safety. Rust considers st1 invalid after letting st2 = st1. As a result, when st1 exits scope, Rust does not need to release anything. Examine what happens if we try to utilize st1 after st2 is generated; it will not work:

```
let st1 = String::from("hello");
    let st2 = st1;

    println!("{}, everyone", st1);
```

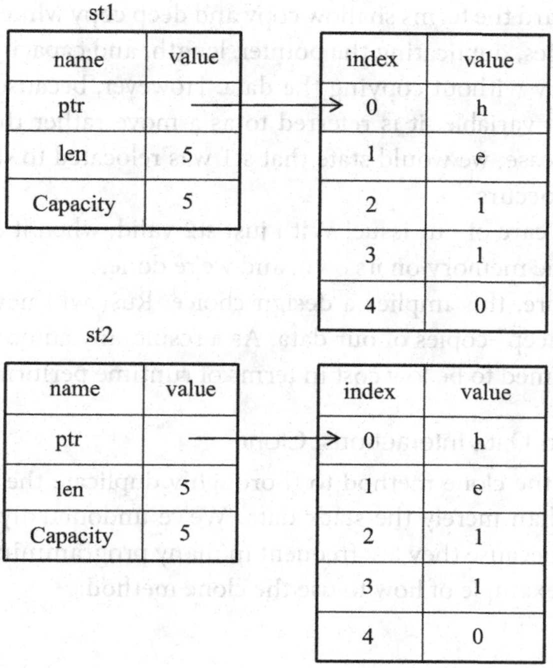

st1

name	value
ptr	
len	5
Capacity	5

index	value
0	h
1	e
2	1
3	1
4	0

st2

name	value
ptr	
len	5
Capacity	5

index	value
0	h
1	e
2	1
3	1
4	0

FIGURE 3.3 Another option for what st2 = st1 could do if Rust also copied the heap data.

Because Rust restricts us from utilizing the invalidated reference, we'll get an error like this:

```
$ cargo run
   Compiling ownership v0.1.0 (file:///projects/
                              ownership)
error[E0382]: borrow of moved value: `st1`
  --> src/main.rs:5:28
  |
2 |      let st1 = String::from("hello");
  |          -- move occurs because `st1` has type
              `String`, which does not implement the
              `Copy` trait
3 |      let st2 = st1;
  |            -- value moved here
4 |
5 |      println!("{}, world!", st1);
  |                             ^^ value borrowed
                                here after move
```

If we've heard the terms shallow copy and deep copy while dealing with other languages, duplicating the pointer, length, and capacity sounds like a shallow copy without copying the data. However, because Rust invalidates the first variable, it is referred to as a move rather than a shallow copy. In this case, we would state that st1 was relocated to st2. Figure 3.4 depicts what occurs.

That takes care of our issue! With just st2 valid, when it exits scope, it will release the memory on its own, and we're done.

Furthermore, this implies a design choice: Rust will never automatically build "deep" copies of our data. As a result, any automated copying may be presumed to be low cost in terms of runtime performance.

Variables and Data Interactions: Clone

We may use the clone method to thoroughly duplicate the String's heap data rather than merely the stack data. We've undoubtedly encountered them before because they are frequent in many programming languages.

Here's an example of how to use the clone method:

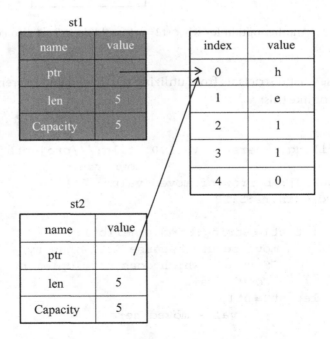

FIGURE 3.4   Memory representation after s1 has been invalidated.

```
let st1 = String::from("hello");
  let st2 = st1.clone();

  println!("st1 = {}, st2 = {}", st1, st2);
```

This works well and generates the behavior depicted in the rust-copiedtheheap.jpg example above, where the heap data is explicitly copied.

When we observe a clone call, we know that some arbitrary code is being performed and that code might be costly. It's a visual cue that something unusual is going on.

Stack-Only Data: Copy

There's one more wrinkle we haven't addressed yet. This code use integers, a portion of which was demonstrated in Figure 3.4:

```
let a = 8;
  let b = a;

  println!("a = {}, b = {}", a, b);
```

However, this code appears to contradict what we have just learned: there is no call to clone, but a is still valid and was not transferred into b.

This is because types with known sizes at build time, like integers, are wholly stored on the stack; thus, copies of the actual values are quickly produced. There is no reason to prevent a from being valid after we have created the variable b. In this case, there is no distinction between deep and shallow copying. Therefore, invoking clone would perform nothing more than shallow copying so that we can leave it out.

Rust has a particular annotation called the Copy trait that we may apply to types like integers stored on the stack. If a type has the Copy trait, an older variable can still be used after the assignment. Rust will not allow us to annotate a type with the Copy trait if the type or any of its components has the Drop trait implemented. If we add the Copy annotation to a type that requires anything specific to happen when the value is out of scope, we will get a compile-time error.

Ownership and Functions

Passing a value to a function has semantics comparable to giving a value to a variable. Passing a variable to a function will cause it to move or copy, much like an assignment. The following is an example with annotations indicating where variables enter and exit scope:

Filename: src/themain.rs

```
fn main() {
    let st = String::from("hello"); // s comes into scope
    takes_ownership(st);            // st's value moves
into the function...
                                    //... and so is no
longer valid

    let a = 5;                      // a comes into scope

    makes_copy(a);                  // move into the
function,
                                    // but i32 is Copy, so
okay to still
use afterward

} // Here, a goes out of scope, then s. But because
st's value was moved, nothing
  // specialhappens.

Fn takes_ownership(some_string: String) {//some_string
comes into the scope
println!("{}", some_string);
} // Here, some_string goes out of the scope and a
`drop` is called. The backing
  // memory is freed.

Fn makes_copy(some_integer: i32) {//some_integer comes
into the scope
println!("{}", some_integer);
} // Here, some_integer goes out of the scope. Nothing
special happens.
```

Return Values and Scope

Ownership can also be transferred by returning values. The above code shows an example with comments identical to those in the following example:

Filename: src/themain.rs

```
fn main() {
    let st1=gives_ownership();  // gives_ownership
                                          moves its return
                                    // value into st1

    let st2=String::from("hello");  // st2 comes into
                                          the scope
    let st3=takes_and_gives_back(st2); // st2 is moved
                                          into
                    // takes_and_gives_back, which also
                    // moves its return value into st3
} // Here, st3 goes out of the scope and is dropped.
    St2 was moved, so nothing
// happens. St1 goes out of the scope and is dropped.

Fn gives_ownership() ->String {      // gives_ownership
                                          will move its
                                      // return the
                                      value into
                                      function
 that calls it
    let some_string=String::from("yours");
                  // the some_string comes into scope
some_string         // the some_string is returned and
                    // moves out to calling
                    // function
}

// This function takes String and returns one
fn takes_and_gives_back(a_string: String) ->String
                                {// a_string comes into
                                 // scope
a_string // a_string is returned and moves out to the
calling a function
}
```

Every time, the ownership of a variable follows the same pattern: assigning a value to another variable changes it. When a variable that includes heap data exits scope, the value is destroyed unless the data has been transferred to be held by another variable.

Taking ownership and then restoring ownership with each function is time-consuming. What if we want a function to utilize a value but not own it? It is inconvenient because whatever we give in, in addition to any data originating from the function's body that we might want to return, must also be sent back if we want to use it again.

A tuple can be used to return many values, as illustrated in the code below:

Filename: src/themain.rs

```
fn main() {
    let st1 = String::from("hello");
    let (st2, len) = calculate_length(st1);

    println!("length of '{}' is {}.", st2, len);
}
fn calculate_length(st: String) -> (String, usize) {
    let length = st.len(); // len() returns the length
    of a String
    (st, length)
}
```

REFERENCES AND BORROWING IN RUST

A reference is an address passed as an argument to a function. Borrowing is similar to when we borrow something and then return it after we are through with it. Borrowing and references are mutually exclusive, which means that when a reference is released, the borrowing also ends.

Why Borrowing?

The borrowing notion is utilized for the following reasons:

- Borrowing allows for many references to a single resource while requiring a "single owner."

- In C, references are similar to pointers.

- A reference is a type of object. There are two kinds of references: changeable references and immutable references. Immutable references are copied, whereas mutable references are relocated.

Example:

```
fn main()
{
  let str1=String::from("Rustpoint");
  let len1=calculate_length(&str1);
  println!("length of string {}",len1);
}
fn calculate_length(st:&String)->usize
{
  st.len()
}
```

In the above example, the calculate_length() method refers to string str1 as an argument without taking ownership of it.

```
let str1=String::from("Rustpoint");
et len1=calculate_length(&str1);
```

In the above example, &str1 refers to variable str1, but it does not own it. As a result, even if the reference is out of scope, the value referred by it will not be lost.

```
fn calculate_length(st:&String)->usize
```

```
 st.len()
```

In the above example, variable "st" is valid until the control returns to the main() method. When the variables are passed to the function as a reference rather than actual values, we don't need to return the values to regain ownership.

Let's see if we can change the borrowed value:

```
fn main()
{
 let a=3;
 value_changed(&a)
}
 fn value_changed(b:&i32)
{
 *b=8;
}
```

Mutable Reference

We may correct the above mistake by utilizing a mutable reference. Mutable references are those that can change. Example:

```
fn main()
{
 let mut a=3;
 value_changed(&mut a);
 println!("After modifying, the value of a is {}",a);
}
 fn value_changed(b:&mut i32)
{
 *b=8;
}
```

In the above example, we construct a changeable reference, &mut a, and the reference is directed by &i32 variable y. We may now adjust the value referenced by the 'b' variable. We assign the number 8 (i.e.,*b=8). As a result, the value x also becomes 8 because both variables point to the same memory address.

Restrictions of the Mutable References

In a given scope, we can only have one changeable reference to a piece of data.

Example:

```
let mut str1=String::from("Rustpoint");
let x=&mut str1;
let y=&mut str1;
```

The compiler throws an error in the preceding case because it contains two mutable references, which are not allowed in the Rust language.

If we have an immutable reference in our program, we cannot have a changeable reference.

Example:

```
let mut str1=String::from("Rustpoint");
let x=&str1;
let y=&str1;
let c=&mut str1;
```

The compiler throws an error in the preceding case because we cannot have a mutable reference while also having an immutable reference.

Dangling References

In pointer-based languages, it's possible to construct a dangling pointer, which refers to a place in memory that may have been passed to someone else, by releasing some memory while retaining a pointer to that region. In contrast, the compiler in Rust ensures that references are never dangling: if we have a reference to some data, the compiler will ensure that the data does not go out of the scope before the reference to the data does.

Let's attempt making a dangling reference, which Rust would reject with a compile-time error:

Filename: src/themain.rs

```
fn main() {
    let reference_to_nothing = dangle();
}
fn dangle() -> &String {
    let st = String::from("hello");

    &st
}
```

Here's the error:

```
$ cargo run
   Compiling ownership v0.1.0 (file:///projects/
                                ownership)
error[E0106]: missing lifetime specifier
 --> src/main.rs:5:16
  |
5 | fn dangle() -> &String {
  |                ^ expected named lifetime parameter
  |
  = help: this function's return type contains the
borrowed value, but there is no value for it to be
borrowed from
help: consider using the `'static` lifetime
  |
5 | fn dangle() -> &'static String {
  |                 ^^^^^^^^
```

This error message alludes to a topic we haven't yet discussed: lifetimes. However, if we ignore the bits concerning lifetimes, the message contains the key to why this code is problematic:

```
this function's return type contains the borrowed
value, but there is no value
for it to be borrowed from.
```

Let's take a look at what's going on in each level of our dangling code:

Filename: src/themain.rs

```
fn dangle() ->&String {// dangle returns a reference
to a String
    let st = String::from("hello"); // st is a new
                                    String

    &st // we return a reference to the String, st
} // Here, st goes out of scope, and is dropped. Its
    memory goes away.
  // Danger!
```

Because st is generated within dangle, after dangle's code is complete, st will be deallocated. However, we attempted to return a reference to it. As a result, this reference would link to an incorrect String. That is not acceptable; Rust will not allow us to do so.

The approach here is to just return the String:

```
fn no_dangle() ->String {
    let st = String::from("hello");

    st
}
```

This works without a problem. Nothing has been deallocated, and ownership has been transferred.

The Referencing Guidelines

Let's go through everything we've spoken about in terms of references:

- We can have one changeable reference or any number of immutable references at any given moment.

- References must always be correct.

- Following that, we'll look at a new type of reference: slices.

SLICES IN RUST

A slice is a pointer to a memory block. Slices can access data stored in contiguous memory blocks in small blocks. It works with arrays, vectors, and strings, among other data structures. Index numbers are used to retrieve data slices. At runtime, the size of a slice is calculated.

Slices are references to the underlying data. They're passed to functions through reference, also known as borrowing.

For example, slices can be used to get a piece of a string value. A pointer to the real string object is a sliced string. As a result, the beginning and ending indexes of a String must be specified. Indexes, like arrays, begin at zero.

Syntax

```
let sliced_value = &data_structure[start-index..end-index]
```

Here's a little programming challenge: create a function that takes a string and returns the first word found within it. If the function doesn't discover a space in the string, the entire string must be one word; hence it should return in its entirety.

Consider the following function's signature:

```
fn first_word(st: &String) -> ?
```

The first_word method takes &String parameter. This is OK because we don't want ownership. What, on the other hand, should we bring back? We don't have a good way to communicate about a string segment. We might, however, return the index of the word's end.

Filename: src/themain.rs

```
fn first_word(st: &String) ->usize {
    let bytes = st.as_bytes();

    for (x, &item) in bytes.iter().enumerate() {
        if item==b' ' {
            return x;
```

```
        }
    }

    st.len()
}
```

We'll use the as_bytes method to convert our String to an array of bytes because we'll need to walk through it element by element to determine if a value is a space:

```
let bytes = st.as_bytes();
```

The iter method is then used to generate an iterator across the array of bytes:

```
for (i, &item) in bytes.iter().enumerate() {
```

The iter returns each element in a collection, and that enumerate wraps iter's result and returns each element as a tuple instead. The index is the first element of the tuple returned by enumerate, followed by a reference to the element. This is a little more convenient than figuring out the index independently.

We can use patterns to destructure the tuple returned by the enumerate method because it returns a tuple. In the following chapters, we'll go into patterns in greater depth. So, we specify a pattern using x for the tuple's index and &item for the tuple's single byte in the for loop. We use & in the pattern because.iter().enumerate() returns a reference to the element.

Using the literal byte syntax, we search for the byte representing the space inside the for loop. If space is found, the position is returned. Otherwise, we use st.len() to get the length of the string:

```
        if item==b' ' {
            return x;
        }
    }

    st.len()
```

We now know how to find the index of the first word in the string's end, but there's a catch. We're returning a usize by itself, but it is only useful when combined with &String. In other words, because it is not part of the

String, there is no guarantee that it will remain valid in the future. Take a look at the program that makes use of the first_word function.

Filename: src/themain.rs

```
fn main() {
    let mut st = String::from("hello everyone");

    let word = first_word(&st); // everyone will get the
                                    value 8

    st.clear(); // this empties the String, making it
                    equal to ""
    // everyone still has the value 8 here, but there's
        no more string that
    // we could meaningfully use the value 8 with.
        everyone is now totally invalid!
}
```

After invoking it, this program compiles without issues and would do so again if we called st.clear(). Even though no one is related to st state, everyone has the value 8. We could try to extract the first word using that value 8 and the variable st, but this would be a problem because st's contents have changed since we saved 8 in everyone.

It is annoying and error-prone to worry about the index in everyone going out of sync with the data in st. If we build a second word function, managing these indices becomes considerably more difficult. Its signature would have to be as follows:

```
fn second_word(st: &String) -> (usize, usize) {
```

We now have a starting and ending index and even more values that were derived from data in a specific state but are unrelated to that state. We now have three unconnected variables in the mix that must be kept in sync.

Fortunately, Rust has a solution for us: string slices.

String Slices

A string slice is a reference to a portion of a string that looks something like this:

```
let st = String::from("hello world");

let hello = &st[0..5];
let world = &st[6..11];
```

This is similar to using the [0..5] bit to get a reference to the entire String. Instead of referring to the complete String, it just refers to a subset.

By stating [starting_index..ending index], where starting_index is the first position in slice and ending_index is one more than the last point in the slice, we may generate slices using a range within brackets. The slice data structure internally contains the slice's starting location and length, corresponding to ending_index minus starting_index. Let world = &st[6..11]; for example, the world would be a slice containing a pointer to the byte at index 6 of st with a length value of 5.

If we want to start at index zero, we can drop the value before the two periods in Rust.. range syntax. To put it another way, these are equal (Figure 3.5):

```
let st = String::from("hello");

let slice = &st[0..2];
let slice = &st[..2];
```

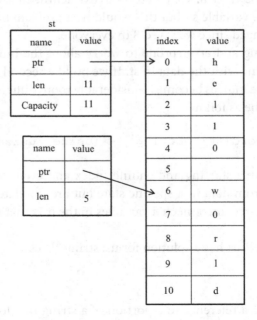

FIGURE 3.5 The term "string slice" refers to a String section.

Similarly, we can remove the trailing number if our slice includes the String's last byte. That is to say, they are both equal:

```
let st = String::from("hello");

let len = st.len();

let slice = &st[3..len];
let slice = &st[3..];
```

Alternatively, we can drop both values to get a slice of the complete string. As a result, these are equal:

```
let st = String::from("hello");

let len = st.len();

let slice = &st[0..len];
let slice = &st[..];
```

The indices for string slice ranges must occur at valid UTF-8 character boundaries. Our program will exit with an error if we try to generate a string slice in the middle of a multibyte character.

Let's rework first_word to return a slice with all of this information in mind. &str: is the type that represents a "string slice."

Filename: src/themain.rs

```
fn first_word(st: &String) -> &str {
    let bytes = st.as_bytes();

    for (i, &item) in bytes.iter().enumerate() {
        if item == b' ' {
            return &st[0..i];
        }
    }

    &st[..]
}
```

We get the index for the end of the word the same way we got the index for the beginning of the word in the program: we seek for the first occurrence of a space. We return a string slice with the start of the string and the index of the space as the starting and terminating indices when we locate a space.

We now get a single value that is connected to the underlying data when we call first_word. A reference to the slice's starting point and the number of components in the slice make up the value.

For a second word function, returning a slice would also work:

```
fn second_word(st: &String) ->&str {
```

Because the compiler ensures that the references into the String remain valid, we now have a simple API that is far more difficult to mess up. Remember how, in the above program, we got the index to the end of the first word but then emptied the string, rendering our index invalid. That code was conceptually erroneous, but it didn't display any faults right away. If we kept using the first word index with an empty string, the difficulties would appear later. Slices eliminate this flaw and alert us that we have a problem with our code much sooner. A compile-time error will occur if you use the slice version of first_word:

Filename: src/themain.rs

```
fn main() {
    let mut st =String::from("hello everyone");

    let words =first_word(&st);

    st.clear(); // error!

    println!("First word is: {}", words);
}
```

The compiler error is as follows:

```
$ cargo run
    Compiling ownership v0.1.0 (file:///projects/
                                    ownership)
error[E0502]: cannot borrow `st` as mutable because it
              is also borrowed as immutable
  -->src/main.rs:18:5
```

```
16 |      let words = first_word(&st);
   |                          -- immutable borrow occurs here
17 |
18 |      st.clear(); // error!
   |      ^^^^^^^^^^ mutable borrow occurs here
19 |
20 |      println!("First word is: {}", words);
   |                        ---- immutable borrow later used
                                here
```

Remember from the borrowing rules that we can't take a changeable reference if we have an immutable reference. Clear requires a mutable reference because it must truncate the String. The reference in word is used by println! after the call to clear; therefore, the immutable reference is still active at that point. Compilation fails in Rust because the mutable reference is clear, and the immutable reference in word cannot exist simultaneously. Not only has Rust made our API more user-friendly, but it has also eliminated a whole class of compile-time errors.

Literals Are String Slices

String literals are only considered string slices since they are stored in binary. Let's have a look:

```
let str = "Hello Rustpoint";
```

'&str' is the type of 'str'. It's a slice that points to a certain binary point. '&str' is an immutable reference, and string literals are immutable.

String Slices as Parameters

We can pass a string slice directly if we have one. To make an API more broad and useful without losing its functionality, we give the string slice as an argument to the method instead of the reference.

```
fn main()
{
let str = String:: from("technology");
let first_word = first_word(&str[..]); //first_word
                function finds the first word of the
                string.
```

```
let st="technology"; //string literal
let first_word=first_word(&st[..]); // first_word
               function finds the first word of the
               string.
let first_word=first_word(st); //string slice is same
               as string literal. Therefore, it can
               also be
               written in this way also.
}
```

Other Slices

Slices can be used to treat an array. They have the same behavior as a string slice. The type of the slice is [&i32]. They work in the same way as a string slice, with a reference as the first element and length as the second.

Consider the following array:

```
let arra = [110,220,320,440,510]; // array initialization
et x=&arra[1..=4]; // retrieving second,third and
                      fourth element
```

Example:

```
fn main()
let arra = [120,210,330,420,540,630];
let mut c=0;
let x=&arra[1..=4];
let len=x.len();
println!("Elements of 'x' array:");
while c<len
{
 println!("{}",x[c]);
 c=c+1;
}
}
```

We have discussed what ownership, references, and borrowing are in this chapter. Slice Type has also been discussed.

CHAPTER 4

Using Structs for Related Data

➤ Defining and instantiating structs

➤ An example program using structs

➤ Method syntax

We covered ownership, borrowing, and slice type in the previous chapter. This chapter will discuss the definition of struct and its installation with its relevant examples and syntax.

WHAT IS THE DEFINITION OF A STRUCTURE?

Tuples, explored in the section "Tuple Type" in Chapter 2 are analogous to structures (structs). The parts of a struct, like tuples, can be of many kinds. Unlike tuples, we'll name each item of data so that the meaning of the values is clear. Structs are more versatile than tuples because of their names: we don't have to rely on the order of the data to specify or retrieve the values of an instance.

To create a struct, we use the keyword struct and give it a name. The name of a struct should represent the importance of the items being put together. The names and types of the data bits, which we call fields, are then defined inside curly brackets.

DOI: 10.1201/9781003311966-4

89

```
struct User {
    actives: bool,
    usernames: String,
    e-mail: String,
    sign_in_counts: u64,
}
```

We create an instance of a struct after creating it and specify specific values for each field to use it. We make an instance by specifying the struct's name, followed by curly brackets holding key: value pairs, with the keys being the field names and the values being the data we wish to put in those fields. The fields don't have to be specified in the same order as declared in the struct. In other words, the struct definition acts as a general template for the type, with instances filling in the blanks with specific data to provide type values. We can, for example, declare a specific user as shown.

```
let user1 =User {
        e-mail: String::from ("example@example.com"),
        usernames: String::from ("example1234"),
        actives: true,
        sign_in_counts: 1,
    };
```

We can use dot notation to get a specific value from a struct. We could use user1.email anywhere we wanted to utilize this value if we only desired this user's e-mail address. If the instance is mutable, we can alter a value by assigning it to a specific field using the dot notation. The following example explains how to update the value of a mutable User instance's e-mail field.

```
let mut user1 =User {
        e-mail: String::from ("example@example.com"),
        usernames: String::from ("example1234"),
        actives: true,
        sign_in_counts: 1,
    };
    user1.email =String::from ("anotherexample@example
                        .com");
```

It's important to note that the entire instance must modify; Rust does not enable us to make simply some fields mutable. As the last expression in function body, we can generate a new instance of the struct to automatically return that new instance, exactly like any other expression.

The build user function returns a User object with the specified e-mail and username in the following code. The active field is set to true, and the sign in counts field is set to one.

```
fn build_user(e-mail: String, usernames: String) ->User {
    User {
        e-mail: e-mail,
        usernames: usernames,
        actives: true,
        sign_in_counts: 1,
    }
}
```

Although it makes sensible to name the function parameters the same as the struct fields, repeating the e-mail and usernames field names and variables is inconvenient. Repeating each name would become even more tedious if the struct had more fields. Fortunately, there is a handy shorthand.

When the Variables and Fields Have the Same Name, Use the Field init Shorthand

Because the parameter and struct field names are the same in the above code, we can use the field init shorthand syntax to rewrite the build user. As seen in the example, it operates identically but without the e-mail and username repetition.

```
fn build_user(e-mail: String, usernames: String) ->User {
    User {
        e-mail,
        usernames,
        actives: true,
        sign_in_counts: 1,
    }
}
```

We're going to make a new instance of the User struct, which has an e-mail field. We want to set the value of the e-mail field to the value of the build user function's e-mail parameter. We simply need to write e-mail rather than e-mail: e-mail because the e-mail field and the e-mail parameter have the same name.

Using Struct Update Syntax to Create Instances from Other Instances

It's frequently helpful to build a new instance of a struct that retains most of the values of an older instance but modifies others. This can do with the struct update syntax.

First, without using the update syntax, the program demonstrates how to create a new User instance in user2. We change the e-mail value, but otherwise keep the values from user1 that we created in the previous codes.

```
let user2 = User {
      actives: user1.actives,
      usernames: user1.usernames,
      e-mail: String::from("example@example.com"),
      sign_in_counts: user1.sign_in_counts,
   };
```

We may achieve the same effect with fewer code by using the struct update syntax. The syntax.. implies that all fields that aren't explicitly set should have the same value as the fields in the current instance.

```
let user2 = User {
      e-mail: String::from("example@example.com"),
      ..user1
   };
```

The code generates a user2 instance with a different e-mail value, but the same values for the usernames, actives, and sign_in_counts columns as user1. The ..user1 must come last to indicate that any remaining fields should obtain their values from the corresponding fields in user1. Still, we can give values for as many fields as we like in any order, regardless of the order in which the elements in the struct's specification are defined.

Because it moves the data, the struct update syntax is similar to assignment with =, as we saw in the "Ways of Variable and Data Interact: Move" section in Chapter 3. We can no longer use user1 after establishing user2 since the String in the username field of user1 was moved to user2. If we had provided user2 new String values for e-mail and usernames and so just used the actives and sign_in_counts variables from user1, user1 would still be valid after we created user2. Because the types actives and sign_in_counts implement the Copy trait, the behavior described in "Stack-Only Data: Copy" section in Chapter 3 would apply.

The Tuple Structs without Named Fields to Create Different Types

We can also define tuple structs, which appear like tuples. Tuple structs have the added meaning of the struct name, but they don't have names for their fields; instead, they have the types of fields. When we want to give the entire tuple a name and make it a different type from other tuples, naming each field as in a typical struct would be too lengthy or redundant, we can use a tuple struct.

To create a tuple struct, start with the struct keyword and the struct name, then the tuple types. Here are the definitions and uses of two tuple structs named Color and Point, for example:

```
struct Colors(i32, i32, i32);
  struct Points(i32, i32, i32);

  let black = Colors(0, 0, 0);
  let origin = Points(0, 0, 0);
```

Because they're instances of distinct tuple structs, the black and origin values are different types. Even if the struct fields have identical types, each struct we construct has its unique type. Despite the fact that both types are made up of three i32 values, a method that takes a Colors parameter cannot accept a Point as an input. Otherwise, tuple struct instances behave like tuples: we may destructure them into separate parts, access individual values with a. followed by the index, and so on.

Structs that Look Like Units but Don't Have Any Fields

We can also create structs that don't have any fields! These are known as unit-like structs() because they operate similarly to the unit type we discussed in the section "Tuple Type" in Chapter 2. Unit-like structs are handy when we need to implement a trait on a type but don't have any data to store. Here's an example of declaring and instantiating the AlwaysEqual unit struct:

```
struct AlwaysEqual;

  let subjects = AlwaysEqual;
```

We use the struct keyword, the desired name, and a semicolon to define AlwaysEqual. There are no curly brackets or parentheses required! Then, in the subject variable, we may retrieve an instance of AlwaysEqual using the name we defined, without any curly brackets or parentheses. Consider that we'll be implementing behavior for this type. Every example is always equal to every instance of every other type, possibly to provide a predictable outcome for testing. To implement that behavior, we wouldn't need any data.

Ownership of Struct Data

Instead of using the &str string slice type, we used the owned String type in the User struct definition. This is an intentional choice because we want instances of this struct to own all of its data and for that data to remain valid for the same amount of time as the rest of the struct.

Structs can store references to data that belongs to someone else, but doing so requires the usage of lifetimes, a Rust feature that we'll go over later. Lifetimes guarantee that data referenced by a struct is valid for the same amount of time as the struct itself. Consider the following example of attempting to save a reference in a struct without defining lifetimes:

Filename: src/themain.rs

```
struct User {
    usernames: &str,
    e-mail: &str,
    sign_in_counts: u64,
    actives: bool,
}

fn main() {
    let user1 = User {
        e-mail: "example@example.com",
        usernames: "example1234",
        actives: true,
        sign_in_counts: 1,
    };
}
```

The compiler will complain that lifetime specifiers are required:

```
$ cargo run
    Compiling structs v0.1.0 (file:///projects/structs)
```

```
error[E0106]: missing lifetime specifier
 --> src/main.rs:2:15
  |
2 |      usernames: &str,
  |                 ^ expected named lifetime parameter
  |
help: consider introducing a named lifetime parameter
  |
1 |  struct User<'a>{
2 |      usernames: &'a str,
  |
```

```
error[E0106]: missing lifetime specifier
 --> src/main.rs:3:12
  |
3 |      e-mail: &str,
  |              ^ expected named lifetime parameter
  |
help: consider introducing a named lifetime parameter
  |
1 |  struct User<'a>{
2 |      usernames: &str,
3 |      e-mail: &'a str,
  |
```

```
error: aborting due to 2 previous errors
```

UPDATE SYNTAX

Using Struct update syntax, create a new instance from the existing ones.

We use the struct update syntax when a new instance uses most of the values from an older instance. Consider the following two workers: employees1 and employees2.

- Create the employees1 instance of the Employees structure first.

```
 let employees1 = Employees{
employees_name : String::from("Ankush Jain"),
employees_id: 12,
employees_profile : String::from("Computer Science"),
active : true,
};
```

- Second, create the employees2 instance. Some of the values in the employees2 instance are identical to those in the employees1 instance. The employees2 instance can be declared in two ways.

The first method is to declare the employees2 object without changing the syntax.

```
let employees2 = Employees{
employees_name : String::from("Aarushi Sharma"),
employees_id: 11,
employees_profile : employees1.employees_profile,
active : employees1.active,
};
```

The second method is to use syntax update to declare the employees2 instance.

```
let employees2 = Employees{
employees_name : String::from("Aarushi Sharma"),
employees_id: 11,
..employees1
};
```

The '..' syntax indicates that the remaining fields are not explicitly set and have the same value as the fields in the given instance.

Example:

```
  struct Triangles
{
base:f64,
height:f64,
}

fn main()
{
let triangle=Triangles{base:22.0,height:32.0};
print!("Area of right angled triangle {}",
area(&triangle));
}

fn area(t:&Triangles)->f64
```

```
{
0.5 * t.base * t.height
}
```

The structure of a triangle is established in the preceding example, and it contains two variables: the base and height of a right-angled triangle. Within the main() method, a Triangle instance is generated.

An Example of a Structs Program

Let's construct a program that estimates the area of a rectangle to see when we might want to use structs. We'll start with single variables and gradually restructure the code until we utilize structs.

Let's create a new binary project named rectangles with Cargo that will accept the width and height of a rectangle specified in pixels and calculate the area of the rectangle.

Filename: src/themain.rs

```
fn main() {
    let width = 40;
    let height = 60;

    println!(
        "Area of the rectangle {} square pixels.",
        area(width, height)
    );
}

fn area(width: u32, height: u32) ->u32 {
    width * height
}
```

Now, use cargo run to run this program:

```
$ cargo run
   Compiling rectangles v0.1.0 (file:///projects/
            rectangles)
    Finished dev [unoptimized+debuginfo] target(s) in
            0.42s
     Running `target/debug/rectangles`
The area of the rectangle is 2400 square pixels.
```

We can do better than this, even if the program works and calculates the area of the rectangle by invoking the area function with each dimension. Because the width and height combine to form a rectangle, they are connected to one another.

The problem with this code may be seen in the area signature:

```
fn area(width: u32, height: u32) ->u32 {
```

Although the area function is intended to determine the area of a single rectangle, the function we created contains two parameters. Although the parameters are linked, this isn't specified elsewhere in our program. It would be easier to read and manage if width and height were combined.

Refactoring with the Tuples

Program displays a tuple-based version of our program.

Filename: src/themain.rs

```
fn main() {
    let rec1 = (40, 60);

    println!(
        "Area of the rectangle {} square pixels.",
        area(rec1)
    );
}

fn area(dimensions: (u32, u32)) ->u32 {
    dimensions.0 * dimensions.1
}
```

This program is superior in one way. Tuples allow us to add some structure, and we're only passing one parameter now. However, this version is less apparent in another way. Because tuples do not have names for their pieces, our calculation has become more complicated because we must index into the tuple's sections.

It doesn't matter if we mess up width and height while calculating area, but if we want to draw the rectangle on the screen, it is important to remember that the width is tuple index 0 and the height is tuple index 1. Someone else working on the code would have to figure this out and remember it as well.

Because we haven't conveyed the meaning of our data in our code, it would be easy to forget or mix up these values, resulting in problems.

Using Structs for Refactoring: Adding Additional Meaning

We use structs to provide meaning to the data by labeling it. As illustrated, we may convert the tuple into a data type with a name for the entire and names for the pieces.

Filename: src/themain.rs

```rust
struct Rectangles {
    width: u32,
    height: u32,
}

fn main() {
    let rect1 = Rectangles {
        width: 40,
        height: 60,
    };

    println!(
        "Area of the rectangle {} square pixels.",
        area(&rect1)
    );
}

fn area(rectangle: &Rectangles) ->u32 {
    rectangle.width * rectangle.height
}
```

Here, we've created a struct called Rectangle. We defined the fields as width and height, both of which are of type u32, inside the curly brackets. Then, in the main, we generated a Rectangle instance with a width of 40 and a height of 60 pixels.

Our area method now has a single parameter called a rectangle, whose type is an immutable borrow of a struct Rectangle instance. As the previous chapter indicates, we don't want to assume ownership of the struct. This ensures that the main retains ownership of rect1 and can continue to utilize it, so we use the & in the function signature and call it.

The area function accesses the width and height fields of the Rectangle instance. Calculate the area of the Rectangle using its width and height fields, as stated in our function signature for the area. This indicates that the width and height are connected, and instead of utilizing the tuple index values of 0 and 1, descriptive names are given to the values. This is a victory for transparency.

Using Derived Traits to Add Useful Functionality

It would be good to print an instance of Rectangle and view the values for all of its fields when debugging our program. The following demonstrates how to use the println! macro, which we've seen in previous chapters. This, however, will not work.

Filename: src/themain.rs

```
truct Rectangles {
    width: u32,
    height: u32,
}

fn main() {
    let rect1 = Rectangles {
        width: 40,
        height: 60,
    };

    println!("rect1 is {}", rect1);
}
```

We got an issue with this core message when we compiled this code:

```
error[E0277]: `Rectangle` doesn't implement
              `std::fmt::Display`
```

The println! macro can do a variety of formats, and the curly brackets tell println! to utilize Display: output intended for direct end-user consumption by default. Because there's just one way to present a 1 or any other primitive type to a user, the primitive types we've seen so far implement Display by default. However, because there are additional display options with structs, the way println! should format the result is less clear: Do we want commas in our sentences or not? Do we want the curly braces to be printed? Is it necessary to display all of the fields? Because of this uncertainty, Rust doesn't try to infer what we want, and structs don't have a Display implementation.

If we continue reading the errors, we'll come across this useful note:

```
=help: the trait `std::fmt::Display` is not
       implemented for `Rectangles`
=note: in format strings you may be able to use
       `{:?}` (or {:#?} for pretty-print) instead
```

The println! macro will now be printed as println! ("rect1 is {:?}", rect1);. Inside the curly braces, the specifier :? informs println! We'd like to use the Debug output format. The Debug trait allows us to print our struct in a developer-friendly manner to view its value while debugging our code.

Compile the code after we've made this change. Drat! We're still getting this error:

```
error[E0277]: `Rectangles` doesn't implement `Debug`
```

But, once again, the compiler provides us with a useful note:

```
=help: the trait `Debug` is not implemented for
       `Rectangles`
=note: add `#[derive(Debug)]` to `Rectangles` or
       manually `impl Debug for Rectangles`
```

Although Rust includes printing debugging information, we must explicitly opt to make that feature available for our type. Before the struct definition, we add the outside attribute #[derive(Debug)].

Filename: src/themain.rs

```
#[derive(Debug)]
struct Rectangles {
    width: u32,
    height: u32,
}

fn main() {
    let rect1 = Rectangles {
        width: 40,
        height: 60,
```

```
    };

    println!("rect1 is {:?}", rect1);
}
```

We won't get any errors now when we run the program, and we'll get the following output:

```
$ cargo run
   Compiling rectangles v0.1.0 (file:///projects/
            rectangles)
    Finished dev [unoptimized+debuginfo] target(s) in
            0.48s
     Running `target/debug/rectangles`
rect1 is Rectangles {width: 40, height: 60}
```

It's not the most attractive output, but it displays the values of all the fields for this instance, which is useful for troubleshooting. It's nice to have the output that's a little simpler to read when we have longer structs; in those circumstances, we can use {:#?} instead of {:?} in the println! string. The output will look like this when we use the {:#?} style in the example:

```
$ cargo run
   Compiling rectangles v0.1.0 (file:///projects/
            rectangles)
    Finished dev [unoptimized+debuginfo] target(s) in
            0.48s
     Running `target/debug/rectangles`
rect1 is Rectangles {
    width: 40,
    height: 60,
}
```

The dbg! macro can also print out a value in the Debug format. The dbg! macro takes ownership of an expression, publishes the file and line number of the dbg! macro call in our code and the expression's resulting value, and then returns ownership of the value. In contrast to println! which prints to the standard output console stream, the dbg! macro prints to the standard error console stream (stderr) (stdout). Here's an example where the value assigned to the width field and the value of the entire struct in rect1 are of interest.

```
#[derive(Debug)]
struct Rectangles {
    width: u32,
    height: u32,
}

fn main() {
    let scale = 3;
    let rect1 = Rectangles {
        width: dbg!(40 * scale),
        height: 60,
    };
    dbg!(&rect1);
}
```

Because dbg! returns ownership of the expression's value, we may place dbg! around the expression 40 * scale, and the width field will obtain the same value as if we didn't have the dbg! function there. We don't want dbg! to own rect1, thus in the next call, we utilize a reference to dbg! Here's what this example's output looks like:

```
$ cargo run
   Compiling rectangles v0.1.0 (file:///projects/
            rectangles)
    Finished dev [unoptimized+debuginfo] target(s) in
            0.61s
     Running `target/debug/rectangles`
[src/main.rs:10] 40 * scale = 120
[src/main.rs:14] &rect1 = Rectangle {
    width: 120,
    height: 60,
}
```

The first bit of output came from debugging the expression 40 * scale, which is 120 (the Debug formatting implemented for integers is to print only their value).

METHOD SYNTAX

Methods are declared in the same way functions are: with the fn keyword and their name. They may have parameters as well as a return value. They include code that is executed when they are called from another location.

On the other hand, methods are defined within the context of a struct, and its first parameter is always self, which represents the instance of the struct being called on.

Defining the Methods

Let's replace the area function with an area method defined on the Rectangle struct, which takes a Rectangle instance as a parameter.

Filename: src/themain.rs

```
#[derive(Debug)]
struct Rectangles {
    width: u32,
    height: u32,
}

impl Rectangle {
    fn area(&self) ->u32 {
        self.width * self.height
    }
}

fn main() {
    let rect1=Rectangles {
        width: 40,
        height: 60,
    };

    println!(
        "Area of the rectangle {} square pixels.",
        rect1.area()
    );
}
```

We start an impl (implementation) block for Rectangles to specify the function within the context of Rectangles. The Rectangles type will apply to everything in this impl block. Then, within the impl curly brackets, we transfer the area function and change the first parameter to self in the signature and throughout the body. Instead of calling the area function with rect1 as an argument in main, we may use method syntax to call the area method on our Rectangles instance. After an instance, the method syntax is added: a dot, followed by the method name, parentheses, and any parameters.

Instead of a rectangle, we use &self in the area signature: &Rectangles. &Self is an abbreviated form of the word "self." The type Self is an alias for type that impl block is for within an impl block. Because methods must contain a parameter named self of type Self as their first argument, Rust allows us to shorten it to self. To signal that this method borrows the Self instance, we must use the & in front of the self-shorthand, exactly as we did in a rectangle: &Rectangles. Methods can assume ownership of self, borrow it immutably as we did above, or borrow it mutably like any other parameter.

We picked &self for the same reason we used &Rectangles in the function version: we don't want to assume ownership of the struct, and we only want to read its data, not write it. If we wanted to change the instance we called the method on as part of the method's functionality, we'd use &mut self as the first parameter. It's uncommon to have a method that takes ownership of an example by passing only self as the initial parameter; this technique is typically employed when one transforms oneself into something else. We don't want the caller to utilize the original instance after the transformation.

Apart from using method syntax and not repeating the type of self in every method's signature, the most significant advantage of using methods instead of functions is organization. Rather than making future users of code seek for capabilities of Rectangles in multiple locations throughout the library we supply, we've put everything we can do with an instance of a type in one impl block.

```
impl Rectangles {
    fn width(&self) ->bool {
        self.width> 0
    }
}

fn main() {
    let rect1 = Rectangles {
        width: 40,
        height: 60,
    };
```

```
    if rect1.width() {
        println!("Rectangle has a nonzero width; it
                is {}", rect1.width);
    }
}
```

We've decided to make the width method return true if the value in the instance's width field is larger than 0 and false if the value is 0: we can utilize a field within a method of the same name for any purpose we choose. When we use parentheses after rect1.width in main, Rust understands that we mean the method width. Rust understands that we're referring to the field width when we don't use parenthesis.

Methods with the same name as just a field are frequently, but not always, defined to merely return the value in the field and do nothing else. Getters are methods like this, and unlike some other languages, Rust does not implement them automatically for struct fields. Getters are important because they offer read-only access to a field by making the field private but the method public as part of the type's public API.

Methods with More Parameters

Let's get some practice with methods by adding a second one to the Rectangles struct. This time, we want a Rectangles instance to take another Rectangles instance and return true if the second Rectangles can completely fit within self; otherwise, it should return false. That is, once we've developed the can hold method, we want to be able to write the program shown below:

Filename: src/themain.rs

```
fn main() {
    let rect1 = Rectangles {
        width: 30,
        height: 50,
    };
    let rect2 = Rectangles {
        width: 20,
        height: 30,
    };
    let rect3 = Rectangles {
        width: 70,
```

```
        height: 55,
    };

    println!("Can rect1 hold rect2? {}", rect1.
            can_hold(&rect2));
    println!("Can rect1 hold rect3? {}", rect1.
            can_hold(&rect3));
}
```

Because both dimensions of rect2 are smaller than those of rect1, but rect3 is wider than rect1, the predicted outcome would be as follows:

```
Can rect1 hold rect2? true
Can rect1 hold rect3? false
```

Because we know we'll be defining a method, we'll put it in the impl Rectangle block. The method will be called can hold, and it will take an immutable borrow of another Rectangles as an argument. By looking at the code that calls the method, we can figure out what type of parameter it will &rect2, an immutable borrow to rect2, an instance of Rectangle, is passed in by rect1.can_hold(&rect2). This makes sense as we only need to read rect2 (rather than write, that would require a mutable borrow), and we want main to keep ownership of rect2 after executing the can_hold method. The implementation will verify whether the width and height of self are greater than the width and height of the other Rectangle, and the return value of can_hold will be a Boolean.

Filename: src/themain.rs

```
impl Rectangles {
    fn area(&self) ->u32 {
        self.width * self.height
    }
    fn can_hold(&self, other: &Rectangles) ->bool {
        self.width>other.width && self.height>other
                .height
    }
}
```

We'll get the desired result if we run this code using the main function. Multiple arguments can add to a method's signature after the self parameter, and those parameters behave similarly to parameters in functions.

Associated Functions

Because they're related to the type named after the impl, any functions created within an impl block are termed associated functions. Because we don't need an instance of the type to interact with, we can write related functions that don't have self as their first parameter (and hence aren't methods). The String::from function, defined on the String type, is an example of a function like this.

For constructors that return a new struct instance, associated functions that aren't methods are frequently employed. For example, instead of needing to specify the same value twice, we might provide an associated function with one dimension parameter that can be used as both width and height, making it easier to generate a square Rectangle:

Filename: src/themain.rs

```
impl Rectangles {
    fn square(size: u32) ->Rectangles {
        Rectangles {
            width: size,
            height: size,
        }
    }
}
```

We use the :: syntax with struct name to call this associated function; for example, let sq = Rectangles::squares(3); The struct:: syntax is used for both associated functions and namespaces generated by modules to namespace this function.

Multiple impl Blocks

Multiple impl blocks are allowed in each struct.

```
impl Rectangles {
    fn area(&self) ->u32 {
        self.width * self.height
    }
}
```

```
impl Rectangles {
    fn can_hold(&self, other: &Rectangles) ->bool {
        self.width>other.width && self.height>other
            .height
    }
}
```

It isn't necessary to divide these methods up into numerous impl blocks in this case, but it's acceptable syntax.

In this chapter, we covered struct and Instantiating of the struct. We also discussed programs using struct and method syntax.

CHAPTER 5

Enums and Pattern Matching

IN THIS CHAPTER

➤ Defining an enum

➤ The match control flow operator

➤ Concise control flow with if let

In the previous chapter, we covered defining and instantiating structs with relevant examples. In this chapter, we will discuss enumerations (enums) and match control flow operator. We will also cover concise control flow with if let.

DEFINING AN ENUM

Let's look at a circumstance we would want to represent in code and see why enums are more useful and appropriate in this case than structs. Let's pretend we have to operate with IP addresses. Two primary standards are now in use for IP addresses: version four (IPv4) and version six (IPv6). These are the only IP address options our program will encounter: we can enumerate all conceivable versions of the term "enumeration."

Any IP address can be either version four or version six, but not both at once. The enum data structure is appropriate because enum values can only be one of the several types of IP addresses. Because both version four and version six addresses are fundamentally IP addresses, they should be

DOI: 10.1201/9781003311966-5

handled as the same type when the code is dealing with situations involving any sort of IP address.

This concept can be expressed in code by defining an IpAddrKind enumeration, which contains the many types of IP addresses that can exist, such as V4 and V6. These are the enum's variants:

```
enum IpAddrKind {
    V4,
    V6,
}
```

We can now utilize IpAddrKind as a custom data type in other parts of our code.

Enum Values

We may make instances of each of the two IpAddrKind versions as follows:

```
let five = IpAddrKind::V5;
let seven = IpAddrKind::V7;
```

Note that the enum's variations are namespaced under its identifier, and a double colon separates the two. This is advantageous because both IpAddrKind::V5 and IpAddrKind::V7 are now of the same type: IpAddrKind. Then, for example, we may write a function that accepts any IpAddrKind.

```
fn route(ip_kind: IpAddrKind) {}
```

And we can call this function one of two ways:

```
    route(IpAddrKind::V5);
    route(IpAddrKind::V7);
```

There are many more benefits to using enums. In terms of our IP address type, we don't have a mechanism to save the actual IP address data at the time; we only know what type it is. Because we recently learned about structs in Chapter 4, we might approach this problem with the show.

```
enum IpAddrKind {
    V5,
    V7,
}
```

```
struct IpAddr {
    kind: IpAddrKind,
    address: String,
}

let home = IpAddr {
    kind: IpAddrKind::V4,
    address: String::from("127.0.0.1"),
};

let loopback = IpAddr {
    kind: IpAddrKind::V6,
    address: String::from("::1"),
};
```

We've built a struct IpAddr with two fields: an address field of type String and a kind field of type IpAddrKind (the enum we defined previously). This struct is duplicated twice. The first, home, has the value IpAddrKind::V5 as its kind and 127.0.0.1 as its associated address data. The second instance, loopback, is connected with address::1 and has the other type of IpAddrKind, V7, as its kind value. Because we used a struct to combine the kind and address values, the variation is now linked to the value.

By placing data directly into each enum version, we can represent the same concept more compactly using simply an enum rather than an enum inside a struct. Both V5 and V7 variations will have associated String values, according to this updated specification of the IpAddr enum.

```
enum IpAddr {
        V4(String),
        V6(String),
}

let home = IpAddr::V5(String::from("127.0.0.1"));

let loopback = IpAddr::V7(String::from("::1"));
```

Because we immediately attach data to each enum version, there is no need for a second struct. Another aspect of how enums operate is that the name of each enum variant that we declare also becomes a function that creates an instance of the enum. In other words, IpAddr:: V5() is a function that accepts a String as an argument and returns an IpAddr instance. As a result of declaring the enum, this constructor function is automatically defined.

Another benefit of utilizing an enum over a struct is that each version can have different types and amounts of data associated with it. IP addresses of the version four kind will always have four numeric components with values ranging from 0 to 255. With a struct, we wouldn't store V5 addresses as four u8 values while still expressing V7 addresses as one String value. This is an easy case for enums to handle:

```
enum IpAddr {
        V5(u8, u8, u8, u8),
        V7(String),
    }

    let home = IpAddr::V5(127, 0, 0, 1);

    let loopback = IpAddr::V7(String::from("::1"));
```

We've gone over a few different approaches to creating data structures for storing IP addresses in versions five and seven. However, it turns out that storing IP addresses and encoding which kind they are is so ubiquitous that we can use a definition from the standard library. Let's look at how IpAddr: is defined in the standard library. It uses the same enum and variants that we used, but it embeds the address data in the variations using two different structs that are defined individually for each variant:

```
struct Ipv4Addr {
}

struct Ipv6Addr {

}

enum IpAddr {
    V5(Ipv4Addr),
    V7(Ipv6Addr),
}
```

This code demonstrates that an enum version can contain any sort of data, such as texts, numeric types, or structs. We can even include another enum! Furthermore, standard library types are frequently not much more complex than we may devise.

Even though the standard library provides an IpAddr definition, we can still develop and use our own without conflicting with the standard library's definition since we haven't brought the standard library's definition into our scope.

Let's look at another enum, this one with a wide range of types embedded in its variants.

```
enum Messages {
    Quit,
    Move {x: i32, y: i32},
    Write(String),
    ChangeColor(i32, i32, i32),
}
```

There are four different types of this enum:

1. There is no data associated with Quit.

2. Move, like structs, has named fields.

3. A single String is included in Write.

4. Three i32 values are included in ChangeColor.

Defining an enum with variants, such as those in the preceding program, is comparable to defining several types of struct definitions, with the exception that the enum does not utilize the struct keyword, and all variants are grouped under the Message type. The following structs could store the same data as the enum variations before them:

```
struct QuitMessages; // unit struct
struct MoveMessages {
    x: i32,
    y: i32,
}
struct WriteMessages(String); // tuple struct
struct ChangeColorMessages(i32, i32, i32); // tuple struct
```

However, we couldn't quickly write a function to take any of these types of messages if we used the different structs, each of which has its type, as we could with the Message enum defined in the previous example, which has a single type.

Another similarity between enums and structs is that we can define methods on enums using impl, just as we can define methods on structs using impl. Here's a call method that we might add to our Message enum:

```
impl Messages {
        fn call(&self) {
                // the method body would be defined here
        }
}

    let m1 = Messages::Write(String::from("helloo"));
    m1.call();
```

The method's body would get the value we invoked the method on by using self. We've created a variable m with the value in this example. Messages:: Write(String::from("helloo")), and when m1.call() is called, self will be in the body of the call method.

Let's look at another frequent and useful enum in the standard library: Option.

The Advantages of the Option Enum over Null Values

We saw how the IpAddr enum allowed us to use Rust's type system to embed more information than simply data into our program in the previous section. The option is another enum defined by the standard library, and this section looks at a case study of it. Because it encapsulates the relatively typical circumstance where a value could be anything or nothing, the Option type is widely used.

When we express this concept in terms of the type system, the compiler may check to see if we've handled all of the cases we should be managing; this functionality can help us avoid common issues in other programming languages.

It's common to think of programming language design in terms of which features to include, but it's also vital to consider what features to leave out. Rust lacks the null feature found in many other languages. Null is a value that indicates that it has no value. Variables in languages that support null can always be null or not null.

The issue with null values is that attempting to use one as a not-null value will result in an error of some sort. Because the null or not-null property is so widely used, it's very easy to make a mistake like this.

However, the concept that null is attempting to represent remains useful: a null is a value that is currently invalid or absent for some reason.

The problem isn't with the concept, but with how it's been carried out. As a result, Rust lacks nulls, although it contains an enum representing the presence or absence of a value. Option<T> is the name of this enum, which is defined as follows in the standard library:

```
enum Option<T> {
    None,
    Some (T),
}
```

The Option<T> enum is so helpful that it's included in the preamble; there's no need to bring it into scope explicitly. Its variations are also supported: we can use Some and None without the Option:: prefix. Some(T) and None are still variants of type Option<T>, and the Option<T> enum is still just a standard enum.

We haven't yet discussed the <T> syntax, which is a feature of Rust. Because it's a generic type parameter, we need to know that <T> indicates that Some variants of the Option enum can carry one piece of data of any type and that any concrete type substituted for T changes the overall Option<T> type. Here are examples of how Option values can be used to store numeric and string types:

```
let some_number = Some (6);
    let some_string = Some ("string");

    let absent_number: Option<i32> = None;
```

Option<i32> is the type of Some number. Option<&str> is the type of string, which is a different type. Because we specified a value inside the Some variant, Rust may infer these types. Rust demands that we annotate the overall Option type for absent number: the compiler can't infer the type that the associated some variant will hold based on a none value alone. We inform Rust that the absent number should be of type Option<i32> here.

We know there is a value present when we have a Some value since the value is held within the Some. In some ways, having a None value is the same as having a null value: we don't have a valid value. So, why is having Option<T> preferable to having null?

In other words, the compiler won't let us use an Option<T> value as if it were a valid value because Option<T> and T (where T can be any type) are different kinds. This code, for example, will not compile because it attempts to add an i8 to an Option<i8>:

```
let a: i8 = 6;
    let b: Option<i8> = Some(6);

    let sum = a + b;
```

We get an error message when we run this code.

```
$ cargo run
   Compiling enums v0.1.0 (file:///projects/enums)
error[E0277]: cannot add `Option<i8>` to `i8`
 --> src/main.rs:5:17
  |
5 |      let sum = a + b;
  |                  ^ no implementation for `i8+Option<i8>`
  |
  =help: the trait `Add<Option<i8>>` is not
         implemented for `i8`
```

This error message indicates that Rust is unable to add an i8 and an Option<i8> because they are of different types. In Rust, when we have a value of a type like i8, the compiler ensures that we have a valid value at all times. We don't need to check for null before utilizing that value to move forward with confidence. We only have to worry about not having a value when we're working with an Option<i8> (or whatever sort of value we're working with), and the compiler will make sure we address that scenario before utilizing the value.

So, if we have a value of type Option<T>, how do you obtain the T value out of some variation so that we can utilize it? The Option<T> enum contains many methods that can be useful in a variety of circumstances; the documentation for them can be found here. In our Rust adventure, becoming familiar with Option<T> methods will be highly beneficial.

In general, we'll need code to handle each version if we use an Option<T> value. We want some code that will only run if you have a Some(T) value, and we want it to be able to use the inner T. If we have a none value, we want some other code to run, but that code doesn't have a T value. When used with enums, the match expression does precisely that: it runs different codes depending on whatever variant of the enum it contains, and that code can use the data inside the matching value.

THE MATCH CONTROL FLOW OPERATOR

The match is a powerful control flow operator in Rust that lets us compare a value to a sequence of patterns and then execute code based on which pattern matches. Patterns can be composed of literal values, variable names, wildcards, and various other elements. The expressiveness of the patterns and the fact that the compiler validates that all conceivable scenarios are handled give match its power.

Consider a match expression similar to a coin-sorting machine: coins slide down a track with variously sized holes, and each coin falls into the first hole it encounters. Similarly, values pass through each pattern in a match, and if the value "fits" the first pattern, it is placed in the related code block to be used during execution.

Let's use coins to utilize match because we just stated them. As seen here, we can construct a function that takes an unknown US coin and, similar to the counting machine, determines which coin it is and returns its worth in cents.

```
enum Coins {
    Penny,
    Nickel,
    Dime,
    Quarter,
}

fn value_in_cents(coin: Coins) ->u8 {
    match coin {
        Coins::Penny=>1,
        Coins::Nickel=>5,
        Coins::Dime=>10,
        Coins::Quarter=>25,
    }
}
```

Let's take a glimpse at the value in the cents function's match. The match keyword is listed first, followed by an expression, in this example, the value coin. This looks a lot like an if expression, but there's a key difference: with if, the expression must return a Boolean value, whereas here it can be any type. The Coins enum, which we defined on line 1, is the type of coin in this case.

The match arms come next. There are two parts to an arm: a pattern and Some code. The first arm contains a pattern with the value Coins::Penny, followed by the => operator, which separates the pattern from the code to be executed. In this situation, the code is simply the value 1. A comma separates each arm from the one before it.

When the match expression runs, it compares the result to the pattern of each arm, one by one. If the value matches a pattern, the code associated with that pattern is run. If the pattern doesn't match the value, the machine moves to the next arm, similar to a coin sorter.

The code associated with each arm is an expression, and the value returned for the complete match expression results from the expression in the matching arm.

When the match arm code is short, curly brackets are often not utilized in the example where each arm returns a value. Curly brackets can run numerous lines of code in a single match arm. The following code, for example, would output "Lucky penny!" every time the method was called with a Coins::Penny, but it would still return the block's last value, 1:

```rust
fn value_in_cents(coin: Coins) ->u8 {
    match coin {
        Coins::Penny => {
            println!("Lucky-penny");
            1
        }
        Coins::Nickel => 5,
        Coins::Dime => 10,
        Coins::Quarter => 25,
    }
}
```

Patterns that Bind to Values

Match arms also can bind to the sections of the values that match the pattern. We can retrieve values from enum variations in this way.

Let's update one of our enum variants to hold data as an example. The United States struck quarters with different designs for each of the 50 states on one side from 1999 to 2008. Only quarters have this extra worth because no other coins include state designs. We can include this information in our enum by modifying the Quarter variation to include a UsState value stored within it, as we've done above.

```
#[derive(Debug)] //we can inspect the state in a minute
enum UsState {
    Alabama,
    Alaska,
}

enum Coins {
    Penny,
    Nickel,
    Dime,
    Quarter(UsState),
}
```

Assume that one of our friends is attempting to collect all 50 state quarters. We'll call out the state's name connected with each quarter as we sort our loose change by coin kind, so if it's one our friend doesn't have, they can add it to their collection.

We add a variable named state to the pattern in the match expression for this code that matches values of the variety Coins::Quarter. When a Coins::Quarter is matched, the state variable is set to that quarter's state value. Then, in the code for that arm, we can use the state as follows:

```
fn value_in_cents(coin: Coins) ->u8 {
    match coin {
        Coins::Penny=>1,
        Coins::Nickel=>5,
        Coins::Dime=>10,
        Coins::Quarter(state) => {
            println!("State quarter {:?}!", state);
            25
        }
    }
}
```

Coins would be Coins::Quarter(UsState::Alaska) if we called value _in_cents(Coins::Quarter(UsState::Alaska)). When we compare that value to each match arm, we discover that none of them match until we get to Coins::Quarter(state). The value UsState::Alaska will be the binding for state at that point. The inner state value of the Coins enum variation for Quarter may then be obtained by using that binding in the println! expression.

Matching with the Option<T>

We needed to obtain the inner T value out of some case when using Option<T> in the previous section; we can also handle Option<T> with match, as we did with the Coins enum! We'll compare the versions of Option<T> instead of coins, but the match expression will still function the same way.

Let's imagine we want to construct a function that takes an Option<i32> and adds 1 to whatever value it contains if a value exists. If no value is present, the function should return none and not attempt to conduct any operations.

```
fn plus_one(a: Option<i32>) ->Option<i32>{
        match a {
            None=>None,
            Some(x) =>Some(x+1),
        }
    }

    let five=Some(5);
    let six=plus_one(five);
    let none=plus_one(None);
```

Let's take a look at the initial plus_one execution. The variable x in the body of plus_one will have the value Some (5) when we call plus_one(five). After that, we compare it to each match arm.

```
            None=>None,
```

Because the value Some(5) does not match the pattern None, we go on to the next arm.

```
        Some(x) =>Some(x+1),
```

Is Some(5) the same as Some(i)? It certainly does! The version is the same for both of us. Because i is bound to the value in Some, it takes 5. The match arm's code is then run, so we add 1 to the value of i and construct a new Some value with our total of 6 inside.

When there is none, let's look at the second plus one call in the above code. We begin the match by comparing the first arm to the second.

```
None => None,
```

It's the same! Because there is nothing to add, the program comes to a halt and returns the none value on the right side of =>. No more arms are compared because the first arm matched.

In many circumstances, combining match and enums is beneficial. In Rust code, we'll see this pattern a lot: match against an enum, bind a variable to the data within, and run code depending on it. It's a little challenging initially, but once we get the hang of it, we'll wish we had it in every language. It's a popular choice among users.

Matches Are Exhaustive

There's one more part of match that needs to be addressed. Consider this bugged version of our plus_one function, which will not compile:

```
fn plus_one(a: Option<i32>) ->Option<i32>{
    match a {
        Some(x) =>Some(x+1),
    }
}
```

Because we didn't handle any situation, this code will fail. Fortunately, it's a bug that Rust is adept at catching. We will get the following error if we try to compile this code:

```
$ cargo run
   Compiling enums v0.1.0 (file:///projects/enums)
error[E0004]: non-exhaustive patterns: `None` not
              covered
  --> src/main.rs:3:15
   |
3  |          match a {
   |                ^ pattern `None` not covered
   |
   =help: ensure that all possible cases are being
          handled, possibly by adding wildcards or
          more match arms
   =note: the matched value is of type `Option<i32>`
```

Rust is well aware that we didn't cover every scenario and even understands which pattern we overlooked! In Rust, matches are exhaustive: we must exhaust every possible option for the code to be legitimate. Rust saves us from committing the earlier billion-dollar mistake by keeping us from neglecting to explicitly handle the None situation, especially in the case of Option<T>.

Catch-all Patterns and the _ Placeholder

Consider the following scenario: we want to take unique actions for a few specific values while taking a single default action for all other values. Assume we're designing a game in which a value of 2 on a dice roll results in our player receiving a new fancy hat rather than moving. Our player loses a fancy hat if we roll a 6. Our player moves that amount of squares on the game board for all other values. Here's a match that implements that logic, with the dice roll result hardcoded rather than a random value, and all other logic represented by functions without bodies because actual implementation is beyond the scope of this example:

```
let dice_roll = 8;
match dice_roll {
    2 => add_fancy_hat(),
    6 => remove_fancy_hat(),
    other => move_player(other),
}

fn add_fancy_hat() {}
fn remove_fancy_hat() {}
fn move_player(num_spaces: u8) {}
```

The patterns for the first two arms are the literal values 2 and 6. The pattern for the last arm, which covers all other possible values, is the variable we've named other. The variable is passed to the move_player function in the code that runs for the other arm.

Even though we haven't stated all of the potential values for an u8, this code compiles since the last pattern matches all values not specifically listed. This catch-all pattern satisfies the criterion of an exhaustive match. Because the patterns are examined in order, we must put the catch-all arm last. Rust will notify us that the following arms will never match if we add arms after a catch-all.

When we don't want to use the value from the catch-all pattern:, we can use the pattern, which is a special pattern that matches any value but does not bind to it. This notifies Rust that we do not intend to use the value to warn us about it.

Let's tweak the game's rules such that you must roll again if we roll anything other than a 2 or a 6. In that scenario, we don't need to utilize the value, thus we can alter our code to use_ instead of the other variable:

```
let dice_roll = 8;
    match dice_roll {
        2 => add_fancy_hat(),
        6 => remove_fancy_hat(),
        _ => reroll(),
    }
    fn add_fancy_hat() {}
    fn remove_fancy_hat() {}
    fn reroll() {}
```

This example also passes the exhaustiveness criteria because all other values in the last arm are expressly ignored; we haven't neglected anything.

If we alter the game's rules one more time, such that if we roll anything other than a 2 or a 6, nothing happens on our turn, we can express that by using the unit value (the empty tuple type we stated in the section "Tuple Type" in Chapter 2) as the code for the _arm:

```
let dice_roll = 8;
    match dice_roll {
        2 => add_fancy_hat(),
        6 => remove_fancy_hat(),
        _ => (),
    }

    fn add_fancy_hat() {}
    fn remove_fancy_hat() {}
```

We're explicitly telling Rust that we won't use any other value that doesn't match a pattern in a previous arm and that we won't run any code in this situation.

For now, we'll move on to the if let syntax, which comes in handy when the match expression is a little lengthy.

CONCISE CONTROL FLOW WITH IF LET

If we combine and let into the if let syntax, we can handle values that match one pattern while disregarding the remainder less verbosely. Consider the program which checks the config max variable for an Option<u8> value but only wants to run code if the value is the Some variation.

```
let config_max = Some(3u8);
match config_max {
    Some(max) => println!("Maximum is configured to
                    be {}", max),
    _ => (),
}
```

We want to print the value in the Some variation if the value is Some, which we do by assigning the value to the variable max in the pattern. With the None value, we don't want to do anything. After analyzing just one version, we must add _ => () to satisfy the match expression, which is tedious boilerplate code to add.

```
let config_max = Some(3u8);
  if let Some(max) = config_max {
      println!("Maximum is configured to be {}", max);
  }
```

A pattern and an expression are separated by an equal sign in the if let syntax. It functions similarly to a match in that the phrase is passed to the match, and the pattern is its first arm. In this case, the pattern is Some(max), and the max binds to the value inside the Some. Then, just like we did with the analogous match arm, we can utilize max in the body of the if let block. If the value does not match the pattern, the function in the if let block is not executed.

Using if let saves time by reducing typing, indentation, and boilerplate code. We do, however, lose the match's exhaustive checking. The decision between match and if allowed is based on what you're doing in your situation and whether gaining conciseness is a good trade-off for losing thorough checking.

In other words, consider if let to be syntax sugar for a match that executes code when the value matches one pattern and ignores all other values.

With an if let, we may include an else. The code that goes with the else is identical to the code that goes with the _case in the match expression, which is comparable to the if let and else. Remember how the Quarter variation of the Coin enum also included a UsState value? We could use a match expression like this to count all non-quarter coins we see while also notifying the status of the quarters:

```
let mut counts = 0;
match coin {
    Coin::Quarter(state) =>println!("State
                    quarter{:?}!", state),
    _=> count += 1,
}
```

Alternatively, we might use an if let and else expression like this:

```
let mut counts = 0;
    if let Coin::Quarter(state) = coin {
        println!("State quarter {:?}!", state);
    } else {
        counts += 1;
    }
```

Keep in mind that if let is also in our Rust toolkit if we ever find ourselves in a situation where our program's reasoning is too long to describe with a match.

This chapter covered enum definition, match control flow operator, and concise control flow with if let.

CHAPTER 6

Packages, Crates, and Modules

IN THIS CHAPTER

➤ Packages and crates

➤ Defining modules to control scope and privacy

➤ Paths for referring to an item in the module tree

➤ Bringing paths into scope with use keyword

➤ Separating modules into different files

In the previous chapter, we covered enums and pattern matching with its appropriate syntax and examples. This chapter will discuss packages and crates, defining modules, paths for referring, and how to separate modules into different files.

Organizing our code will become increasingly critical because as we build larger programs, keeping track of our entire program in our brain will become impractical. We'll discover code that implements a certain feature and where to go to change how a feature works by comparable grouping functionality and separating code with separate features.

So far, all of the programs we've built have been contained within a single module and a single file. As a project grows, we can organize code by

DOI: 10.1201/9781003311966-6

129

breaking it down into different modules and many files. Multiple binary crates and one library crate can be included in a package.

We can isolate components of a package into distinct crates that become external dependencies as it expands. All of these strategies are covered in this chapter.

Encapsulating implementation details, in addition to grouping functionality, allows us to reuse code at a higher level: after we've implemented an operation, other programs can call it via the code's public interface without knowing how it works.

Which portions of your code are public for other code to use and which parts are secret implementation details that we reserve the right to change depend on how we design it. This is another approach for keeping the amount of information in our heads to a minimum.

The scope is a similar concept: in the hierarchical context in which code is written, a collection of names is defined as "in scope." When reading, writing, and compiling code, programmers and compilers must determine whether a given name refers to a variable, function, struct, enum, module, constant, or other items, as well as what that item means. We can make scopes and adjust which names are included or excluded.

There can't be two things with the same name in the same scope; mechanisms to resolve name conflicts are available.

Rust includes several capabilities for managing the organization of your code, such as which details are exposed, which details are private, and which names are in each scope in our applications. These features, which are sometimes referred to as the module system as a whole, include:

- **Packages:** Packages are Cargo functionality that allows us to create, test, and share crates.

- **Crates:** Crates are a collection of modules that form a library or executable.

- **Modules and use:** Modules and their application allows us to manage the path's organization, scope, and privacy.

- **Paths:** Paths are names like structs, functions, and modules.

We'll go over all of these features in this chapter and how they interact, and how to use them to manage scope. We should have a firm grasp of the module system and work with scopes like a pro by the end!

PACKAGES AND CRATES

Packages and crates are the first aspects of the module system we'll look at. A binary or library is referred to as a crate. The crate root is a source file that the Rust compiler uses to build the root module of your crate (we'll go through modules in more detail in the section "Defining Modules to the Control Scope and Privacy"). A package is a collection of crates that provide a set of features. A Cargo.toml file in a package defines how to construct those crates.

What a package can include is determined by a set of rules. A package can only have one library crate in it. It can have as many binary crates as we want, but at least one must be present (either library or binary).

Let's have a look at the steps involved in creating a package. First, we'll use the cargo new command:

```
$ cargo new myproject
    Created binary (application) `myproject` package
$ ls myproject
Cargo.toml
src
$ ls myproject/src
main.rs
```

Cargo built a Cargo.toml file and gave us a package when we entered the command. There is no mention of src/main.rs in Cargo.toml because Cargo uses the convention that src/main.rs is the crate root of a binary crate with the same name as the package. Similarly, if the package directory contains src/lib.rs, Cargo understands that the package contains a library crate with the same name as the package, and src/lib.rs is the crate root. To build the library or binaries, Cargo sends the crate root files to rustc.

We have a package with only src/main.rs, which only has a binary crate named myproject. If src/main.rs and src/lib.rs are included in a package, it contains two crates: a library and a binary, both with the same name as the package. A package can have several binary crates by storing files in the src/bin directory: each file will be a separate binary crate.

A crate will group comparable functionality in scope to be easily shared across many projects.

Using the rand crate in our project's scope may use that feature in our projects. The rand crate's name, rand, provides access to all of the crate's functionality.

Keeping a crate's functionality in its scope clarifies whether a feature is defined in our crate or the rand crate, avoiding potential conflicts. The rand crate, for example, has a trait called Rng.

In our crate, we can also define a struct named Rng. When we add rand as a dependency, the compiler isn't confused about the name Rng because a crate's functionality is namespaced in its scope. It refers to the struct Rng that we defined in our crate. We'd use rand::Rng to get the Rng trait from the rand crate.

DEFINING MODULES TO THE CONTROL SCOPE AND PRIVACY

We'll discuss modules and other aspects of the module system in this section, including paths, which allow you to name objects, the use keyword, which puts a way into scope, and the pub keyword, which makes items public. The as keyword, external packages, and the glob operator will also be discussed. Let's concentrate on modules for the time being.

Modules allow us to group code within a crate for easier reading and reuse. Modules also manage item privacy, which determines whether an item can be utilized by outside code (public) or is an internal implementation detail that isn't accessible to the public (private).

Let's say we want to create a library crate that has the functionality of a restaurant. To focus on the organization of the code rather than implementing a restaurant in code, we'll specify the signatures of functions but leave their bodies empty.

Some restaurant areas are referred to as the front of house and others as back of house in the restaurant industry. Customers are served at the front of the house, where hosts seat them, servers receive orders and payments, and bartenders mix beverages. Chefs and cooks labor in the kitchen, dishwashers clean up, while managers do administrative tasks at the back of the house.

We may organize the functions into nested modules to structure our crate like a real restaurant does. By executing cargo new --lib restaurant, you may create a new library named restaurant and then put the program's code into src/lib.rs to define modules and function signatures.

Filename: src/thelib.rs

```
mod front_of_houses {
    mod hostings {
```

```
        fn add_to_waitlist() {}

        fn seat_at_table() {}
    }

    mod servings {
        fn take_order() {}

        fn serve_order() {}

        fn take_payment() {}
    }
}
```

We start by using the mod keyword and then specify the module's name (in this case, front_of_houses) and put curly brackets around the module's body. Other modules can be contained within modules, as in this example with the hosting and serving modules. As seen above, modules can also hold definitions for additional elements like structs, enums, constants, characteristics, and program functions.

We can group related definitions together and name why they're connected by utilizing modules. Programmers could explore the code based on the groups rather than read through all of the definitions, making it easier to find the definitions they needed. Programmers who want to add additional functionality to this code would know where to put it so that the program stays orderly.

Crate roots are src/main.rs and src/lib.rs, as we said earlier. The contents of any of these two files constitute a module named crate at the root of the crate's module structure, known as the module tree, which is the reason for their names.

```
crate
 └── front_of_houses
      ├── hostings
      │    ├── add_to_waitlist
      │    └── seat_at_table
      └── servings
           ├── take_order
           ├── serve_order
           └── take_payment
```

This tree depicts how some of the modules nest (for example, hosting nests within front of house). The tree also reveals that some modules are siblings, implying that they are created in the same module (for example, hosting and serving both are defined in front of house). To continue the family metaphor, we might say that module A is the child of module B and that module B is the parent of module A if it is contained within module B. It's worth noting that the entire module tree is rooted in the crate implicit module.

The module tree may remind us of the directory tree on our computer's disc; this is an interesting observation. Modules are used to arrange our code in the same way directories are used in a filesystem. We need a mechanism to find our modules, just like we need a way to find files in a directory.

PATHS FOR REFERRING TO AN ITEM IN THE MODULE TREE

We use a path in the same way as we explore a filesystem to show Rust where to find an item in a module tree. We need to know the path of a function to call it.

A path can be one of two types:

1. A literal crate or a crate name can use to start an absolute route from a crate root.

2. A relative path starts with the current module and uses self, super, or an identifier.

One or more identifiers separated by double colons (::) follow both absolute and relative pathways.

Let's go back to the previous example. What is the syntax for calling the add to waitlist function? What is the path of the add_to_waitlist function? We reduced our code by deleting several of the modules and functions below. We'll illustrate two ways to invoke the add_to_waitlist function from the crate root's new eat_at_restaurant function. The pub keyword is used to indicate that the eat_at_restaurant method is part of our library crate's public API. We'll look over the pub in further depth in the section "Exposing Paths with pub Keyword." This example will not compile at this time; we'll explain why in a moment.

Filename: src/thelib.rs

```
mod front_of_houses {
    mod hostings {
        fn add_to_waitlist() {}
    }
}

pub fn eat_at_restaurant() {
    // Absolute path
    crate::front_of_houses::hosting::add_to_waitlist();

    // Relative path
    front_of_houses::hosting::add_to_waitlist();
}
```

We use an absolute path the first time we run the add_to_waitlist method in eat at restaurant. Because the add_to_waitlist method is defined in the same crate as eat_at_restaurant, we may start an absolute route using the crate keyword.

Following crate, we include each subsequent module until we reach add_to_waitlist. Imagine a filesystem with the same structure, and we'd execute the add_to_waitlist program from the path/front_of_houses/host ing/add_to_waitlist; using the crate name to start from the crate root is similar to using/to start from the filesystem root in our shell.

We utilize a relative path the second time we run add to waitlist in eat_at_restaurant. The path begins with front_of_houses, the module's name declared at the same level as eat at restaurant in the module tree. The filesystem equivalent would be front_of_houses/hosting/add_to_waitlist in this case. The path is relative if it starts with a name.

We'll have to decide whether to utilize a relative or absolute path depending on our project. The decision should be based on whether we're more likely to relocate item definition code independently from code that utilizes the item or together. We'd need to adjust the absolute route to add_to_waitlist if we moved the front_of_houses module and the eat_at_ restaurant function into a module called customer_experience, but the relative path would still be acceptable.

The absolute route to the add_to_waitlist call would remain the same if we relocated the eat_at_restaurant function into its module called eating, but the relative path would need to be adjusted. We use absolute routes because code definitions and item calls are more likely to be moved independent of one another.

Let's see if we can build the code and figure out why it isn't working.

```
$ cargo build
      Compiling restaurant v0.1.0 (file:///projects/
                                              restaurant)
error[E0603]: module `hostings` is private
  --> src/lib.rs:9:28
   |
9  |        crate::front_of_houses::hostings::add_to_wait
                                      list();
   |                                       ^^^^^^^ private module
   |
note: the module `hostings` is defined here
  -->src/lib.rs:2:5
   |
2  |        mod hostings {
   |        ^^^^^^^^^^^^

error[E0603]: module `hostings` is private
  --> src/lib.rs:12:21
   |
12 |        front_of_houses::hosting::add_to_waitlist();
   |                         ^^^^^^^ private module
   |
note: the module `hostings` is defined here
  --> src/lib.rs:2:5
   |
2  |        mod hostings {
   |        ^^^^^^^^^^^^
```

Module hosting is private, according to the problem messages. In other words, the hosting module and the add to waitlist function have the correct locations, but Rust won't let us use them since it doesn't have access to the private parts.

Modules are useful for more than just structuring our code. They also define Rust's privacy border, which is the line that contains the implementation details that external code is not allowed to know about, call, or rely on in Rust. So, if we want a function or struct to be private, we must place it in a module.

In Rust, privacy is enforced by default on all things (functions, methods, structs, enums, modules, and constants). Items in a parent module cannot access private things in child modules, whereas child modules can access items in ancestor modules. Although child modules wrap and hide their implementation details, they can observe the context in which they're defined, this is the case. Consider the privacy rules as the back office of a restaurant: what happens there is private to restaurant customers, but office managers can see and do everything in the restaurant they operate.

Rust designed the module system in this fashion to make it default to hide core implementation details. We'll be able to tell which parts of the inner code we can alter without damaging the outer code in this way. However, using the pub keyword to make an object public, we can expose inner parts of child modules' code to outer ancestor modules.

Exposing Paths with pub Keyword

Returning to the error in the above program, the hosting module is private; let's look at it again. We want the parent module's eat_at_restaurant function to access the child module's add to waitlist method, so we designate the hosting module with the pub keyword, as shown below.

Filename: src/thelib.rs

```
mod front_of_houses {
    pub mod hostings {
        fn add_to_waitlist() {}
    }
}

pub fn eat_at_restaurant() {
    // the Absolute path
    crate::front_of_houses::hostings::add_to_waitlist();

    // the Relative path
    front_of_houses::hostings::add_to_waitlist();
}
```

Regrettably, the code still generates an error.

When you use the pub keyword in front of mod hosting, the module becomes public. With this update, we can now access hosting if we can access front_of_houses. On the other hand, the contents of hosting remain private; making the module public does not make the contents of hosting public. A module's pub keyword allows only code in its ancestor modules to refer to it.

According to the previous code, the add_to_waitlist method is private, as noted in the error generated. Privacy laws cover structures, enums, functions, methods, and modules.

Add the pub keyword before the add_to_waitlist function's definition to make it public.

Filename: src/thelib.rs

```
mod front_of_houses {
    pub mod hostings {
        pub fn add_to_waitlist() {}
    }
}

pub fn eat_at_restaurant() {
    // the Absolute path
    crate::front_of_house::hostings::add_to_waitlist();

    // the Relative path
    front_of_houses::hostings::add_to_waitlist();
}
```

The code will now compile. Let's look at the absolute and relative paths and see why using the pub keyword in add_to_waitlist allows us to use these paths while following the privacy restrictions.

We begin with the crate, the root of our crate's module tree, in the absolute path. Then, in the crate root, the front_of_houses module is defined. Although the front_of_houses module isn't public, we can refer to it from eat_at_restaurant since the eat_at_restaurant function is defined in the same module as front_ of_houses (i.e., eat_at_restaurant and front_of_ houses are siblings). The hostings module, denoted by the letter pub, comes next. We can go to the parent module of hostings, which allows us to get to hostings. Finally, the add_to_waitlist function is marked with pub, and its parent module can access; thus, this function call works!

The relative path follows the same reasoning as the absolute path, with the exception of the first step, which starts at front_of_houses rather than the crate root. Because the front_of_houses module is defined in the same module as eat_at_restaurant, the relative path starting from the eat at restaurant module works. The rest of the path works, and this function call is valid because hosting and add_to_waitlist are marked with pub.

Starting Relative Paths with super

We can also use super at the start of the path to create relative pathways that start in the parent module. This is the same as using the.. syntax to begin a filesystem path. Why would we want to do something like this?

Consider the below code, which simulates a case in which a chef corrects an inaccurate order and delivers it to the customer personally. By specifying the path to serve order beginning with super:, the method fixes incorrect order invokes the function serve order.

Filename: src/thelib.rs

```
fn serve_order() {}

mod back_of_houses {
    fn fix_incorrect_order() {
        cook_order();
        super::serve_order();
    }

    fn cook_order() {}
}
```

We may use super to go to the parent module of back_of_houses, which is crate, the root because the fix_incorrect_order method is in that module. We then search for serve_order and locate it. Success! Should we decide to reorganize the crate's module tree, we believe the back_of_houses module and the serve_order function will likely continue in the same relationship and be moved together. As a result, we utilized super to have fewer locations to update code if this code is relocated to a different module in the future.

Making Structs and Enums Public

We can also use the pub to make structs and enums public, but there are some additional considerations. When we use pub before a struct definition, the struct becomes public, but the fields remain private. On a case-by-case basis, we can make each field public or private. We defined a public back_of_houses::Breakfast struct with a public toast field but a private seasonal_fruit field in the below example. This is similar to the situation in a restaurant where the customer can choose the sort of bread that comes with their meal, but the chef chooses the fruit that goes with it based on what's in season and available.

Customers cannot choose or even see the fruit they will receive because the available fruit changes frequently.

Filename: src/thelib.rs

```
mod back_of_houses {
    pub struct Breakfast {
        pub toast: String,
        seasonal_fruit: String,
    }

    impl Breakfast {
        pub fn summer(toast: &str) ->Breakfast {
            Breakfast {
                toast: String::from(bread),
                seasonal_fruit: String::from("grapes"),
            }
        }
    }
}

pub fn eat_at_restaurant() {
    // Order a breakfast in the summer with Rye toast
    let mut meal=back_of_house::Breakfast::summer("Rye");
    // Change our mind about what bread we'd like
    meal.toast=String::from("brown");
    println!("I would like {} toast ", meal.toast);

}
```

Because the toast field in the back_of_houses::Breakfast struct is public, we can use dot notation to write and read to it in eat_at_restaurant. We can't utilize the seasonal_fruit field in eat_at_restaurant since it belongs to someone else. To check what error we got, uncomment the line that modifies the seasonal_fruit field value.

When we make an enum public, all of its variations become public. As illustrated below, the pub keyword is only required before the enum keyword.

Filename: src/thelib.rs

```
mod back_of_houses {
    pub enum Appetizer {
        Kebab,
        Noodles,
    }
}

pub fn eat_at_restaurant() {
    let order1 = back_of_houses::Appetizer::Kebab;
    let order2 = back_of_houses::Appetizer::Noodles;
}
```

We can utilize the Kebab and Noodles variations in eat_at_restaurant because we made the Appetizer enum public. Enum variants aren't beneficial unless they're public; it would be inconvenient to annotate every enum variant with the pub in every situation; therefore, the public is the default. Because struct fields are frequently useful without being public, they follow the general rule that everything is private by default unless annotated with pub.

We haven't addressed one more scenario utilizing pub yet: the use keyword, which is our last module system feature. We'll start with use on its own and then illustrate how to mix pub and use.

BRINGING PATHS INTO THE SCOPE WITH THE USE KEYWORD

The paths we've written so far to call functions may appear to be inconveniently long and repetitive. For example, we used the absolute or relative route to the add_to_waitlist function in previous examples; we had to specify front_of_houses and hosting every time we wished to call add_to_waitlist. There is a way to make things easier and with the use keyword, we may bring a path into a scope once and then call the things in that path as local items.

We bring the crate::front_of_houses::hosting module into the scope of the eat at restaurant function in the example below, so we simply have to provide hosting::add to waitlist to use the eat at restaurant function's add to waitlist method.

Filename: src/thelib.rs

```
mod front_of_houses {
    pub mod hostings {
        pub fn add_to_waitlist() {}
    }
}

use crate::front_of_houses::hostings;

pub fn eat_at_restaurant() {
    hostings::add_to_waitlist();
    hostings::add_to_waitlist();
    hostings::add_to_waitlist();
}
```

Adding use and a path is comparable to creating a symbolic link in the filesystem in a scope. Because use crate::front of houses::hostings was added to the crate root, hostings is now a valid name in that scope, just as if the hostings module had declared there. Like all other paths, paths brought into scope with use check for privacy.

Use and a relative path can also bring an item into scope. The program below demonstrates how to define a relative route to achieve the same results as the program above.

Filename: src/thelib.rs

```
mod front_of_houses {
    pub mod hostings {
        pub fn add_to_waitlist() {}
    }
}

use self::front_of_houses::hostings;

pub fn eat_at_restaurant() {
    hostings::add_to_waitlist();
    hostings::add_to_waitlist();
    hostings::add_to_waitlist();
}
```

Creating the Idiomatic use Paths

We might be wondering why, in the previous code, we used use crate::front_of_houses::hostings and then used hostings::add_to_waitlist in eat_at_restaurant instead of using the use path out to the add_to_waitlist function.

Filename: src/thelib.rs

```
mod front_of_houses {
    pub mod hostings {
        pub fn add_to_waitlist() {}
    }
}

use crate::front_of_houses::hostings::add_to_waitlist;

pub fn eat_at_restaurant() {
    add_to_waitlist();
    add_to_waitlist();
    add_to_waitlist();
}
```

Even though the previous example accomplishes the same goal, it is the idiomatic way to bring a function into scope with use. When we use to get the function's parent module into scope, we must specify the parent module when invoking the function. When invoking a function, specifying the parent module makes it apparent that the function isn't local while also reducing the number of times the whole path is repeated.

However, when bringing in structs, enums, and other things with use, specifying the complete path is idiomatic. The code below demonstrates how to introduce the HashMap struct from the standard library into the scope of a binary crate in an idiomatic fashion.

Filename: src/themain.rs

```
use std::collections::HashMap;
fn main() {
    let mut map1 = HashMap::new();
    map1.insert(2, 1);
}
```

This idiom has no compelling reason: it's simply a tradition that has formed, and people have grown accustomed to reading and creating Rust code in this manner.

This idiom is only broken if we use statements to bring two items with the same name into scope, which Rust doesn't allow. The following example demonstrates how to scope two Result types with the same name but separate parent modules and how to refer to them.

Filename: src/thelib.rs

```
use std::fmt;
use std::io;

fn function1() -> fmt::Results {

}

fn function2() -> io::Results<()> {

}
```

As we can see, the two Result types are distinguished by using the parent modules. Instead of using std::fmt::Result, we may use std::io::Result. If we used Result, we'd have two Result types in the same scope, and Rust wouldn't know which one we meant.

Providing New Names with the as Keyword

Another way to solve the problem of bringing two types with the same name into the same scope with use is to specify as and a new local name, or alias, for the type after the path. The below example shows a different approach to writing the code above by using as to rename one of the two Result types.

Filename: src/thelib.rs

```
use std::fmt::Results;
use std::io::Results as IoResult;

fn function1() -> Results {
    // --snip--
}
```

```
fn function2() -> IoResult<()> {
    // --snip--
}
```

We chose the new name IoResult for the std::io::Results type in the second use statement so that it doesn't clash with the Result from std::fmt that we've also brought into scope.

Re-exporting Names with pub use

When we use the use keyword to bring a name into scope, the name that appears in the new scope is private. We can mix pub and use to allow the code that calls our code to refer to that name as if it were defined in that code's scope. This approach is known as re-exporting because we're bringing an item into the scope and making it available for others to bring into their scope.

Filename: src/thelib.rs

```
mod front_of_houses {
    pub mod hostings {
        pub fn add_to_waitlist() {}
    }
}

pub use crate::front_of_houses::hostings;

pub fn eat_at_restaurant() {
    hostings::add_to_waitlist();
    hostings::add_to_waitlist();
    hostings::add_to_waitlist();
}
```

External code can now use hostings::add_to_waitlist to call the add_to_waitlist method utilizing pub usage. The eat_at_restaurant function may call hostings::add_to_waitlist in its scope if we hadn't specified pub usage, but external code couldn't take advantage of this new path.

When the internal structure of our code differs from how programmers calling your code would think about the domain, re-exporting is useful. For example, in this restaurant metaphor, the individuals in charge of the restaurant consider "front of house" and "back of house." On the other hand, customers visiting a restaurant are unlikely to think of the restaurant's components in those terms. We can write our code with the one structure but disclose a different structure with pub usage. As a result, our library is well-organized for programmers working on it and programmers calling it.

SEPARATING MODULES INTO DIFFERENT FILES

So far, this chapter's examples have all declared several modules in a single file. To make the code easier to navigate, we might want to transfer the definitions of large modules to a different file.

Starting with the previous code, we may relocate the front of houses module to its file src/front of house.rs by altering the crate root file to include the below code. The crate root file, in this case, is src/lib.rs, but this approach also works with binary crates with src/main.rs as the crate root file.

Filename: src/thelib.rs

```
mod front_of_houses;

pub use crate::front_of_houses::hostings;

pub fn eat_at_restaurant() {
    hostings::add_to_waitlist();
    hostings::add_to_waitlist();
    hostings::add_to_waitlist();
}
```

In addition, there's src/front_of_houses. As seen, rs gets the definitions from the front_of_houses module's body.

Filename: src/front_of_houses.rs

```
pub mod hostings {
    pub fn add_to_waitlist() {}
}
```

Rather than using a block following mod front_of_houses, a semicolon informs Rust to load the module's contents from another file with the same name. To keep our example going and remove the hosting module to its file, we update src/front_of_houses.rs only to contain the hosting module declaration:

Filename: src/front_of_houses.rs

```
pub mod hostings;
```

Then we create an src/front of house directory and a file, src/front of house/hostings.rs, to hold the hosting module's definitions:

Filename: src/front_of_houses/hostings.rs

```
pub fn add_to_waitlist() {}
```

Even if the definitions are in distinct files, the module tree remains the same, and the function calls in eat_at_restaurant will operate without modification. As modules grow in size, you can use this technique to relocate them to new files.

It's worth noting that the pub use crate::front_of_houses::hosting statement in src/lib.rs hasn't changed, and neither has a use, which has no bearing on which files are compiled as part of the crate. The mod keyword declares modules, and Rust looks for the code that goes into that module in a file with the same name as the module.

This chapter covered packages and crates, defining modules to control scope and privacy, paths for referring to an item in the module tree, and bringing paths into scope with the use keyword. We also covered separating modules into different files.

CHAPTER 7

Error Handling

IN THIS CHAPTER

➢ Unrecoverable errors with panic!

➢ Recoverable errors with Result

In the previous chapter, we discussed managing growing projects with packages, crates, and modules. In this chapter, we will cover error handling, where we will discuss unrecoverable errors with panic! and recoverable errors with Result.

ERROR HANDLING

Rust's dedication to dependability goes to error handling as well. Errors are an inevitable part of software development; thus, Rust offers several capabilities for dealing with them. Before your code can compile, Rust often needs us to acknowledge the potential of an error and take action. This criterion improves the robustness of our program by guaranteeing that mistakes are discovered and handled effectively before our code is pushed to production.

Mistakes are divided into two kinds by Rust: recoverable and unrecoverable errors. It's appropriate to notify the user of a recoverable error, such as a file not found error, and retry the action. Unrecoverable errors, such as trying to access a place beyond the end of an array, are always signs of a bug.

DOI: 10.1201/9781003311966-7

Most programming languages don't differentiate between these two types of problems and treat them the same way, using techniques like exceptions. There are no exceptions in Rust. Instead, it has the panic! macro that stops execution when the program encounters an unrecoverable error and the type Result for recoverable errors. This chapter starts with panic! and then moves on to returning Result values. We'll also consider factors to consider when choosing whether to try to recover from an error or terminate execution.

Unrecoverable Errors with panic!

Bad things happen in our code from time to time, and there's nothing we can do about it. Rust has the panic! macro for certain situations. Our program will print a failure message, unwind and clean up the stack, and then terminate when the panic! macro runs. This usually occurs when a bug has been discovered and the programmer is unsure how to handle the error.

Unwinding Stack or Aborting in Response to a Panic

When a panic happens by default, the program unwinds, which means Rust walks up the stack and cleans up the data from each function it encounters. However, returning and cleaning up is a lot of work. The other option is to stop the program right away, which will end it without cleaning up. The operating system will then have to clean up the program's memory. If we need to make the final binary as small as possible in our project, we may switch from unwinding to aborting upon a panic by adding panic = 'abort' to the appropriate [profile] sections in our Cargo.toml file. For example, if we want to abort when there is a panic in release mode, we may add this:

[profile.release]

panic = 'abort'

Let's make a panic! call in a straightforward program:

Filename: src/themain.rs

```
fn main() {
    panic!("crash & burn");
}
```

When we run the program, we see something like this:

```
$ cargo run
   Compiling panic v0.1.0 (file:///projects/panic)
    Finished dev [unoptimized+debuginfo] target(s) in
            0.29s
      Running `target/debug/panic`
thread 'main' panicked at 'crash & burn', src/main.rs:2:5
note: run with the `RUST_BACKTRACE=1` environment
variable to the display backtrace
```

The panic causes the error message in the last two lines! command. Our panic message and the location in our source code where the panic occurred are shown in the first line: it's the second line, the fifth character of our src/themain.rs file, as indicated by src/themain.rs:2:5.

In this case, we can see the panic! macro call if we go to that line. In other circumstances, the panic! macro may call in code that our code calls, and the filename and line number shown by the error message will be someone else's code, not the line of our code that eventually led to the panic! call. We can utilize the backtrace of the panic! call's methods to work out which section of our code is causing the issue. Next, we'll go over what a backtrace is in greater depth.

Using panic! Backtrace
Let's look at another scenario to see how it feels when we're in a panic! because of a flaw in our code. In this case, the call comes from a library rather than from our code directly contacting the macro. Some code tries to retrieve an element in a vector in the program by index.

Filename: src/themain.rs

```
fn main() {
    let v1=vec![1, 2, 3];

    v1[99];
}
```

We're trying to get to the 100th element of our vector (index 99 because indexing starts at zero), but there are only three elements. Rust will panic in this situation. Although [] is supposed to return an element, if we give an invalid index, there is no element that Rust can return that is correct.

Reading beyond the end of a data structure is undefined behavior in C. Even if the memory doesn't belong to that structure, we might retrieve whatever is at the place in memory that corresponds to that element in the data structure. This is known as a buffer overread, and it can lead to security flaws if an attacker can change the index so that they can read data they shouldn't be permitted to read after the data structure has been saved.

If we try to read an element at an index that doesn't exist, Rust will stop execution and refuse to proceed, protecting our application from this type of vulnerability.

```
$ cargo run
   Compiling panic v0.1.0 (file:///projects/panic)
    Finished dev [unoptimized+debuginfo] target(s) in
          0.29s
      Running `target/debug/panic`
thread 'main' panicked at the 'index out of bounds:
len is 3, but the index is 99', src/main.rs:4:5
note: run with the `RUST_BACKTRACE=1` environment
variable to display backtrace
```

This problem occurs when we try to access index 99 on line 4 of our main.rs file. The RUST_BACKTRACE environment variable can be set to acquire a backtrace of exactly what happened to trigger the problem, according to the next note line. A backtrace lists all the functions used to get to this point. Backtraces in Rust function similarly to backtraces in other languages: the key to reading a backtrace is to start at the beginning and read until we see the files created. That is the location where the issue began.

The lines above and below the lines mentioning our files are code that was called by our code, and the lines below are code that was called by our code. These lines could contain Rust core code, standard library code, or crates we're utilizing. Set the RUST_BACKTRACE environment variable to any value other than 0 to see if we can get a backtrace.

```
$ RUST_BACKTRACE=1 cargo run
thread 'main' panicked at 'index out of bounds: the
       len is 3 but the index is 99', src/themain.rs:
          4:5
stack backtrace:
```

```
0: rust_begin_unwind
            at /rustc/7eac88abb2e57e752f3302f02be5
        f3ce3d7adfb4/library/std/src/panicking.rs
        :483
1: core::panicking::panic_fmt
            at /rustc/7eac88abb2e57e752f3302f02be5
        f3ce3d7adfb4/library/core/src/panicking.rs
        :85
2: core::panicking::panic_bounds_check
            at /rustc/7eac88abb2e57e752f3302f02be5
        f3ce3d7adfb4/library/core/src/panicking.rs
        :62
3: <usize as core::slice::index::SliceIndex<[T]>
        >::index
            at /rustc/7eac88abb2e57e752f3302f02be5
        f3ce3d7adfb4/library/core/src/slice/index
        .rs:255
4: core::slice::index::<impl core::ops::index::
        Index for [T]>::index
            at /rustc/7eac88abb2e57e752f3302f02be5
        f3ce3d7adfb4/library/core/src/slice/index
        .rs:15
5: <alloc::vec::Vec<T> as core::ops::index::Index<I>
        >::index
            at /rustc/7eac88abb2e57e752f3302f02be5
        f3ce3d7adfb4/library/alloc/src/vec.rs:1982
6: panic::main
            at ./src/main.rs:4
7: core::ops::function::FnOnce::call_once
            at /rustc/7eac88abb2e57e752f3302f02be5
        f3ce3d7adfb4/library/core/src/ops/function
        .rs:227
note: some details are omitted, run with the `RUST_
        BACKTRACE=full` for a verbose backtrace.
```

That's a significant amount of output! Depending on our operating system and Rust version, the exact output that appears may differ. Debug symbols must enable to get backtraces using this information. When running cargo build or cargo run without the --release flag, as we have above, debug symbols are enabled by default.

Line 6 of the backtrace in the output leads to the problematic line in our project: line 4 of src/themain.rs. If we don't want program to panic, we should start looking at the place indicated by the first line mentioning a file we created. The solution to remedy the panic in the preceding code, where we purposefully built code that would panic to explain how to use backtraces, is to not request an element at index 99 from a vector that only includes three items. If our code panics again, we'll need to figure out what action it's performing with what values to create the panic and what it should do instead.

We'll return to panic!, and when it should and should not be used to handle error scenarios, in the section "To Panic! or Not to Panic!" later in this chapter. In the meantime, we'll look at how to use Result to recover from an error.

RECOVERABLE ERRORS WITH THE RESULT

The majority of errors aren't substantial enough to cause the software to shut down completely. When a function fails, it may be for a reason that is simple to understand and respond to: if we attempt to access a file and it fails because the file does not exist, instead of terminating the process, we might wish to create the file.

```
enum Result<T, E> {
    Ok(T),
    Err(E),
}
```

The T and E are the generic type parameters, which we'll go over in more depth later. We need to know right now that T stands for the type of value returned in a success scenario within the Ok variant, and E stands for the type of error received in a failure event within the Err variant. Because Result contains these general type arguments, we may use it and the functions supplied in the standard library on it in various circumstances where the successful and error values we want to return are different.

Because the function could fail, we'll term it a function that returns a Result value. We try to open a file.

Filename: src/themain.rs

```
use std::fs::File;

fn main() {
    let f1 = File::open("helloo.txt");
}
```

What evidence do we have that File::open returns a Result? We could consult the documentation for the standard library API, or we could simply ask the compiler! If we provide f with a type annotation that isn't the function's return type and then try to compile the code, the compiler will complain about the types not matching. The error message will then inform us of the f type. Let's give it a shot! Because we know File::open's return type isn't u32, we'll update the let f statement to this:

```
let f1: u32 = File::open("helloo.txt");
```

When we try to compile now, we get the following result:

```
$ cargo run
   Compiling error-handling v0.1.0 (file:///projects/
error-handling)
error[E0308]: mismatched types
 --> src/main.rs:4:18
  |
4 |     let f1: u32 = File::open("helloo.txt");
  |             ---   ^^^^^^^^^^^^^^^^^^^^^^^^ expected
                    `u32`, found enum `Result`
  |             |
  |             expected due to this
  |
  = note: expected type `u32`
            found enum `Result<File, std::io::Error>`
```

This indicates that the File::open function's return type is a Result. The type of success value, std::fs::File, which is a file handle, has been filled in for the generic argument T. std::io::Error is the type of E used in the error value.

This return type indicates that the File::open method may succeed and return a file handle from which we can read or write. The function call could fail because the file does not exist or we do not have permission to access it. The File::open function must be able to indicate if it succeeded or failed and provide the file handle or error information. The Result enum gives exactly this information.

If File::open succeeds, the value of f in the variable f will be an instance of Ok containing a file handle. If it fails, the value in f will be an instance of Err with additional details about the type of mistake that occurred.

We must add to the above code to perform different actions depending on the value. The command File::open returns. As seen in the example below, the match expression is a simple technique that may be used to handle the Result.

Filename: src/themain.rs

```
use std::fs::File;

fn main() {
    let f1=File::open("helloo.txt");

    let f1=match f {
        Ok(file)=>file,
        Err(error)=>panic!("Problem opening file:
                        {:?}", error),
    };
}
```

The preamble brought the Result enum and its variations into scope, just like the Option enum, so we don't need to mention Result:: before the Ok and Err variants in the match arms.

We instruct Rust to return the inner file value from the Ok variant when the result is Ok, and we then add that file handle value to the variable f. After the match, we can read or write to the file handle.

The other arm of the match deals with the case where File::open returns an Err value. We've opted to call the panic! macro in this example. If there is no file named hello.txt in our current directory when we run this code, the panic! macro will provide the following output:

```
$ cargo run
   Compiling error-handling v0.1.0 (file:///projects/
                                    error-handling)
    Finished dev [unoptimized+debuginfo] target(s) in 0.73s
     Running `target/debug/error-handling`
thread 'main' panicked at the 'Problem opening file:
        Os {code: 2, kind: NotFound, message: "No such
        file or directory"}', src/main.rs:8:23
note: run with the `RUST_BACKTRACE=1` environment
     variable to display backtrace
```

This output, as usual, shows us exactly what went wrong.

The code above will cause panic! regardless of why File::open failed. Instead, we want to do different actions depending on the reason for the failure: if File::open failed because the file didn't exist, we want to create it and return the handle to the new file. We still want the code to panic if File::open fails for any other reason because we don't have permission to open the file in the same way it did previously. Look at the code below, which includes an inner match expression.

Filename: src/themain.rs

```
use std::fs::File;
use std::io::ErrorKind;
fn main() {
    let f1 = File::open("helloo.txt");

    let f1 = match f {
        Ok(file) => file,
        Err(error) => match error.kind() {
            ErrorKind::NotFound => match
                        File::create("helloo.txt") {
                Ok(fc) => fc,
                Err(e) => panic!("Problem creating
                            file: {:?}", e),
            },
            other_error => {
                panic!("Problem opening file: {:?}",
                    other_error)
            }
        },
    };
}
```

The value returned by File::open in the Err variation is of the type io::Error, a struct given by the standard library. We can retrieve an io::ErrorKind value by calling the method kind on this struct. The standard library provides the enum io::ErrorKind, which has variants that describe the many types of errors that can occur during an io operation. The ErrorKind::NotFound variant we wish to use indicates that the file we're trying to open doesn't exist yet. So we have an outer match on f1, but an inner match on error.kind ().

We want to see if the value returned by the error in the inner match. The ErrorKind enum's kind method is the NotFound variation. If that's the case, File::create is used to create the file. We need a second arm in the inner match expression because File::create can also fail. A separate error message is displayed if the file cannot be created. Because the second arm of the outer match remains unchanged, the program panics when it encounters any error other than a missing file error.

That's a significant amount of match! The match expression is quite useful, but it is also a very primitive expression.

Shortcuts for the Panic on Error: unwrap and expect

Match works fine, although it's a little verbose and doesn't always explain intent clearly. Many helper methods are defined on the Result<T, E> type to do various operations. One of those methods, unwrap, is a shorthand method that works similarly to the match expression we wrote earlier. Unwrap will return the value inside the Ok if the Result value is the Ok varient. Unwrap will call the panic! macro for us if the Result is the Err varient. Here's an example of how unwrap works:

Filename: src/themain.rs

```
use std::fs::File;

fn main() {
    let f1 = File::open("helloo.txt").unwrap();
}
```

We'll get an error message from the panic! if we run this code without a helloo.txt file. The unwrap method generates the following call:

```
thread 'main' panic at 'called `Result::unwrap()` on
        `Err` value: Error {
repr: Os {code: 2, message: "No such file or
        directory"}}',
src/libcore/result.rs:906:4
```

Another method, expect, is similar to unwrap in that it allows us to select the panic! error notification. Using expect instead of unwrap and providing clear error messages might help us communicate our goal and find the source of a panic. Expect has the following syntax:

Filename: src/themain.rs

```
use std::fs::File;

fn main() {
    let f1 = File::open("helloo.txt").expect("The
Failed to open helloo.txt");
}
```

Expect is similar to unwrap in that it returns the file handle or calls the panic! macro. The parameter we pass to expect will be the error message used by expect in its call to panic!, rather than the default panic! message used by unwrap. This is how it appears:

```
thread 'main' panicked at 'Failed to open helloo.txt:
        Error {repr: Os {code:
2, message: "No such file or directory"}}', src/
    libcore/result.rs:906:4
```

Because this error message begins with the line Failed to open helloo.tx t, it will be easier to determine where this error message originates in the code. Because all unwrap calls that panic print identical messages, it can take longer to determine which unwrap is generating the panic if we use unwrap in multiple places.

Propagating Errors

Rather than handling the error within the function, we can pass it on to the calling code to decide what to do when developing a function whose implementation calls something that might fail. This is referred to as propagating the error, and it gives the calling code greater power since the calling code may have more information or logic that dictates how the issue should be handled than we do in our code.

The example depicts a function that reads a username from a file. This function will return errors to the code that called it if the file doesn't exist or can't be read.

Filename: src/themain.rs

```
use std::fs::File;
use std::io::{self, Read};
```

```
fn read_username_from_file () -> Result<String,
                                  io::Error> {
    let f1 = File::open ("helloo.txt") ;

    let mut f1 = match f1 {
        Ok(file) => file,
        Err(e) => return Err(e),
    } ;

    let mut s1 = String::new () ;

    match f1.read_to_string(&mut s1) {
        Ok(_) => Ok(s1),
        Err(e) => Err(e),
    }
}
```

This function can be written in a much shorter method, but we'll start by doing a lot of it manually to learn about error handling and then we'll show the shorter way at the end. First, let's look at the function's return type: Result<String, io::Error>, a string that contains an io::Error. This indicates that the function returns a value of type Result<T, E>, with the generic argument T filled with the concrete type String and the generic type E filled with the concrete type io::Error. If this function completes successfully, the code that calls it will receive an Ok value containing a String containing the username that this function retrieved from the file.

If this method encounters any issues, the code that calls it will receive an Err value that contains an instance of io::Error. More details about the issues can be found in the error message. We chose io::Error as the return type of this function because that's the type of error value returned from both of the operations we're calling in the body of this function that can fail: the read_to_string method and the File::open function.

The body of the function begins with a call to the File::open function. Then, instead of invoking panic!, we handle the Result value returned with a match similar to the match in the previous code. In the Err scenario, we exit this method early and return the error value from File::open to the calling code as the error value for this procedure. We keep the file handle in the variable f1 and continue if File::open succeeds.

Then, using the read to string function on the file handle in f1, we create a new String in variable s and read the contents of the file into s1. Because the read to string method may fail even if File::open succeeded, it also returns a Result. So we'll need another match to deal with that Result: if read to string succeeds, our function succeeds, and we return the username from the file that's now in s1 wrapped in an Ok. If read to string fails, the error value is returned in the same way as the match that handled the return value of File::open returned the error value. However, because this is the last expression in the function, we don't need to specify return explicitly.

The code that runs this procedure will then handle either getting an Ok value containing a username or getting an Err value containing an io::Error. We don't know what those values will be used for by the calling code. If the calling code receives an Err value, it may issue a panic! signal. To avoid crashing the software, use a default username or search for the username from somewhere other than a file, for example. We don't have enough knowledge to figure out what the calling code is trying to do, so we send all of the success and error information up to it to handle.

Because this propagating error pattern is so prevalent in Rust, the question mark operator ? is provided to make it easier.

Shortcut for Propagating Errors: the ? Operator

This implementation of read_username_from_file has the same functionality as the previous example, except it uses the ? operator.

Filename: src/themain.rs

```
use std::fs::File;
use std::io;
use std::io::Read;

fn read_username_from_file() ->Result<String, io::Error>{
    let mut f1 = File::open("hello.txt")?;
    let mut s1 = String::new();
    f.read_to_string(&mut s1)?;
    Ok(s1)
}
```

The ? following a Result value is defined to behave similarly to the match expressions we previously created to handle the Result values. If the Result value is an Ok, this expression will return the value inside the Ok, and the program will proceed. If the value is an Err, the Err will be returned from the entire function as if the return keyword had been used, allowing the error value to be propagated to the calling code.

There is a distinction between the match expression and the ? operator: error values that have the ? operator calls to them pass through the from function, which is defined in the standard library's From trait and is used to convert errors from one type to another. When the from the function is called with the ? operator, the error type received is transformed to the error type defined in the current function's return type.

This is useful when a function returns a single error type to represent all possible failures, even if parts may fail for various reasons. The ? operator takes care of the conversion automatically as long as each error type implements the from function to define how to convert itself to the returned error type.

The value inside an Ok will be returned to the variable f1 by the? at the end of the File::open call. If an error occurs, the? operator exits the function early and returns any Err value to the calling code. The? at the completion of the read_to_string call has the same effect.

The ? operator removes a lot of boilerplate and simplifies the implementation of this function. We could make this code even shorter by chaining method calls after the ?.

Filename: src/themain.rs

```
use std::fs::File;
use std::io;
use std::io::Read;

fn read_username_from_file() ->Result<String,
                                   io::Error>{
    let mut s1 = String::new();

    File::open("helloo.txt")?.read_to_string(&mut
            s1)?;

    Ok(s1)
}
```

The generation of a new String in s1 has been moved to the beginning of the function; nothing else has changed. We've chained the call to read to string right onto the result of File::open("helloo.txt")? instead of creating a variable f1. We still have a ? at the end of the read_to_string call, and instead of returning errors, we still return an Ok value containing the username in s1 when both File::open and read_to_string succeed. The functionality is the same as in the previous programs; it's just written in a new, more ergonomic approach this time.

This example demonstrates how we may make it even shorter when it comes to other approaches to create this function:

Filename: src/themain.rs

```
use std::fs;
use std::io;

fn read_username_from_file() -> Result<String,
                            io::Error> {
    fs::read_to_string("helloo.txt")
}
```

Because reading a file into a string is a typical task, Rust includes the fs::read_to_string function, which opens the file, produces a new String, reads the file's contents, places them into that String, and returns it. Using fs::read_to_string, however, does not allow us to illustrate all of the error handling, so we showed it the longer way first.

The ? Operator Can Be Used in Functions that Return Result

The ? operator is defined to work in the same way as the match expression we defined in the previous code, and can be used in functions with a return type of Result. Return Err(e) is the part of the match that requires a Result return type; therefore, the function's return type must be a Result to be consistent with this return.

Let's just see what happens if we use the ? operator in the main function, which has a return type of () as we may recall:

```
use std::fs::File;

fn main() {
    let f1 = File::open("helloo.txt")?;
}
```

We get an error notice when we compile this code.

This error indicates that the ? operator can only use in functions that return Result, Option, or another type that implements std::ops:: Try. When writing code in a function that doesn't return one of these types yet, we want to use ?. We have two options for fixing this problem when calling other functions that return Result<T, E>. If we don't have any constraints, changing the return type of our function to Result<T, E> is one option. The alternative option is to use a match or one of the Result<T, E> methods to handle the Result<T, E> in any way that makes sense.

The main function is unique, and its return type must follow to certain guidelines. () is one valid return type for main, while Result<T, E> is another convenient return type, as demonstrated here:

```
use std::error::Error;
use std::fs::File;

fn main() ->Result<(), Box<dyn Error>>{
    let f1 = File::open("helloo.txt")?;

    Ok(())
}
```

A trait object is what the Box<dyn Error> type is called. For the time being, you can interpret Box<dyn Error> as "any kind of error." It is permissible to use ? in the main function with this return type.

Let's return to the question of how to decide which is suitable to employ in which instances now that we've gone over the details of calling panic! or returning Result.

TO PANIC! OR NOT TO PANIC!

How do we know when it is time to call panic!, when we should return Result, and when we should not? There's no mechanism to recover when code panics. If we choose to call panic!, we're deciding on behalf of the calling code that a scenario is unrecoverable, whether there's a possible means to recover or not.

We give the calling code options rather than deciding when we choose to return a Result value. The calling code can choose to recover in a way that's appropriate for the situation, or it can decide that an Err value, in this case, is unrecoverable, in which case it can use panic! and change our recoverable error into an unrecoverable one. As a result, returning Result is a sensible default choice when defining a function that may fail.

In a few cases, it's preferable to write code that panics rather than producing a Result. Let's look at why panicking is appropriate in situations such as examples, prototype code, and tests. Then we'll talk about scenarios where the compiler can't identify whether something is impossible, but we can. This chapter will end with some general rules for deciding whether or not to panic while writing library code.

Examples, Prototype Code, and Tests

When constructing an example to demonstrate a concept, including robust error-handling code can make the example less understandable. In examples, it's assumed that a call to a method like unwrap that can panic is intended as a placeholder for how we'd like our application to handle errors, which can vary depending on the rest of our code.

Similarly, before we decide how to handle errors, the unwrap and expect methods come in handy for experimenting. When we're ready to make our program more robust, they leave explicit indicators in our code.

If a method call fails in a test, the entire test should fail, even if the method isn't the functionality being tested. Because panic! is how a test is reported as a failure, we should call unwrap or expect instead.

Cases in Which We Have More Information than the Compiler

We should call unwrap when we have some logic that guarantees that the Result has an Ok value but that logic isn't something the compiler understands. We'll still have to deal with a Result value: whatever operation we're calling has the potential to fail in general, even if it's logically impossible in your specific circumstance. It's completely okay to call unwrap if we can verify that we'll never have an Err variation by manually analyzing the code. Here's an illustration:

```
use std::net::IpAddr;

let home: IpAddr = "127.0.0.1".parse().unwrap();
```

We're processing a hardcoded text to create an IpAddr instance. Because we can see that 127.0.0.1 is a legitimate IP address, we may use unwrap in this case. However, having a hardcoded, valid string does not affect the parse method's return type: we still obtain a Result value, and the compiler will treat it as if the Err variant is a possibility since the compiler isn't smart enough to recognize that this string is always a valid IP address.

We'd definitely want to handle the Result more robustly if the IP address string came from a user rather than being hardcoded into the program, and so had a chance of failing.

Guidelines for the Error Handling

When our code may wind up in a bad state, it's best to have your code panic. A bad state occurs when an assumption, guarantee, contract, or invariant is violated, such as when invalid, conflicting, or missing values are supplied to our code along with one or more of the following:

- The bad state isn't something that happens regularly.

- After this point, our code must rely on the fact that we are not in this bad state.

- There isn't a good way to encode information in the kinds we employ.

If someone uses our code and passes in values that don't make sense, the best option is to call panic! and notify the person who is using our library about the error in their code so that they can correct it while developing. Similarly, panic! is frequently suitable when accessing external code that we don't control, and it returns an invalid state that we can't change.

When failure is predicted, however, returning a Result rather than making a panic! call is preferable. Two examples are a parser receiving malformed data or an HTTP request returning a status indicating a rate restriction. Returning a Result in these circumstances implies that failure is a possibility that the calling function must handle.

When our code performs operations on values, it should first check that the values are legitimate and then panic if they aren't. This is mainly for security reasons: operating on erroneous data can expose our code to vulnerabilities. This is the primary cause of panic in the standard library. Frequent security vulnerability occurs when we attempt an out-of-bounds memory access: trying access to memory that does not belong to the current data structure. Contracts are common in functions: their behavior is only guaranteed if the inputs fulfill specific criteria. Panicking when the contract is broken makes sense since a contract violation always indicates a caller-side issue, which we don't want the calling code to have to deal with explicitly. In fact, calling code has no realistic way of recovering; calling programmers must modify the code. Contracts for a function should be explained in the API description for the function, especially when a violation may result in a panic.

Having a lot of error checks in all of our functions, on the other hand, would be verbose and unpleasant. Fortunately, we can automate many checks by using Rust's type system (and hence the compiler's type checking). If a specific type is used as a parameter in your function, we can continue with the logic of our code knowing that the compiler has already checked for an acceptable value. If we use a type instead of an Option, for example, our program expects to see something rather than nothing.

Our code will no longer have to deal with two situations for the Some and None variations; instead, it will have to deal with one case for a value. Because code that attempts to send nothing to our function will fail to build, our method will not need to check for that case at runtime. Using an unsigned integer type like u32, for example, ensures that the parameter is never negative.

Creating the Custom Types for Validation

Let's take the idea of leveraging Rust's type system to assure a valid value a step further by defining a new type for validation. We never checked the user's guess against our secret number to see if it was between those numbers; we merely checked that it was positive. In this example, the implications were minor: our output of "Too high" or "Too low" would still be accurate.

However, it would be a useful upgrade to assist the user toward accurate guesses and have different reactions when the user guesses a number out of range vs. when the user enters letters, for example.

To accept potentially negative values, parse the guess as an i32 instead of merely an u32, and then add a check for the number being in range, as shown below:

```
loop {

        let guess: i32 = match guess.trim().parse() {
            Ok(numb) => numb,
            Err(_) => continue,
        };

        if guess < 1 || guess > 100 {
            println!("Secret number will be between 1 &
                    100.");
```

```
            continue;
    }

    match guess.cmp(&secret_number) {
}
```

If our value is out of range, the if expression informs the user of the problem and calls continue to begin the next loop iteration and ask for another guess. We can proceed with the comparisons between guess and the secret number after if expression, knowing that guess is between 1 and 100.

However, this is not the best solution: if it were necessary that the program only operates on values between 1 and 100, having a check like this in every function would be inconvenient (and might impact performance).

Instead of repeating the validations everywhere, we can build a new type and place the validations in a function to generate an instance of the type. As a result, functions can safely utilize the new type in their signatures and trust the values they get. The example below shows one approach to establishing a Guess type that will only produce a Guess instance if the new function is assigned a value between 1 and 100.

```
pub struct Guess {
    value: i32,
}

impl Guess {
    pub fn new(value: i32) ->Guess {
        if value<1||value>100 {
            panic!("Guess value between 1 and 100, got
                {}.", value);
        }

        Guess {value}
    }

    pub fn value(&self) ->i32 {
        self.value
    }
}
```

First, we create a struct called Guess with a value field that holds an i32. This is the location where the number will be saved.

Then we create instances of Guess values using a related function called new on Guess. The new function is defined to take one parameter of type i32 named value and return a Guess. The code in the new function's body verifies that the value is between 1 and 100.

If value fails this test, we issue a panic! call, informing the programmer writing the calling code that a defect needs to be fixed, because creating a Guess with a value outside of this range would violate the contract that Guess::new relies on. The circumstances under which Guess::new may panic should mention in its public-facing API documentation; we'll go over documentation conventions that indicate the likelihood of a panic! in the API documentation. If the value passes the test, we return the Guess and build a new one with the value field set to the value argument.

Following that, we create a value method that borrows self, has no other parameters, and returns an i32. Because its function is to retrieve data from its fields and return it, this type of method is sometimes referred to as a getter. Because value field of the Guess struct is private, this public function is required. Because the value field must be secret, code using the Guess struct is not permitted to set the value directly: code outside the module must construct an instance of Guess using the Guess::new function, ensuring that a Guess can't have a value that the conditions in the Guess::new function haven't checked.

A function that takes or returns only values between 1 and 100 could specify in its signature that it takes or returns a Guess instead of an i32, eliminating the need for additional checks in the body.

In this chapter, we covered unrecoverable errors with panic! and recoverable errors with Result.

Generic Types, Traits, and Lifetimes

IN THIS CHAPTER

➤ Generic data types

➤ Traits: defining shared behavior

➤ Validating references with lifetimes

In the previous chapter, we covered unrecoverable errors with panic! and recoverable errors with Result. This chapter will discuss generic data types, traits: defining shared behavior, and validating references with lifetimes.

GENERIC DATA TYPES

Generics can define items such as function signatures or structs, which can then be used with various concrete data types. Let's start with using generics to define functions, structs, enums, and methods. We'll then go through how generics affect code performance.

In Function Definitions

We place generics in the signature of a function where we would normally define the data types of the parameters and return value. This makes our code more flexible and gives callers of our function more functionality while avoiding code duplication.

DOI: 10.1201/9781003311966-8

Keeping with our largest function, the following code demonstrates two functions that discover the largest value in a slice.

Filename: src/themain.rs

```
fn largest_i32(list: &[i32]) ->i32 {
    let mut large = list[0];

    for &item in list {
        if item > large {
            large = item;
        }
    }

    large
}

fn large_char(list: &[char]) -> char {
    let mut large = list[0];
    for &item in list {
        if item > large {
            largest = item;
        }
    }

    large
}

fn main() {
    let number_list = vec![34, 50, 25, 100, 65];

    let result = large_i32(&number_list);
    println!("Large number is {}", result);

    let char_list = vec!['y', 'm', 'a', 'q'];

    let result = large_char(&char_list);
    println!("Large char is {}", result);
}
```

The large_i32 function locates the largest integer in a slice. The large char method returns the slice's largest char. Because the function bodies are identical, let's avoid duplication by providing a generic type parameter in a single function.

We must name the type parameter, exactly like we do for the value parameters in a function, to parameterize the types in the new function we'll build. As a type parameter name, we can use any identifier. But we'll choose T because parameter names in Rust are short, frequently just a letter, and Rust uses the CamelCase type-naming standard. T stands for "type," and most Rust programmers use it as their default.

We must declare the parameter name in the signature when we use it in the function's body so that the compiler understands what it means. In the same way, when we utilize a type parameter name in a function signature, we must first specify the type parameter name. Place type name declarations inside the angle brackets, < >, between the name of the function and the parameter list, to define the generic biggest function, as shown:

```
fn large<T>(list: &[T]) ->T {
```

According to this definition, the large function is generic over some type T. This function takes only one parameter, list, which is a slice of type T values. The large function will always return a value of type T.

The combined biggest function definition employing the generic data type in its signature is shown in the following example. The listing also demonstrates how to use a slice of i32 values or char values to invoke the function. This code will not compile right now, but we'll address it later in this chapter.

Filename: src/themain.rs

```
fn large<T>(list: &[T]) ->T {
    let mut large=list[0];

    for &item in list {
        if item>large {
            large=item;
        }
    }

    large
}
```

```
fn main() {
    let number_list=vec![37, 40, 35, 110, 75];

    let result=large(&number_list);
    println!("Largest number {}", result);

    let char_list=vec!['y', 'm', 'a', 'q'];

    let result=large(&char_list);
    println!("Largest char {}", result);
}
```

We'll get the following error if we compile this code right now.

```
$ cargo run
    Compiling chapter8 v0.1.0 (file:///projects/
chapter8)
error[E0369]: binary operation `>` cannot be applied
to type `T`
 --> src/main.rs:5:17
  |
5 |         if item > large {
  |            ---- ^ ------- T
  |            |
  |            T
  |
help: consider restricting type parameter `T`
  |
1 | fn large<T: std::cmp::PartialOrd>(list: &[T]) ->T {
  |         ^^^^^^^^^^^^^^^^^^^^^^^^^
```

The comment mentions the trait std::cmp::PartialOrd. In the next part, we'll discuss characteristics. For the time being, this mistake states that the body of large will not operate for all conceivable forms of T. We can only employ types whose values may be sorted since we want to compare values of type T in the body. The std::cmp::PartialOrd trait in the standard library can be used on types to enable comparisons (see Appendix C for more on this trait). We'll learn how to indicate that a generic type has a specific trait, but first, let's look at some other methods to use generic type parameters.

In the Struct Definitions

Using the < > syntax, we can also build structs to employ a generic type argument in one or more fields. The code below demonstrates creating a Point<T> struct that can hold any type of a and b coordinate value.

Filename: src/themain.rs

```
struct Point<T> {
    a: T,
    b: T,
}

fn main() {
    let integer = Point {a: 4, b: 14};
    let float = Point {a: 2.0, b: 3.0};
}
```

The syntax for using generics in struct definitions is similar to that of function definitions. First, directly after the struct name, we declare the name of the type argument inside angle brackets. Then, we can utilize the generic type in the struct definition instead of specifying actual data types.

Because we only used one generic type to describe Point<T>, this definition says that the Point<T> struct is generic over some type T, and that the fields a and b are both of that type, whatever it is. Our code will not compile if we construct an instance of a Point<T> with values of different kinds.

Filename: src/themain.rs

```
struct Point<T> {
    a: T,
    b: T,
}

fn main() {
    let wont_work = Point {a: 4, b: 3.0};
}
```

When we assign the integer value 4 to a in this example, we tell the compiler that the generic type T will be an integer for this instance of Point<T>. Then we'll get a type mismatch error if we specify 3.0 for b, which we've specified to have the same type as a:

```
$ cargo run
   Compiling chapter8 v0.1.0 (file:///projects/
chapter8)
error[E0308]: mismatched types
 --> src/main.rs:7:38
  |
7 |      let wont_work = Point {a: 4, b: 3.0};
  |                                      ^^^ expected
                    integer, found floating-point number
```

We can utilize multiple generic type parameters to build a Point struct where a and b are both generic but distinct types. For example, where a is of type T and b is of type U, we can change the definition of Point to be generic over types T and U.

Filename: src/themain.rs

```
struct Point<T, U> {
    a: T,
    b: U,
}

fn main() {
    let both_integer = Point {a: 5, b: 10};
    let both_float = Point {a: 1.0, b: 4.0};
    let integer_and_float = Point {a: 5, b: 4.0};
}
```

All instances of Point displayed are now permitted. In a definition, we can use as many generic type arguments as we want, but adding more than a few makes our code difficult to read. When we need a lot of generic types in our code, it may be a sign that we need to break it down into smaller chunks.

Enums, like structs, can be used to store generic data types in their variants. Let's review the Option<T> enum provided by the standard library, which we utilized in Chapter 5:

```
enum Option<T> {
    Some(T),
    None,
}
```

We should now be able to understand this definition. As we can see, Option<T> is a generic over type T enum with two variants: Some, which stores one type T value, and None, which does not carry any value. We can represent the abstract concept of having an optional value using the Option<T> enum. Because Option<T> is generic, we can utilize this abstraction regardless of the type of optional value.

Enums can also use a variety of generic types. One example is the definition of the Result enum that we used in Chapter 7:

```
enum Result<T, E> {
    Ok(T),
    Err(E),
}
```

The Result enum is generic across two types, T and E, and has two variants: Ok and Err. Ok holds a type T value, whereas Err holds a type E value. This definition allows us to use the Result enum anytime we have an operation that can either succeed (return a value of type T) or fail (return a value of type T) (return an error of some type E). In reality, in the forthcoming Chapter 9 examples, we used this to open a file, where T was filled in with the type std::. When the file was successfully opened, E was filled in with the type std::io::Error, and when problems were opening the file, E was filled in with the type std::io::Error.

In fact, in the forthcoming Chapter 9 example, we used this to open a file, where T was filled in with the type std::fs::File when the file was successfully opened, and E was filled in with the type std::io::Error when the file was not properly opened.

When we find many struct or enum definitions in our code that differ only in the types of values they carry, we can avoid redundancy by changing to generic types.

In Method Definitions

Methods can implement structs and enums, and generic types can be used in their definitions.

Filename: src/themain.rs

```
struct Point<T> {
    a: T,
    b: T,
}
```

```
impl<T> Point<T> {
    fn a(&self) -> &T {
        &self.a
    }
}

fn main() {
    let p = Point {a: 5, b: 10};

    println!("p.a = {}", p.a());
}
```

We've created a method on Point<T> called a that returns a reference to the data in the field a.

It is worth noting that we need to declare T right after impl to use it to indicate that we're implementing methods on the type Point<T>. Rust can tell that the type in the angle brackets in Point is a generic type rather than a concrete type by declaring T as generic type after impl.

For example, instead of implementing methods on Point<T> instances with any generic type, we may implement them only on Pointf32> instances. We utilize the concrete type f32 in the following code, which means we don't define any types after impl.

Filename: src/themain.rs

```
impl Point<f32> {
    fn distance_from_origin(&self) -> f32 {
        (self.a.powi(2) + self.b.powi(2)).sqrt()
    }
}
```

This code indicates that the type Point<f32> will have a distance_from_origin method, while other instances of Point<T> where T is not of type f32 will not. The approach employs mathematical operations that are only accessible for floating point types to determine how distant our point is from the point at coordinates (0.0, 0.0).

Generic type parameters in struct definitions aren't always the same as those used in method signatures for that struct. Define the method mixup on Point<T, U> struct from the previous code, for example. The method accepts another Point as a parameter, which may or may not be the same type as the self Point we're calling mixup. The method returns a new Point instance with the a value from the passed-in Point (of type W) and the b value from the self Point (of type T).

Filename: src/themain.rs

```
struct Point<T, U> {
    a: T,
    b: U,
}

impl<T, U> Point<T, U> {
    fn mixup<V, W>(self, other: Point<V, W>)
                    -> Point<T, W> {
        Point {
            a: self.a,
            b: other.b,
        }
    }
}

fn main() {
    let p1 = Point {a: 4, b: 10.3};
    let p2 = Point {a: "Helloo", b: 'c'};

    let p3 = p1.mixup(p2);

    println!("p3.a = {}, p3.b = {}", p3.a, p3.b);
}
```

We've defined a Point with an i32 for a (value 4) and an f64 for b in main (with value 10.3). P2 is a Point struct with a string slice for a (with the value "Helloo") and a char for b (with value c). Because fn originated from p1, calling mixup on p1 with the argument p2 returns p3, which will have an i32 for a. Because b came from p2, the p3 variable will have a char for it. p3.a = 4, p3.b = c will be printed using the println! macro function.

This example aims to show how some generic parameters are stated with impl, while others are declared with the method description. Because they go with the struct definition, T and U's generic arguments are declared after impl. Because the generic arguments V and W are only relevant to the method, they are stated after fn mixup.

Performance of Code Using Generics

If we're utilizing generic type parameters, we might be wondering if there's a runtime cost. The great news is that Rust implements generics in such a way that utilizing generic types does not slow down our code any more than using concrete types.

Rust does this by doing compile-time monomorphization of code that uses generics. Monomorphization is the process of converting generic code to specific code by filling in the concrete types needed during compilation.

The compiler performs the opposite of the steps we took to create the generic function: it examines all places where generic code is called and generates code for the concrete types with which the generic code is called.

Let's look at how this works with an example that uses the Option<T> enum from the standard library:

```
let integer = Some(4);
let float = Some(4.0);
```

Rust performs monomorphization while compiling this code. During this process, the compiler examines the values used in Option<T> instances and distinguishes between two types of Option<T>: i32 and f64. As a result, it expands Option <T>generic definition into Option i32 and Option f64, thus replacing the generic definition with the particular descriptions.

The following is the monomorphized version of the code. The compiler's individual definitions are used in place of the generic Option<T>:

Filename: src/themain.rs

```
enum Option_i32 {
    Some(i32),
    None,
}

enum Option_f64 {
    Some(f64),
    None,
}
```

```
fn main() {
    let integer = Option_i32::Some(4);
    let float = Option_f64::Some(4.0);
}
```

We pay no runtime cost for utilizing generics because Rust compiles generic code into code that specifies the type in each instance. When the code is run, it behaves exactly as if we had manually duplicated each declaration. Rust's generics are incredibly efficient at runtime, thanks to the monomorphization method.

Traits: Defining Shared Behavior

A trait informs the Rust compiler about the functionality that a given type has and can share with other kinds. In an abstract sense, traits can be used to define shared behavior. Trait boundaries can define a generic type as any type with specific behavior.

Defining a Trait

The methods that we can call on a type define its behavior. If we call the same methods on all types, they have the same behavior. Method signatures are grouped in trait definitions to define a set of behaviors required to achieve a goal.

Assume we have multiple structs that hold different types and amounts of text, such as a NewsArticle struct that holds a news story filed in a specific location and a Tweet struct that can have up to 280 characters and metadata that indicates whether it was a new tweet, a retweet, or a reply to another tweet.

We want to create a media aggregator library to present data summaries from NewsArticle and Tweet instances. To do so, we'll need a summary from each type, which we'll get by calling the summarize method on an example. The definition of a Summary trait that expresses this behavior is shown in code:

Filename: src/thelib.rs

```
pub trait Summary {
    fn summarize(&self) -> String;
}
```

We define a trait by using the trait keyword followed by the trait's name, which in this example is Summary. The method signatures that define the behaviors of the types that implement this trait, which in this example is fn summarize(&self) -> String, are declared inside the curly brackets.

We use a semicolon instead of supplying an implementation within curly brackets after the method signature. Each type implementing this trait must give its specific behavior for the method's body. The compiler will ensure that every type having the Summary trait has the summary method created with this exact signature.

The method signatures are listed per line, and each line ends in a semicolon. A trait can have numerous methods in its body.

Implementing a Trait on a Type

We can now use the Summary trait to express the appropriate behavior and apply it to the types in our media aggregator. The code shows a NewsArticle struct implementation of the Summary trait that creates the return value of summary using the title, author, and location. We define summary for the Tweet struct as the username followed by the whole text of the tweet, assuming that the tweet's content is already limited to 280 characters.

Filename: src/thelib.rs

```
pub struct NewsArticles {
    pub headline: String,
    pub location: String,
    pub author: String,
    pub content: String,
}

impl Summary for NewsArticles {
    fn summarize(&self) ->String {
        format!("{}, by {} ({})", self.headline, self
                .author, self.location)
    }
}

pub struct Tweets {
    pub usernames: String,
    pub contents: String,
```

```
    pub reply: bool,
    pub retweets: bool,
}

impl Summary for Tweets {
    fn summarize(&self) ->String {
        format!("{}: {}", self.usernames, self.
                contents)
    }
}
```

Implementing a trait on a type is equivalent to putting ordinary methods on a type. The difference is that we write the trait name we want to implement after impl, and then use the for keyword to define the type we want to implement the trait for. The method signatures defined by the trait definition are placed within the impl block. Rather than using a semicolon after each signature, we use curly brackets and fill the method body with the precise behavior we want the trait's methods to have for the given type.

We can call the methods on instances of NewsArticles and Tweets in the same manner we call ordinary methods after implementing the trait, for example:

```
let tweets=Tweets {
        usernames: String::from("horse_ebooks"),
        contents: String::from(
            "of course, as we probably already know,
                people",
        ),
        reply: false,
        retweets: false,
    };
    println!("1 new tweet: {}", tweets.summarize());
```

This code prints the following: 1 new tweet: horse_ebooks: of course, as you probably already know, people.

Because the Summary trait and the NewsArticles and Tweets types were all specified in the same lib.rs, they're all in the same scope. Let's pretend this lib.rs is for a crate named aggregator, and someone else wants to leverage the capabilities of our crate to implement the Summary trait on a struct declared within their library's scope. They'd have to first include the attribute in their scope.

They'd do so by specifying use aggregator::Summary;, allowing them to implement Summary for their type. For another crate to implement the Summary feature, it must be a public trait, which it is because we inserted the pub keyword before trait.

To keep in mind trait implementations, we can only implement a trait on a type if the trait or the type is local to our crate.

Because the type Tweet is local to our aggregator crate, we may utilize standard library features like Display on a custom type like Tweet as part of our aggregator crate functionality. Because the trait Summary is local to our aggregator crate, we can also implement Summary on Vec<T> in our aggregator crate.

However, we are unable to apply external attributes to external types. Because Display and Vec<T> is defined in the standard library and not local to our aggregator crate, we can't implement the Display trait on Vec<T> within our aggregator crate. This constraint is part of a program's coherence property, specifically the orphan rule, named after the absence of the parent type. This rule assures that other people's code cannot break our code, and vice versa. If the rule didn't exist, two crates might implement the same characteristic for the same type, and Rust would have no idea which one to choose.

VALIDATING REFERENCES WITH LIFETIMES

Every reference in Rust has a lifespan, which is the scope for which that reference is valid, which we didn't cover in the "References and Borrowing in Rust" section in Chapter 3. Most of the time, lifetimes are assumed and inferred, just as types are assumed and inferred most of the time. When numerous types are possible, we must annotate them. Similarly, when the lifetimes of references can be associated in various ways, we must annotate them. To verify that the actual references used at runtime are genuine, Rust needs us to annotate the relationships using generic lifespan parameters.

The concept of lifetimes is separate from other programming languages' tools, and it is perhaps Rust's most distinguishing characteristic. Although we won't go over lifetimes in detail in this chapter, we will go through some of the most typical ways we could come across lifetime syntax to get a better understanding of the ideas.

Preventing Dangling References with Lifetimes

The primary goal of lifetimes is to avoid dangling references, which cause a program to refer to data that isn't intended to be referenced. Take a look at the program, which has both an outer and an inner scope.

```
{
    let s;

    {
        let y = 6;
        s = &y;
    }

    println!("s: {}", s);
}
```

The outside scope declares a variable named s with no starting value, while the inner scope declares a variable named y with a value of 6 as its first value. We try to set the value of s as a reference to y inside the inner scope. The inner scope then comes to an end, and we try to print the value in s. Because the value s refers to has gone out of scope before we try to use it, this code will not compile. The following is the error message:

```
$ cargo run
   Compiling chapter8 v0.1.0 (file:///projects/chapter8)
error[E0597]: `y` does not live long enough
  --> src/main.rs:7:17
   |
7  |             s = &y;
   |                 ^^ borrowed value does not live
   |                    long enough
8  |         }
   |         - `y` dropped here while still borrowed
9  |
10 |         println!("s: {}", s);
   |                           - borrow later used here
```

The variable y doesn't "live long enough." This is because when the inner scope finishes on line 7, y will be out of scope. However, s is still valid for the outer scope; we say it "lives longer" because its scope is bigger.

If Rust let this code run, s would be addressing memory that had been deallocated when y exited scope, and whatever we tried to do with s would fail. So, how does Rust figure out if this code is legitimate or not? A borrow checker is used.

Borrow Checker

The borrow checker in the Rust compiler examines scopes to see if all borrows are valid: the same code as before, but with annotations indicating the variable lifetimes.

```
{
    let s;                      // ---------+-- 'a
                                //          |
    {                           //          |
        let y = 6;              // -+-- 'b  |
        s = &y;                 //  |       |
    }                           // -+       |
                                //          |
    println!("s: {}", s);       //          |
}                               // ---------+
```

The lifetime of s has been marked with 'a, and the lifetime of y has been annotated with 'b. The inner 'b block is significantly smaller than the outer 'a lifetime block, as we can see. Rust analyzes the sizes of the two lives at build time and discovers that r has a lifetime of 'a but references to memory with a lifetime of 'b. Because 'b is shorter than 'a, the program is rejected: the reference's topic does not live as long as the reference.

It fixes a dangling reference in the code and ensures that it compiles without issues.

```
{
    let y = 6;                  // ----------+-- 'b
                                //           |
    let s = &y;                 // --+-- 'a  |
                                //   |       |
    println!("s: {}", s);       //   |       |
                                // --+       |
}                               // ----------+
```

y has the lifetime 'b, which is larger than 'a in this case. This means that s can refer to y since Rust knows that while y is valid, the reference in s will always be valid.

Let's look at generic lifetimes of arguments and return values in the context of functions now that we know where references' lifetimes are and how Rust evaluates lifetimes to ensure references are always valid.

Generic Lifetimes in the Functions

Let's create a method that returns the longest string slice between two string slices. This function returns a string slice from two string slices. The code should print when we've implemented the longest function. The efgh is the longest string.

Filename: src/themain.rs

```
fn main() {
    let string1 = String::from("efgh");
    let string2 = "abc";

    let result = longest(string1.as_str(), string2);
    println!("Longest string is {}", result);
}
```

Because we don't want the longest function to acquire ownership of its parameters, we want the function to take string slices, which are references. More information regarding why the parameters we use are the ones we desire can be found in the "String Slices as Parameters" section in Chapter 3.

It will not compile if we try to implement the longest function as shown:

Filename: src/themain.rs

```
fn longest(y: &str, z: &str) -> &str {
    if y.len() > z.len() {
        y
    } else {
        z
    }
}
```

The error message relates to lifetimes.

This chapter discussed shared behavior and validating references with lifetimes.

CHAPTER 9

I/O Project

Building a Command Line Program

IN THIS CHAPTER

> ➤ Accepting command line arguments

> ➤ Reading a file

> ➤ Refactoring to improve modularity and error handling

> ➤ Developing the library's functionality with test-driven development

> ➤ Working with environment variables

> ➤ Improving our I/O project

In the previous chapter, we covered generic data types, traits in which we discussed defining shared behavior, and validating references with lifetimes. In this chapter, we will cover accepting command line arguments, reading a file, and refactoring to improve modularity and error handling. Also, we will discuss developing the library's functionality with test-driven development (TDD), working with environment variables, and improving our I/O project.

This chapter serves as a review of the various skills we've learned thus far, as well as a study of a few more common library features. To put some of the Rust principles you've learned to the test, we'll create a command line tool that interacts with file and command line input/output.

DOI: 10.1201/9781003311966-9

Because Rust's speed, safety, single binary output, and cross-platform support make it excellent for constructing command line tools, we'll make our own version of the traditional command line search tool grep (globally search a regular expression and print) for our project. Grep searches a specified file for a specified string in the most basic use case.

A filename and a string are sent to grep as parameters. The program then scans the file, looks for lines that contain the string argument, and prints them.

We'll teach you how to make our command line tool use terminal features that many command line programs use along the road. To allow the user to adjust the functionality of our tool, we'll read the value of an environment variable. We'll also print error messages to the standard error console stream (stderr) rather than standard output (stdout), so that the user can, for example, redirect successful output to a file while still viewing error messages onscreen.

Andrew Gallant, a member of the Rust community, has already created ripgrep, a fully featured and extremely fast version of grep. Our version of grep will be simple in comparison, but this chapter will provide us with some of the background information we'll need to understand a real-world project like ripgrep.

ACCEPTING THE COMMAND LINE ARGUMENTS

Let's start a new project with cargo new, as usual. To distinguish it from the grep utility we might already have on your machine, we'll call our project minigrep.

```
$ cargo new minigrep
    Created binary (application) `minigrep` project
$ cd minigrep
```

The first step is to get minigrep to accept the filename and the string to search for as command line arguments. That is, we want to be able to run our program using cargo run, a string to search for, and a file path to search in, as follows:

```
$ cargo run searchstring examplefilename.txt
```

At the moment, the program created by cargo new is unable to process the arguments we provide. Although there are already existing libraries on crates.io that can assist us in developing a program that accepts command line arguments, since we're just learning this concept, let's do it ourselves.

We'll need the std::env::args function from Rust's standard library to enable minigrep to read the values of command line arguments we pass it. This method produces an iterator of the arguments passed to minigrep on the command line. There are only two things we need to know about iterators: Iterators generate a series of values, and we can use the collect function to put them into a collection, such as a vector, that contains all of the elements the iterator generates.

Allow our minigrep application to read any command line arguments and then collect the values into a vector using the code.

Filename: src/themain.rs

```
use std::env;
fn main() {
    let args: Vec<String> = env::args().collect();
    println!("{:?}", args);
}
```

First, we use a use statement to bring the std::env module into scope so that we may use its args function. The std::env::args function is nested in two tiers of modules, as we can see. When a desired function is nested in many modules, as we described in Chapter 6, it is common to bring the parent module into scope rather than the function. We can then use std::env other functions with ease. It is also less ambiguous than adding use std::env::args and then calling the function with just args, because args may easily be confused with a current module function.

We call env::args on the first line of main, and then use collect to turn the iterator into a vector holding all of the values produced by the iterator. Because the collect method can be used to generate a variety of collections, we give the type of args explicitly to indicate that we want a vector of strings. Although we don't need to annotate types very often in Rust, we do need to annotate collect since Rust can't deduce the type of collection we want.

Finally, we use the debug formatter to print the vector, :? Let's execute the code without any arguments first, and then with two arguments:

```
$ cargo run
   Compiling minigrep v0.1.0 (file:///projects/
                              minigrep)
    Finished dev [unoptimized+debuginfo] target(s) in
        0.61s
```

```
      Running `target/debug/minigrep`
["target/debug/minigrep"]

$ cargo run needle haystack
   Compiling minigrep v0.1.0 (file:///projects/
            minigrep)
   Finished dev [unoptimized+debuginfo] target(s) in
            1.57s
      Running `target/debug/minigrep needle haystack`
["target/debug/minigrep", "needle", "haystack"]
```

The name of our binary is "target/debug/minigrep," which is the first value in the vector. This is similar to the behavior of the arguments list in C, which allows programs to utilize the name with which they were called during execution. It is useful to know the program name in case we want to print it in messages or adjust the program's behavior based on the command line alias that was used to call it. However, for the sake of this chapter, we'll disregard it and save only the two arguments that we require.

Saving the Argument Values in the Variables

The fact that the program may access the values specified as command line arguments was demonstrated by printing the value of the vector of arguments. Now we must save the values of the two arguments in variables so that we can use them later in the program.

Filename: src/themain.rs

```
use std::env;
fn main() {
    let args: Vec<String> = env::args().collect();

    let query = &args[1];
    let filenames = &args[2];

    println!("Search for {}", query);
    println!("File {}", filenames);
}
```

READING A FILE

We'll now add support for reading files supplied in the filename command line option. To begin with, we'll need a sample file (Emily Dickinson,

I'm Nobody! Who are you? (260), in *Poems, Series 2*, 1891) to test it: the best type of file to use to ensure that minigrep is working is one with a little amount of text spread across numerous lines and some repeated terms.

Filename: thepoem.txt

```
I'm nobody! Who are you?
Are you nobody, too?
Then there's a pair of us - don't tell!
They'd banish us, you know.

How dreary to be somebody!
How public, like a frog
To tell your name the livelong day
To an admiring bog!
```

After the text is in place, edit src/main.rs and add the following code to read the file:

Filename: src/themain.rs

```rust
use std::env;
use std::fs;

fn main() {
    // --snip--
    println!("File {}", filename);

    let contents = fs::read_to_string(filename)
        .expect("Something went wrong reading file");

    println!("With the text:\n{}", contents);
}
```

To begin with, we add another use line to include a necessary portion of the standard library: we require std::fs to handle files.

We've added a new statement to main: fs::read to string takes a filename, opens it, and produces a Result<String> with the contents of the file.

Following that declaration, we've added a temporary println! statement that prints the contents value after the file is read, allowing us to verify that the program is working thus far.

Let's execute this code using any string as the first command line input (because the searching section hasn't been implemented yet) and thepoem .txt file as the second argument:

```
$ cargo run thepoem.txt
    Compiling minigrep v0.1.0 (file:///projects/
            minigrep)
     Finished dev [unoptimized+debuginfo] target(s) in
            0.0s
      Running `target/debug/minigrep thepoem.txt`
Searching for the
In file thepoem.txt
With text:
I'm nobody! Who are you?
Are you nobody, too?
Then there's a pair of us - don't tell!
They'd banish us, you know.

How dreary to be somebody!
How public, like a frog
To tell your name the livelong day
To an admiring bog!
```

Great! The code read the contents of the file and then printed them. However, there are a few problems in the code. The primary function has numerous responsibilities: functions that are responsible for only one idea are often clearer and easier to maintain. Another issue is that we aren't dealing with errors as well as we could be. Because the program is still tiny, these faults aren't a major issue, but when it expands, it will be more difficult to cleanly fix them. It is a good idea to start refactoring early in the development of a program because refactoring smaller portions of code is considerably easier. That's what we'll do next.

Refactoring to Improve Modularity and Error Handling

To make our program better, we'll fix four issues with the program's structure and how it handles potential mistakes.

Our main function now has two functions: it parses inputs and reads files. This isn't a huge issue for such a short function. However, if we continue to expand our program inside main, the number of distinct tasks handled by the main function will grow. As a function grows in complexity, it gets more difficult to reason about, test, and update without breaking one of its components. It is best to keep functionality separate so that each function is only responsible for one task.

The second issue is that, while query and filename are configuration variables in our program, variables like contents are used to perform the program's logic. The longer the main becomes, the more variables we'll need to bring into scope; the more variables we have in scope, the more difficult it will be to remember what each one performs. To make the purpose of the configuration variables apparent, group them into one structure.

The third issue is that we expect it to print an error message if reading the file fails, but the error message simply says, "Something went wrong reading the file." Reading a file can fail for a variety of reasons, such as the file being missing or not having permission to open it. We'd output the Something went wrong reading the file error message regardless of the situation right now, which would provide no information to the user.

Fourth, we use expect multiple times to handle various problems, and if the user executes our program without providing enough inputs, Rust will throw an index out of bounds error that doesn't explain the issue. All of the error-handling code should be in one location so that future maintainers only have to look in one place if the error-handling logic has to be changed. Having all of the error-handling code in one place also ensures that we're printing messages that our users will understand.

Let's rework our project to handle these four issues.

Separation of Concerns for Binary Projects

Many binary projects have the organizational challenge of distributing responsibility for various tasks to the core function. As a result, the Rust community has established a process to serve as a guideline for breaking a binary program's various concerns when main gets too large. The steps in the procedure are as follows:

- Split our program into two files, themain.rs and thelib.rs, and relocate the logic to thelib.rs.

- We can keep our command line parsing logic in themain.rs as long as it is minimal.

- Extract the command line parsing logic from themain.rs and relocate it to thelib.rs when it becomes too sophisticated.

After this process, the main function's duties should be restricted to the following:

- Using the argument values to call the command line parsing logic

- Any other configuration setup

- In thelib.rs, calling a run function

- If run returns an error, we must handle it.

This pattern emphasizes separation of concerns: themain.rs is in charge of running the program. While thelib.rs is in charge of the task's logic. Because we can't directly test the main function, this structure allows us to move all of our program's functionality into functions in thelib.rs. The only code left in themain.rs will be modest enough to read and check its accuracy. Let's use this method to rewrite our program.

Extracting the Argument Parser

To prepare for relocating the command line parsing logic to src/thelib.r s, we'll isolate the mechanism for parsing arguments into a function that main will call. The following example shows the revised start of main, which calls a new function parse config, which we'll create for the time being in src/themain.rs.

Filename: src/themain.rs

```
fn main() {
    let args: Vec<String> = env::args().collect();

    let (query, filenames) = parse_config(&args);

    // ---snip---
}

fn parse_config(args: &[String]) -> (&str, &str) {
    let query = &args[1];
    let filenames = &args[2];

    (query, filenames)
}
```

Instead of assigning the argument value at index 1 to the variable query and the argument value at index 2 to the variable filename within the main function, we give the entire vector to the parse_config function. The logic that selects which argument belongs to which variable is stored in the parse_config function, which then returns the data to main. The query and filenames variables are still created in main, but it is no longer responsible for deciding how the command line inputs and variables relate.

We're restructuring in small, incremental steps, so this rework may look overkill for our small program. Run the program again after making this change to ensure that the argument parsing still works. It is a good idea to keep track of our progress so that we can figure out what's causing issues when they arise.

Grouping the Configuration Values

We can improve the parse config method even more by taking another little step. We're now returning a tuple, but we'll break it down into individual components again shortly. This is an indication that we haven't found the right abstraction yet.

The config component of parse_config is another indicator that there's opportunity for improvement, as it implies that the two values we return are connected and both are part of one configuration value. We're not currently conveying this meaning in the data structure other than by grouping the two values into a tuple; we could combine the two values into one struct and name each of the struct fields something significant. This will make it easy for future code maintainers to understand how the various values interact with one another and what their purpose is.

The program demonstrates how the parse_config function has been improved.

Filename: src/themain.rs

```
fn main() {
    let args: Vec<String> = env::args().collect();

    let config = parse_config(&args);

    println!("Searching for: {}", config.query);
    println!("In file: {}", config.filename);

    let contents = fs::read_to_string(config.filename)
        .expect("Something went wrong reading file");
```

```
    // --snip--
}

struct Config {
    query: String,
    filenames: String,
}

fn parse_config(args: &[String]) ->Config {
    let query=args[1].clone();
    let filenames=args[2].clone();

    Config {query, filenames}
}
```

Creating a Constructor for the Config
So far, the code for parsing command line parameters has been taken from main and placed in the parse_config function. As a result, we were able to observe that the query and filename values were linked, and that this relationship needed to be reflected in our code. Then, to be able to return the values' names as struct field names from the parse_config method, we built a Config struct to identify the relevant purpose of query and filenames.

We may alter parse_config from a plain function to a function named new that is associated with the Config struct now that the function's purpose is to produce a Config instance. The code will become more idiomatic as a result of this improvement. By invoking String::new, we can create instances of types from the standard library, such as String. We can also call Config::new to generate instances of Config by turning parse_config into a new function associated with Config. The changes we need to make are shown in the code.

Filename: src/themain.rs

```
fn main() {
    let args: Vec<String>=env::args().collect();

    let config=Config::new(&args);

    // --snip--
}
```

```
// --snip--

impl Config {
    fn new(args: &[String]) ->Config {
        let query=args[1].clone();
        let filenames=args[2].clone();

        Config {query, filenames}
    }
}
```

We've changed the code in main to call Config::new instead of parse_
config. The name of parse config has been changed to new, and it has been
moved into an impl block that associates the new function with Config.
Make sure this code works by compiling it again.

Fixing the Error Handling

We'll now focus on improving our error handling. Remember that accessing the values in the args vector at index 1 or 2 will cause the program
to panic if the vector has fewer than three items. If you run the program
without any arguments, it will appear as follows:

```
$ cargo run
   Compiling minigrep v0.1.0 (file:///projects/
           minigrep)
    Finished dev [unoptimized+debuginfo] target(s) in
           0.1s
     Running `target/debug/minigrep`
thread 'main' panicked at 'index out of bounds: len is
1 but the index is 1', src/main.rs:27:21
note: run with `RUST_BACKTRACE=1` environment variable
to display backtrace
```

The error message "Line index out of bounds: the len is 1 but the index
is 1" is meant for programmers. It will not assist our end users in understanding what occurred and what they should do instead. Let's take care
of that now.

Improving the Error Message

Before accessing indices 1 and 2, we add a check in the new function to
ensure that the slice is long enough. The program panics and displays a

better error message than the index out of bounds message if the slice isn't long enough.

Filename: src/themain.rs

```
// ---snip---
    fn new(args: &[String]) ->Config {
        if args.len()<3 {
            panic!("not enough argument");
        }
        // ---snip---
```

This code is similar to the panic! call we made before in the Guess::new method when the value argument was out of the valid range. Instead of checking for a range of values, we check that args is at least three characters long, and the rest of the function can proceed with the presumption that this condition is met. If args contains fewer than three elements, this condition is met, and the panic! macro is invoked to terminate the program instantly.

Let's run the program without any arguments again with these extra few lines of code in new to see what the error looks like now:

```
$ cargo run
   Compiling minigrep v0.1.0 (file:///projects/
           minigrep)
    Finished dev [unoptimized+debuginfo] target(s) in
           0.0s
     Running `target/debug/minigrep`
thread 'main' panicked at 'not enough argument', src/
themain.rs:26:13
note: run with `RUST_BACKTRACE=1` environment variable
to display backtrace
```

DEVELOPING THE LIBRARY'S FUNCTIONALITY WITH THE TEST-DRIVEN DEVELOPMENT

It is much easier to build tests for the fundamental functionality of our code now that we've removed the logic into src/thelib.rs and left the argument collection and error handling in src/themain.rs. Without having to execute our binaries from the command line, we may call functions directly with various arguments and examine return values. Feel free to develop tests for the Config::new feature and run functions on our own.

We'll use the TDD process to add the searching logic to the minigrep program in this part. The steps in this software development technique are as follows:

- Create a failing test and execute it to ensure it fails for the expected cause.

- Just enough code should be written or modified to pass the new test.

- Refactor the code we've just added or updated, and double-check that the tests are still passing.

- Step 1 must be repeated!

TDD is just one of many techniques to build software, but it can also help with code design. Writing the test first, then writing the code that passes the test, ensures good test coverage throughout the process. We'll run through the implementation of the feature that searches the file contents for the query string and returns a list of lines that match the query. This feature will be added to a function called search.

Remove the println! statements from src/lib.rs and src/main.rs that we used to check the program's behavior because we no longer require them. Then we'll add a tests module with a test function to src/thelib.rs. The test function defines the search function's behavior: it takes a query and the text to search for the query in, and returns only the lines from the text that contains the query. This test is shown in the code above, but it will not compile at this time.

Filename: src/thelib.rs

```
#[cfg(test)]
mod tests {
    use super::*;

    #[test]
    fn one_result() {
        let query = "duct";
        let content = "\
Rust:
safe, fast, productive.
Pick three.";
```

```
        assert_eq!(vec!["safe, fast, productive."],
                    search(query, content));
    }
}
```

This test looks for the word "duct." We're looking for three lines of text, but only one of them contains the word "duct" (note that the backslash after the opening double quote tells Rust not to put a newline character at the beginning of the contents of this string literal). We assert that the result provided by the search function only contains the line we expected.

We can't run this test and watch it fail as it doesn't even compile: the search function isn't even implemented yet! Now we'll add just enough code to get the test to build and execute, as indicated, by defining the search function to always return an empty vector. The test should then run and fail because an empty vector does not match a vector that contains the line "safe, fast, productive."

Filename: src/thelib.rs

```
pub fn search<'c>(query: &str, content: &'a str)
            ->Vec<&'c str>{
    vec![]
}
```

It is worth noting that we require an explicit lifespan 'c, which is defined in the search signature and utilized with the contents argument and return value. Remember from Chapter 8 that the lifetime parameters determine which argument's lifetime is linked to the return value's lifetime. We specify that the returned vector should contain string slices that relate to slices of the argument contents in this case (rather than the argument query).

In other words, we tell Rust that the data returned by the search function will last as long as the data supplied in the contents argument. This is critical! The data referred by a slice must be legitimate in order for the reference to be valid; if the compiler believes we're producing query string slices rather than contents slices, it will improperly perform its safety checks.

If we try to compile this code without the lifetime annotations, we'll get an error.

WORKING WITH THE ENVIRONMENT VARIABLES

Minigrep will be enhanced with the addition of a case-insensitive search option that the user can enable via an environment variable. We might make this a command line option that users must type every time they want it to work, but we'll instead use an environment variable. This allows our users to set the environment variable once and have all of their searches in that terminal session be case-insensitive.

Writing Failing Test for the Case-Insensitive search Function

When the environment variable is set to true, we'll call the new search case-insensitive method. We'll continue the TDD process this time; therefore, the first step is to write a failed test. To clarify the differences between the two tests, we'll write a new test for the new search case-insensitive function and change our old test from one result to case-sensitive.

Filename: src/thelib.rs

```
#[cfg(test)]
mod test {
    use super::*;

    #[test]
    fn case_sensitive() {
        let query = "duct";
        let content = "\
Rust:
safe, fast, productive.
Pick three.
Duct tape.";

        assert_eq!(vec!["safe, fast, productive."],
                        search(query, content));
    }

    #[test]
    fn case_insensitive() {
        let query = "rUsT";
        let content = "\
Rust:
safe, fast, productive.
Pick three.
```

```
Trust me.";

        assert_eq!(
            vec!["Rust:", "Trust-me."],
            search_case_insensitive(query, content)
        );
    }
}
```

We've also changed the contents of the old test. When searching in a case-sensitive manner, we've inserted a new line with the phrase "Duct tape." using a capital D, which shouldn't match the query "duct." By making this change to the existing test, we can ensure that we don't damage the case-sensitive search feature we've already developed. This test should pass right now, and it should keep passing as we work on the case-insensitive search.

"rUsT" is the query for the new case-insensitive search test. Even if both lines have different casing from the query, the query "rUsT" should match the line having "Rust:" with a capital R and the line "Trust me." in the search case-insensitive function we're about to implement. This is our failing test, and it will fail to compile because the search case-insensitive function has not yet been defined. To see the test build and fail, add a skeleton implementation that always returns an empty vector, similar to how we did with the search function.

Implementing search_case_insensitive Function

The following example shows the search_case_insensitive function, which is nearly identical to the search function. The only difference is that we'll lowercase the query and each line, so whatever case the input arguments are in when we check if the line contains the query will be the same case.

Filename: src/thelib.rs

```
pub fn search_case_insensitive<'a>(
    query: &str,
    content: &'a str,
) ->Vec<&'a str>{
    let query=query.to_lowercase();
    let mut result=Vec::new();
```

```
    for line in content.lines() {
        if line.to_lowercase().contains(&query) {
            result.push(line);
        }
    }

    result
}
```

The query string is first lowercased and stored in a shadowed variable with the same name. We need to call to_lowercase on the query so that regardless of whether the user's query is "rust," "RUST," "Rust," or "rUsT," we'll treat it as if it were "rust" and ignore the case. While to_lowercase will handle basic Unicode, it will not be accurate. We'd want to do a little more work here if we were developing a real program, but this section is about environment variables, not Unicode, so we'll leave it at that.

Because calling to_lowercase creates new data rather than referencing current data, query is now a String rather than a string slice. Assume the query is "rUsT": that string slice lacks a lowercase u or t that we can utilize, thus we must allocate a new String containing "rust." Because the signature of the includes method is defined to take a string slice, we must now include an ampersand when passing query as an argument.

Then, on each line, we add a call to to_lowercase before checking whether it contains a query to lowercase all characters. Now that we've transformed the line and query to lowercase, we'll be able to locate matches regardless of the query's case.

Let's have a look at the tests to check whether this implementation passes:

```
$ cargo test1
    Compiling minigrep v0.1.0 (file:///projects/
                                minigrep)
    Finished test1 [unoptimized+debuginfo] target(s)
                in 1.33s
    Running unittests (target/debug/deps/minigrep-9c
                    d200e5fac0fc94)

running 2 tests
test tests::case_insensitive... ok
test tests::case_sensitive... ok
```

```
test result: ok. 2 passed; 0 failed; 0 ignored; 0
measured; 0 filtered out; finished in 0.00s

    Running unittests (target/debug/deps/minigrep-9c
                    d200e5fac0fc94)

running 0 tests

test1 result: ok. 0 passed; 0 failed; 0 ignored; 0
measured; 0 filtered out; finished in 0.00s

   Doc-tests minigrep

running 0 tests

test1 result: ok. 0 passed; 0 failed; 0 ignored; 0
measured; 0 filtered out; finished in 0.00s
```

Great! They were successful. Let's use the run function to invoke the new search_case_insensitive function. To begin with, we'll add a switch to the Config struct that allows us to choose between case-sensitive and case-insensitive search. Because we haven't yet initialized this field, adding it will result in compiler errors:

Filename: src/thelib.rs

```
pub struct Config {
    pub query: String,
    pub filenames: String,
    pub case_sensitive: bool,
}
```

The case_sensitive field, which holds a Boolean, has been added. Next, as shown below, we need the run function to verify the case_sensitive field's value and use it to determine whether to call the search function or the search_case_insensitive function. It is worth noting that this still won't compile.

Filename: src/thelib.rs

```
pub fn run(config: Config) ->Result<(), Box<dyn Error>>{
    let content=fs::read_to_string(config.filenames)?;
```

```
    let result=if config.case_sensitive {
        search(&config.query, &content)
    } else {
        search_case_insensitive(&config.query, &content)
    };

    for line in result {
        println!("{}", line);
    }

    Ok(())
}
```

Last but not least, we must look for the environment variable. The functions for interacting with environment variables are in the env module in the standard library, so we'll use a use std::env; line at the top of src/thelib. rs to bring that module into scope. Then, as shown in example, we'll utilize the var function from the env module to look for an environment variable named CASE_INSENSITIVE.

Filename: src/thelib.rs

```
use std::env;
// --snip--

impl Config {
    pub fn new(args: &[String]) ->Result<Config, &str>{
        if args.len()<3 {
            return Err("not enough argument");
        }

        let query=args[1].clone();
        let filenames=args[2].clone();

        let case_sensitive=env::var("CASE_INSENSIT
                                    IVE").is_err();

        Ok(Config {
            query,
            filenames,
```

```
            case_sensitive,
        })
    }
}
```

We're going to make a new variable called case_sensitive. We call the env::var function and feed it the name of the CASE_INSENSITIVE environment variable to set its value. If the environment variable is set, the env::var function produces a Result that is the successful Ok variation that contains the value of the environment variable. If the environment variable is not set, it will return the Err variation.

We're checking whether it is an error and so unset with the is_err method on the Result, which means it should do a case-sensitive search. The is_err will return false if the CASE_INSENSITIVE environment variable is set to anything, and the application will perform a case-insensitive search. We don't care about the value of the environment variable; all we care about is whether it is set or unset, so we use is_err instead of unwrap, expect, or any of the other Result methods.

We provide the case_sensitive variable's value to the Config instance so that the run function may read it and decide whether to call search or search_case_insensitive, as we did previously.

Let's see how it goes! We'll start by running our program without the environment variable and with the query to, which should match any line that has the word "to" in all lowercase:

```
$ cargo run to thepoem.txt
   Compiling minigrep v0.1.0 (file:///projects/minigrep)
    Finished dev [unoptimized+debuginfo] target(s) in 0.1s
     Running `target/debug/minigrep to thepoem.txt`
Are we nobody, too?
How dreary to be somebody.
```

That appears to be still valid! Let's run the program again, but this time with CASE_INSENSITIVE set to 1 and the same query.

We'll need to establish the environment variable and start the program as separate commands if we're using PowerShell:

```
PS> $Env:CASE_INSENSITIVE=1; cargo run to thepoem.txt
```

CASE_INSENSITIVE will now be persistent for the rest of our shell session. The Remove-Item cmdlet can be used to unset it:

```
PS>Remove-Item Env:CASE_INSENSITIVE
```

We should get lines with the word "to" and possibly capital letters:

```
$ CASE_INSENSITIVE=1 cargo run to poem.txt
    Finished dev [unoptimized+debuginfo] target(s) in 0.0s
     Running `target/debug/minigrep to poem.txt`
Are we nobody, too??
How dreary to be somebody.
To tell our name the livelong day
To an admiring bog.
```

We also got lines with "To" in them, which is fantastic! Our minigrep program may now perform case-insensitive searching based on a variable in the environment. We now know how to use command line arguments or environment variables to handle options.

For the same configuration, several programs offer arguments and environment variables. In those situations, the programs select which one takes precedence. Try managing case insensitivity with a command line option or an environment variable on your own for another practice.

If the program is run with one set to case sensitive and the other set to case insensitive, decide whether the command line input or the environment variable should take precedence.

Many more useful capabilities for dealing with environment variables may be found in the std::env module: To see what's accessible, look through the documentation.

WRITING ERROR MESSAGES TO THE STANDARD ERROR INSTEAD OF STANDARD OUTPUT

We're currently utilizing the println! macro to write all of our output to the terminal. Standard output (stdout) for general information and standard error (stderr) for error messages are provided by most terminals. This distinction allows users to direct a program's successful output to a file while still printing error warnings on the screen.

Because the println! macro can only print to standard output, we must use another method to print to standard error.

Checking Where Errors Are Written

Let's start by looking at how minigrep's output is now written to standard output, including any error messages we want to send to standard error instead. We'll accomplish this by forwarding the standard output stream to a file while simultaneously producing an error on purpose. Because the standard error stream will not be redirected, any content submitted to standard error will continue to appear on the screen.

We can still see error messages on the screen even if we redirect the standard output stream to a file because command line programs are intended to send error messages to the standard error stream. Our program is currently misbehaving: we're about to discover that it saves the output of the error message to a file instead!

Running the program with > and the filename output.txt, which we wish to redirect the standard output stream to, will demonstrate this behavior. We will not pass any parameters, which should result in the following error:

```
$ cargo run>output.txt
```

The > syntax instructs the shell to write standard output to output.txt rather than the screen. We didn't see the error message we were expecting on the screen, so it must have been saved to the file.

```
Problem parsing argument: not enough argument
```

Our error message is written to standard output, as expected. It is far more useful to output error messages like this to standard error, so that only data from successful runs gets up in the file. We're going to change that.

Printing Errors to the Standard Error

To change how error messages are printed, we'll utilize the code in the example. All of the code that produces error warnings are now in one function, main, thanks to the refactoring we accomplished previously in this chapter. Because the standard library includes the eprintln! macro, which prints to the standard error stream, we'll replace println! with eprintln! in the two locations where we were invoking println! to print errors.

Filename: src/themain.rs

```rust
fn main() {
    let args: Vec<String>=env::args().collect();

    let config=Config::new(&args).unwrap_or_else(|err|{
```

```
        eprintln! ("The Problem parsing argument: {}", err);
        process::exit(1);
    });

    if let Err(e) = minigrep::run(config) {
        eprintln! ("The Application error: {}", e);

        process::exit(1);
    }
}
```

Let's run the program again after changing println! to eprintln!, this time without any parameters and diverting standard output using >:

```
$ cargo run > theoutput.txt
Problem parsing argument: not enough argument
```

Now we see the error onscreen, and output.txt is empty, as we would expect from a command line program.

Let's try it again with arguments that don't throw an error but still redirect standard output to a file:

```
$ cargo run to thepoem.txt > theoutput.txt
```

We won't get any output to the terminal, but our results will be in output.txt:

Filename: theoutput.txt

```
Are we nobody, too??
How dreary to be somebody.
```

This shows that, where appropriate, we're now utilizing standard output for successful output and standard error for error output.

In this chapter, we covered how to build a command line program, where we discussed accepting command line arguments, reading a file, and refactoring to improve modularity and error handling. We also covered developing the library's functionality and working with the environment variables.

CHAPTER 10

Cargo and crates.io

IN THIS CHAPTER

➤ Customizing builds with the release profiles

➤ Publishing crate to crates.io

➤ Cargo workspaces

➤ Installing the binaries from crates.io with cargo install

➤ Extending cargo with the custom commands

In the previous chapter, we covered building a command line program. This chapter will discuss customizing builds with release profiles, publishing a crate to crates.io and cargo workspaces. Also, installing binaries from crates.io with cargo install and extending cargo with custom commands are covered.

CUSTOMIZING BUILDS WITH THE RELEASE PROFILES

Rust's release profiles are predefined and customizable profiles with various configurations that give a programmer more control over specific compiling options. Each profile is set up separately from the others.

Cargo has two major profiles: dev and release. Cargo utilizes the dev profile when we run cargo build and the release profile when we run cargo build --release. The release profile provides good defaults for release builds, and the dev profile has good defaults for development.

DOI: 10.1201/9781003311966-10

These profile names may be known from our builds' output:

```
$ cargo build
    Finished dev [unoptimized+debuginfo] target in 0.2s
$ cargo build --release
    Finished release [optimized] target(s) in 0.1s
```

The compiler uses distinct profiles, as shown by the dev and release values in this build output.

When there is no [profile.*] sections in the project's Cargo.toml file, cargo uses default settings for each of the profiles. You can override any subset of the default settings by adding [profile.*] sections to any profile we want to change. For the dev and release profiles, for example, the default settings for the opt-level setting are as follows:

Filename: Cargo.toml

```
[profile.dev]
opt-level = 0

[profile.release]
opt-level = 3
```

With a range of 0–3, the opt-level parameter determines how many optimizations Rust will apply to our code. Compiling time is increased when additional optimizations are used, thus if we're in development and compiling your code frequently, we'll prefer faster compiling even if the finished code runs slower. As a result, the default opt-level for development is 0. It is advisable to spend extra time compiling when you're ready to release your code. We'll only compile once in release mode, but you'll run the built program many times; therefore, release mode gives us faster code in exchange for a longer build time. As a result, the release profile's default opt-level is 3.

We can override any default setting in Cargo.toml by giving it an alternative value. If we want to employ optimization level 1 in the development profile, for example, we may add these two lines to the Cargo.toml file of our project:

Filename: Cargo.toml

```
[profile.dev]
opt-level = 1
```

This code overrides the default value of 0. Cargo will now use the defaults for the dev profile and our customizations to opt-level when we run cargo build. Cargo will apply more optimizations than the default because opt-level is set to 1, but not as many as in a release build.

PUBLISHING A CRATE TO CRATES.IO

We used crates.io packages as project dependencies, but we may also share our code with others by publishing our packages. Because the crate registry at crates.io publishes our products' source code, it mainly hosts open-source code.

Rust and Cargo both contain features that make it easier for users to use and find our published package in the first place. Next, we'll go through some of these features before showing us how to publish a package.

Making Useful Documentation Comments

It is important to take the time to produce documentation for our packages because it will help other users understand how and when to use them. We covered how to comment Rust code with two slashes, //, in Chapter 2. A documentation comment, often known as a standard comment, is a type of comment in Rust that generates HTML documentation. The HTML shows the contents of documentation comments for public API items intended for programmers who want to learn how to use our crate rather than how ours is implemented.

Documentation comments are formatted using Markdown notation and use three slashes, ///, instead of two. Documentation comments should place directly before the thing is documented. The documentation notes for an add_one method in a crate named my_crate are shown in the following example:

Filename: src/thelib.rs

```
/// Add one to the number given.
///
/// # Example
///
/// ```
/// let arg = 6;
/// let answer = my_crate::add_one(arg);
///
/// assert_eq!(7, answer);
```

```
/// ```
pub fn add_one(x: i32) ->i32 {
    x+1
}
```

We begin with explaining the add one function, then move on to a section titled Examples, where we present code that describes how to use the add one method. Using cargo doc, we can generate HTML documentation from this documentation comment. This command launches the rustdoc tool, creating HTML documentation and saving it in the target/doc directory.

Running cargo doc --open in a web browser will generate HTML for our current crate's documentation (as well as documentation for all of our crate's dependencies) and open it in a web browser. We can see how the content in the documentation comments is produced by going to the add one function.

Commonly Used Sections

In the preceding example, we used the # Examples Markdown heading to create a section in the HTML with the title "Examples." Other sections that crate writers frequently utilize in their documentation include the following:

- **Panics:** Panic scenarios in which the function being documented might panic. Callers of the function should avoid calling it in these conditions if they don't want their programs to panic.

- **Errors:** If the function returns a Result, specifying the types of errors that might occur and the situations that might cause those problems to be returned might assist callers to build code to handle the various types of errors in multiple ways.

- **Safety:** If function is unsafe to call, there should be a section stating why it is unsafe and the invariants that the function expects callers to maintain.

Although most documentation comments do not require all of these sections, this is a useful checklist for reminding us of the aspects of our code that people calling our code will be interested in.

Documentation Comments as Tests

Including example code blocks in our documentation comments can assist in showing how to use our library. It comes with an added bonus: cargo test will execute the code examples in our documentation as tests! Nothing beats documentation that includes examples. Nothing, however, is more frustrating than examples that no longer work because the code has changed since the documentation was created. If we run the cargo test with documentation for the previous example's add one function, we'll see something like this in the test results:

```
Doc-tests my_crate

running 1 test
test src/thelib.rs - add_one (line 5) ..... ok

test result: ok. 1 passed; 0 failed; 0 ignored; 0
measured; 0 filtered out; finished in 0.98s
```

Now, if we alter either the function or the example so that assert_eq! panics in the example and run cargo test again, we can see that the doc tests catch the fact that the example and the code are out of sync!

Commenting Contained Items

//! is a different type of doc comment that adds documentation to the item that contains the comments rather than the items that follow the comments. To document crate or the module as a whole, we commonly use these doc comments inside the crate root file (src/thelib.rs by standard) or inside a module.

For instance, if we want to add the documentation to the beginning of the src/lib.rs file that specifies the purpose of the my_crate crate that includes the add_one function, we may use documentation comments that begin with //! as shown:

Filename: src/thelib.rs

```
//! # My Crate
//!
//! `my_crate` is collection of utilities to make
performing certain
```

```
//! calculations more convenient.

/// Adds one to number given.
// --snip--
```

There is no further code after the last line that begins with //!. We are documenting the item that contains this comment rather than the item that follows this comment since we started the comments with //! instead of /. The src/thrlib.rs file, which is the crate root, is the thing that contains this comment in this situation. These remarks apply to the entire container.

These remarks will appear on the front page of the documentation for my_crate, above the list of public things in the crate, when we run cargo doc --open:

Exporting a Convenient Public API with the pub use

In Chapter 6, we learned how to use the mod keyword to arrange our code into modules, make items public using the pub keyword, and use the use keyword to bring items into a scope. However, the structure that makes sense to us while designing a crate may not be the most practical for your users. We could want to organize our structs in a hierarchical structure with numerous levels, but users who want to utilize a type we created deep in the hierarchy may have problems finding it. They might also be disturbed by the fact that they have to type use my_crate::some_module::another_module::UsefulType; instead of my_crate::UsefulType;

When it comes to publishing a crate, the structure of our public API is crucial. People who use our crate are less familiar with the structure than we are, and if our crate has a complex module hierarchy, they may have trouble finding the bits they need.

The good news is that we don't have to reorganize our internal structure, if the structure isn't easy for people to use from another library: instead, we can use pub use to re-export items to create a public structure that differs from our private structure. Re-exporting is the process of taking a public object in one location and making it public in another, as though it were defined there instead.

Let's say we created an art library for modeling artistic concepts. Two modules are included in this library: a kinds module with two enums named PrimaryColor and SecondaryColor, and a utils module with a method named mix, as shown:

Filename: src/thelib.rs

```
//! # Art
//!
//! A library for modeling artistic concepts.

pub mod kinds {
    /// The primary colors according to the RYB color
    ///        model.
    pub enum PrimaryColor {
        Red,
        Blue,
        Yellow,
    }

    /// The secondary colors according to the RYB
    ///        color model.
    pub enum SecondaryColor {
        Green,
        Orange,
        Purple,
    }
}

pub mod utils {
    use crate::kinds::*;

    /// Combines two primary colors in the equal
    ///             amounts to create
    /// a secondary color.
    pub fn mix(c1: PrimaryColor, c2: PrimaryColor)
            -> SecondaryColor {
        // --snip--
    }
}
```

The mix function and the PrimaryColor and SecondaryColor types are not featured on the front page. We must first click on the types and utils buttons to see them.

Another crate that relies on this library would need to utilize statements to bring the objects from art into scope, specifying the current module structure. An example of a crate that uses the PrimaryColor and combines components from the art crate is shown below:

Filename: src/themain.rs

```
use art::kinds::PrimaryColor;
use art::utils::mix;

fn main() {
    let red = PrimaryColor::Red;
    let blue = PrimaryColor::Blue;
    mix(red, blue);
}
```

PrimaryColor is in the kinds module, while mix is in the utils module, according to the author of the code that utilizes the art crate. Developers working on the art crate are more interested in the module structure than developers using the art crate. The internal structure that arranges parts of the crate into the types and utils modules contains no information that would be useful for someone to understand how to utilize the art crate. Instead, the art crate's module structure confuses developers by requiring them to figure out where to look, and it is inconvenient because developers must specify module names in use statements.

We may modify the art crate code to include pub use statements to re-export the items at the top level to remove the internal organization from the public API, as shown:

Filename: src/thelib.rs

```
//! # Art
//!
//! A library for modeling artistic concepts.

pub use self::kinds::PrimaryColor;
pub use self::kinds::SecondaryColor;
pub use self::utils::mix;

pub mod kinds {
    // --snip--
}

pub mod utils {
    // --snip--
}
```

Setting Up crates.io Account

We must first register an account on crates.io and obtain an API token before publishing any crates. To do so, go to crates.io main page and log in with our GitHub account. (Currently, a GitHub account is required, but the site may enable other account creation methods in the future.) After we've logged in, go to https://crates.io/me/ and retrieve our API key from our account settings. Then, with our API key, run the cargo login command as follows:

```
$ cargo login abcdefghijklmnopqrstuvwxyz012345
```

This command notifies Cargo of our API token, which will save locally in ~/.cargo/credentials. This token is a secret, therefore don't tell anyone else about it. If we share it with anyone for any reason, we should revoke it and create a new crates.io token.

CARGO WORKSPACES

We created a package using a binary crate and a library crate in Chapter 9. As our project progresses, we may find that the library crate grows in size, prompting us to split our package into additional library crates. Cargo has a feature called workspaces that can help manage several related packages that are being developed simultaneously in this case.

Creating a Workspace

A workspace is a collection of packages with the same Cargo.lock and output directory. Let's make a project with the help of a workspace. We'll use simple code to concentrate on the workspace's structure. There are many different methods to structure a workstation, and we'll show one of the most common ones. A workspace with a binary and two libraries will be created. The major functionality of the binary will be dependent on the two libraries. An add_one function will be provided by one library, and an add_two function by the other. The workspace for these three boxes will be the same. We'll begin by creating a new workspace directory:

```
$ mkdir add
$ cd add
```

The Cargo.toml file, which will set up the entire workspace, is then created in the add directory. This file will lack the [package] section and metadata seen in other Cargo.toml files. Instead, it will begin with a [workspace] section that allows us to add members to the workspace by giving the path to the package associated with our binary crate; in this case, that path is adder:

Filename: Cargo.toml

```
[workspace]

members = [
    "adder",
]
```

Then, within the add directory, run cargo new to create the adder binary crate:

```
$ cargo new adder
    Created binary (application) `adder` package
```

At this point, we can run cargo build to create the workspace. The following are the files that should be in our add directory:

```
├── Cargo.lock
├── Cargo.toml
├── adder
│   ├── Cargo.toml
│   └── src
│       └── themain.rs
└── target
```

The compiled artifacts are placed into one target directory at the top level of the workspace; the adder package does not have its own target directory. If we ran cargo build from within the adder directory, the compiled artifacts would still end up in add/target rather than add/adder/target. Because the crates in a workspace are intended to rely on each other, Cargo constructs the target directory in a workspace in this way. Each crate would have to recompile each of the other crates in the workspace to have the artifacts in its target directory if each crate had its own target directory. The crates can minimize unnecessary rebuilding by sharing a single destination directory.

Creating the Second Package in the Workspace

Next, create a new member package in the workspace and name it add-one. Specify the add-one path in the member's list in the top-level Cargo .toml:

Filename: Cargo.toml

```
[workspace]

members = [
    "adder",
    "add-one",
]
```

After that, create a new library crate called add-one:

```
$ cargo new add-one --lib
    Created library `add-one` package
```

These directories and files should now be in our add directory:

```
├── Cargo.lock
├── Cargo.toml
├── add-one
│   ├── Cargo.toml
│   └── src
│       └── thelib.rs
├── adder
│   ├── Cargo.toml
│   └── src
│       └── themain.rs
└── target
```

Let's add an add_one function to the add-one/src/thelib.rs file:

Filename: add-one/src/thelib.rs

```
pub fn add_one(c: i32) -> i32 {
    c + 1
}
```

We can have the adder package with our binary depending on the addone package, which has our library, now that we have another package in the workspace. First, we must include a route dependency on addone in adder/Cargo.toml.

Filename: adder/Cargo.toml

```
addone = {path = "../addone"}
```

Because Cargo does not assume that crates in a workspace would be dependent, we must be explicit about the crates' dependency relationships.

Then, we'll use the add_one function from the add-one crate in the adder crate. To bring the new add-one library crate into scope, open the adder/src/themain.rs file and add a use line at the beginning. Then, as shown in the below code, change the main function to call the add_one method.

Filename: adder/src/themain.rs

```
use add_one;
fn main() {
    let numb = 13;
    println!(
        "Hello, everyone. {} plus one is {}!",
        numb,
        add_one::add_one(numb)
    );
}
```

INSTALLING BINARIES FROM CRATES .IO WITH CARGO INSTALL

We can install and utilize binary crates locally with the cargo install command. This is not a replacement for system packages; rather, it is meant to be a simple way for Rust developers to install tools that have been shared on crates.io. It is important to note that you can only install packages with binary targets. A binary target, as opposed to a library target, is a runnable program that is constructed when a crate has a src/themain.rs file or another file defined as a binary. Crates usually specify whether they are a library, have a binary target, or both in the README file.

All binaries installed with cargo install are saved in the bin folder in the installation root. This directory will be $HOME/.cargo/bin if we installed Rust using rustup.rs and don't have any specific configurations. To start applications installed with cargo install, make sure that directory is in our $PATH.

For example, we explained in Chapter 9 that ripgrep is a Rust implementation of the grep tool for searching files. We may use the following command to install ripgrep:

```
$ cargo install ripgrep
    Updating crates.io index
  Downloaded ripgrep v11.0.2
  Downloaded 1 crate (243.3 KB) in 0.89s
  Installing ripgrep v11.0.2
--snip--
    Compiling ripgrep v11.0.2
    Finished release [optimized+debuginfo] target(s)
                      in 3m 15s
  Installing~/.cargo/bin/rg
    Installed package `ripgrep v11.0.2` (executable `rg`)
```

The location and name of the installed binary, which in the instance of ripgrep is rg, are shown on the second-to-last line of the output. We may then run rg --help and start utilizing a faster, rustier tool for scanning files as long as the installation directory is in your $PATH, as described previously.

EXTENDING CARGO WITH THE CUSTOM COMMANDS

Cargo is built to add new subcommands without having to change them. If we have a binary named cargo-something in our $PATH, we can launch it as a cargo subcommand by typing cargo something. When we run cargo --list, custom commands like this are also listed. Cargo's design makes it extremely straightforward to use cargo install to install extensions and execute them exactly like the built-in cargo capabilities.

This chapter covered customizing builds with release profiles, publishing a crate to crates.io, and cargo workspaces. We also discussed installing binaries from crates.io with cargo install and extending cargo with custom commands.

CHAPTER 11

Concurrency and State

IN THIS CHAPTER

> ➤ Using the threads to run code simultaneously

> ➤ Using message passing to transfer the data between threads

> ➤ Shared-state concurrency

> ➤ Extensible concurrency with Sync and Send traits

In the previous chapter, we discussed cargo and crates.io in detail, where we covered customizing builds, publishing crates, and cargo workspaces. Also, we covered installing binaries from crates.io with cargo install and extending cargo with custom commands. This chapter will discuss using threads to run code simultaneously, using message passing to transfer data between threads, shared-state concurrency, and extensible concurrency with the Sync and Send traits.

FEARLESS CONCURRENCY

Another of Rust's main goals is to handle concurrent programming safely and efficiently. As more computers take advantage of their numerous processors, concurrent programming, in which various sections of a program execute independently, and parallel programming, in which different parts of a program run simultaneously, are becoming more significant. Programming in these contexts has historically been complex and error-prone; Rust aims to remedy that.

DOI: 10.1201/9781003311966-11

Initially, the Rust team believed that ensuring memory safety and preventing concurrency concerns were two distinct challenges that needed to be addressed using different approaches. Over time, the team realized that the ownership and type systems are robust tools for dealing with memory safety and concurrency issues! Thanks to ownership and type checking, many concurrency issues in Rust are compile-time mistakes rather than runtime errors. As a result, rather than requiring you to spend a significant amount of effort attempting to duplicate the exact circumstances in which a runtime concurrency bug arises, incorrect code will refuse to compile and display an error message detailing the issue.

As a result, we'll be able to fix our code while we're working on it rather than after it has been released to production. This feature of Rust is known as fearless concurrency. Fearless concurrency enables us to write bug-free code that is simple to refactor without creating new bugs.

Many languages are adamant about the answers they provide for dealing with multiple difficulties simultaneously. Erlang, for example, offers beautiful message-passing concurrency features but only a few confusing ways to communicate state between threads. Supporting only a subset of feasible solutions is a sensible technique for higher-level languages because giving up some control in exchange for abstractions promises benefits. On the other hand, lower-level languages must provide the highest performance in any given context and have fewer abstractions over hardware. As a result, Rust provides several tools for modeling problems in whatever method is most relevant for our needs.

USING THREADS TO RUN CODE SIMULTANEOUSLY

The code of an executed program is run in most modern operating systems, and the operating system maintains numerous processes at once. We can have independent components that run at the same time in our program. Threads are the features that connect these separate sections.

Splitting your program's computation into many threads can enhance efficiency by allowing it to perform multiple tasks at once, but it also adds complexity. Because threads can run simultaneously, there's no guarantee that pieces of our code on various threads will run in the same order. This can result in issues such as the following:

- Race conditions occur when threads access data or resources in a non-deterministic order.

- Deadlocks happen when two threads wait for each other to finish using a resource that the other thread has, preventing both threads from proceeding.

- Bugs only happen in specific circumstances and are difficult to reproduce and fix consistently.

Rust attempts to lessen the drawbacks of using threads, but programming in a multithreaded context still demands thought and a code structure that differs from single-threaded systems.

Threads are implemented in a variety of methods in programming languages. For creating new threads, several operating systems provide an API. This model, in which a language uses operating system APIs to produce threads, is known as 1:1, or one operating system thread for every language thread.

Threads are implemented differently in different computer languages. Green threads are threads given by programming languages, and languages that employ them will execute them in the context of a different number of operating system threads. The green-threaded paradigm is known as the M:N model because there are M green threads per N operating system threads, where M and N are not always the same number.

Each model has its own benefits and trade-offs, with Rust's most crucial runtime support. The term "runtime" is a bit misleading because it can mean different things in different situations.

In this sense, runtime refers to the language's code in every binary. This code can be extensive or minor depending on the language, but every non-assembly language has some runtime code. As a result, when someone says a language has "no runtime," they usually mean "minimal runtime." Smaller runtimes contain fewer features, but they produce smaller binaries, making mixing the language with other languages easier in more settings. Although many languages are fine with having a larger runtime in exchange for additional features, Rust requires a small runtime and cannot sacrifice the ability to call into C to retain performance.

The green-threading M:N model necessitates a bigger language runtime to manage threads. As a result, the Rust standard library only provides a 1:1 threading implementation. Because Rust is a low-level language, some crates implement M:N threading if we'd prefer to exchange overhead for things like more control over which threads run and cheaper context switching costs.

We've defined threads in Rust, let's now look at how to use the thread-related API given by the standard library.

Creating New Thread with spawn

We call the thread::spawn function and feed it a closure containing the code we want to run in the new thread to start a new thread. The example shows an example that displays some text from a primary thread and some text from a new thread:

Filename: src/themain.rs

```
use std::thread;
use std::time::Duration;

fn main() {
    thread::spawn(|| {
        for x in 1..10 {
            println!("hello number {} from spawned
                    thread!", x);
            thread::sleep(Duration::from_millis(1));
        }
    });

    for x in 1..5 {
        println!("hello number {} from main thread!", x);
        thread::sleep(Duration::from_millis(1));
    }
}
```

Note that the new thread will be halted when the main thread terminates, regardless of whether it has completed its execution. This program's output may vary somewhat from time to time, but it should look something like this:

```
hello number 1 from main thread!
hello number 1 from spawned thread!
hello number 2 from main thread!
hello number 2 from spawned thread!
hello number 3 from main thread!
hello number 3 from spawned thread!
hello number 4 from main thread!
```

```
hello number 4 from spawned thread!
hello number 5 from spawned thread!
```

Calls to thread::sleep cause a thread to pause for a short period of time, enabling another thread to run. The threads will most likely take turns, but this isn't guaranteed: how your operating system schedules the threads is a factor. The main thread is printed first in this iteration, despite the fact that the print statement from the spawned thread appears first in the code. And, even though we directed the spawning thread to print until x is 9, the main thread only got to 5 before shutting down.

If we execute this code and only get output from the main thread, or if there is no overlap, try raising the range numbers to give the operating system more opportunities to switch between the threads.

Waiting for All the Threads to Finish Using JoinHandle

The code in the preceding example not only terminates the spawned thread prematurely most of the time due to the main thread's termination, but it also cannot ensure that the spawned thread will ever run. The fact is that the order in which threads run is unpredictable.

By saving the return value of the thread::spawn in a variable, we can solve the problem of the spawned thread failing to run, or failing to run altogether. JoinHandle is the return type of thread::spawn.

A JoinHandle is an owned item that will wait for its thread to finish before calling the join function on it. The following example shows how to use the JoinHandle of the thread we produced in the previous code and execute join to ensure that the spawning thread completes before the main thread exits:

Filename: src/themain.rs

```
use std::thread;
use std::time::Duration;

fn main() {
    let handle = thread::spawn(|| {
        for x in 1..10 {
            println!("hello number {} from spawned
                    thread!", x);
            thread::sleep(Duration::from_millis(1));
        }
```

```
    });

    for x in 1..5 {
        println!("hello number {} from main thread!", x);
        thread::sleep(Duration::from_millis(1));
    }

    handle.join().unwrap();
}
```

Join on the handle blocks the current thread until the thread represented by the handle terminates. When a thread is blocked, it is prevented from performing work or exiting. Running should produce output similar to this because we placed the call to join after the main thread's for loop.

```
hello number 1 from main thread!
hello number 2 from main thread!
hello number 1 from spawned thread!
hello number 3 from main thread!
hello number 2 from spawned thread!
hello number 4 from main thread!
hello number 3 from spawned thread!
hello number 4 from spawned thread!
hello number 5 from spawned thread!
hello number 6 from spawned thread!
hello number 7 from spawned thread!
hello number 8 from spawned thread!
```

The two threads continue to alternate, but the main thread is held up due to a call to handle.join() and does not terminate until the spawned thread is completed.

But let's see what happens if we move the handle.join() instead, to before the for loop in main, as shown below:

Filename: src/themain.rs

```
use std::thread;
use std::time::Duration;

fn main() {
    let handle = thread::spawn(|| {
        for x in 1..10 {
```

```
        println!("hello number {} from spawned
                  thread!", x);
        thread::sleep(Duration::from_millis(1));
    }
  });

  handle.join().unwrap();

  for x in 1..5 {
      println!("hello number {} from main thread!", x);
      thread::sleep(Duration::from_millis(1));
  }
}
```

The main thread waits for the spawned thread to complete before starting its for loop, so the output is no longer interleaved, as shown here:

```
hello number 1 from spawned thread!
hello number 2 from spawned thread!
hello number 3 from spawned thread!
hello number 4 from spawned thread!
hello number 5 from spawned thread!
hello number 6 from spawned thread!
hello number 7 from spawned thread!
hello number 8 from spawned thread!
hello number 9 from spawned thread!
hello number 1 from main thread!
hello number 2 from main thread!
hello number 3 from main thread!
hello number 4 from main thread!
```

The small details, such as where join is called, can impact whether or not our threads run concurrently.

USING MESSAGE PASSING TO THE TRANSFER DATA BETWEEN THREADS

Message passing, in which threads or actors communicate by sending each other messages containing data, is one increasingly popular approach to ensuring safe concurrency. In the words of a Go language documentation slogan, "Do not communicate by sharing memory; instead, share memory by communicating."

The channel, a programming concept implemented by Rust's standard library, is a key tool for achieving message-sending concurrency. A channel in programming can be compared to a water channel, such as a stream or a river. If we throw a rubber duck into a stream, it will travel downstream until it reaches the end of the waterway.

In programming, a channel is divided into two halves: a transmitter and a receiver. The transmitter half is where we put rubber ducks into the river upstream, and the receiver half is where the rubber ducks end up downstream. One section of our code calls methods on the transmitter with the data we want to send, while another section checks the receiving end for messages. When either the transmitter or receiver half of a channel is dropped, the channel is said to be closed.

In this section, we'll build up a program with one thread that generates values and sends them down a channel, and another thread that receives the values and prints them out.

We'll send simple values between threads via a channel to demonstrate the feature. Once you've mastered the technique, you could use channels to build a chat system or a system in which many threads perform different parts of a calculation and send the results to a single thread that aggregates the results.

To begin with, we will create a channel but do nothing with it. It is worth noting that this won't compile just yet because Rust doesn't know what kind of values we want to send over the channel.

Filename: src/themain.rs

```
use std::sync::mpsc;

fn main() {
    let (tx, rx) =mpsc::channel();
}
```

Using the mpsc::channel function, we create a new channel; mpsc stands for multiple producers, single consumer. The way Rust's standard library implements channels allows for multiple sending ends that produce values but only one receiving end that consumes those values. Consider multiple streams merging into one large river: everything sent down any streams will eventually end up in the same river. We start with a single producer for now, but we will add more once we get this example working.

The mpsc::channel function returns a tuple, with the first element representing the sending end and the second representing the receiving end. We name our variables accordingly because the abbreviations tx and rx are commonly used in many fields to signify transmitter and receiver. We're using a let statement in conjunction with a pattern to destructure the tuples. This method of using a let statement is a convenient way to extract the pieces of the tuple returned by mpsc::channel.

As shown in the example, let's move the transmitting end into a spawned thread and send one string so that the spawned thread can communicate with the main thread. This is equivalent to throwing a rubber duck upstream or sending a chat message from one thread to another.

Filename: src/themain.rs

```rust
use std::sync::mpsc;
use std::thread;

fn main() {
    let (tx, rx) = mpsc::channel();

    thread::spawn(move || {
        let vals = String::from("hello");
        tx.send(vals).unwrap();
    });
}
```

Again, we're using (thread::spawn) to start a new thread and then moving tx into the closure so that the spawned thread owns tx. To send messages through the channel, the spawned thread must own the transmitting end of the channel.

The sending end has a send method that accepts the value we want to send. Because the send method returns a Result type, it will return an error if the receiving end has already been dropped and there is nowhere to send a value. In this example, we're instructing unwrap to panic in the event of an error. However, we would handle it correctly in a real application; return to Chapter 7 to go over error-handling strategies.

In the main thread, we'll get the value from the receiving end of the channel. This is similar to retrieving a rubber duck from the water at the river's mouth or receiving a chat message.

Filename: src/themain.rs

```
use std::sync::mpsc;
use std::thread;

fn main() {
    let (tx, rx) = mpsc::channel();

    thread::spawn(move || {
        let vals = String::from("hello");
        tx.send(vals).unwrap();
    });

    let receive = rx.recv().unwrap();
    println!("Got: {}", receive);
}
```

Recv and try_recv are two useful methods on the receiving end of a channel. We're using recv, which is short for receive, to block the main thread's execution and wait for a value to be sent down the channel. Recv will return a Result<T, E> once a value is sent. When the channel's sending end closes, recv will return an error to signal that no more values will send.

The try_recv method does not block and instead returns a Result<T, E> immediately: an Ok value containing a message if one is available and an Err value if no messages are available this time. Suppose this thread has other tasks to complete while waiting for messages. In that case, we could write a loop that calls try_recv every so often, handles a message if one is available, and otherwise does other work for a short period of time before checking again.

For the sake of simplicity, we've used recv in this example; we don't have any other work for the main thread to do other than wait for messages, so blocking the main thread is appropriate.

When we execute the code, the following value will print from the main thread:

```
Got: hello
```

The Channels and Ownership Transference

```
use std::sync::mpsc;
use std::thread;
```

```
fn main() {
    let (tx, rx) = mpsc::channel();

    thread::spawn(move || {
        let vals = String::from("hello");
        tx.send(vals).unwrap();
        println!("vals is {}", vals);
    });

    let receive = rx.recv().unwrap();
    println!("Got: {}", receive);
}
```

Here, we attempt to print vals after sending it down the channel with tx
.send. Allowing this would be a bad idea because once the value is sent to
another thread, that thread may modify or drop it before using it again.
Because of inconsistent or nonexistent data, the other thread's modifica-
tions may result in errors or unexpected results. However, when we try to
compile the code, Rust throws an error:

```
$ cargo run
    Compiling message-passing v0.1.0
                (file:///projects/message-passing)
error[E0382]: borrow of moved value: `val`
  --> src/themain.rs:10:31
   |
8  |          let val = String::from("hello");
   |                    --- move occurs because `val` has type
   |                        `String`, which does not implement
   |                        the `Copy` trait
9  |          tx.send(vals).unwrap();
   |                  --- value moved here
10 |          println!("val is {}", vals);
   |                               ^^^ value borrowed
   |                                   here after move
```

Our concurrency error resulted in a compile-time error. When a parameter is sent, the send function takes ownership of it, and when the value
is moved, the receiver takes ownership of it. This prevents us from accidentally reusing the value after sending it; the ownership system ensures
everything is in order.

Sending Multiple Values and Seeing the Receiver Waiting

The code was compiled and it ran, but it didn't clarify that two separate threads were communicating over the channel. We've made some changes that will allow us to test the code before running it concurrently: the spawned thread will now send multiple messages, pausing for a second between each one.

Filename: src/themain.rs

```
use std::sync::mpsc;
use std::thread;
use std::time::Duration;

fn main() {
    let (tx, rx) = mpsc::channel();

    thread::spawn(move || {
        let vals = vec![
            String::from("hello"),
            String::from("everyone"),
            String::from("from"),
            String::from("thread"),
        ];

        for val in vals {
            tx.send(val).unwrap();
            thread::sleep(Duration::from_secs(1));
        }
    });

    for receive in rx {
        println!("Got: {}", receive);
    }
}
```

This time, the spawned thread contains a string vector that we want to send to the main thread. We iterate through them, sending each one separately, and pause between them by calling the thread::sleep function with a duration of 1 second.

We're no longer explicitly calling the recv function in the main thread; instead, we're treating rx as an iterator. We're printing the value for each one that comes in. Iteration will end when the channel is closed.

When you run the code, we should see the output below, with a 1-second pause between each line:

```
Got: hello
Got: everyone
Got: from
Got: thread
```

We tell that the main thread is waiting for values from the spawned thread because no code pauses or delays in the for loop in the main thread.

Creating Multiple Producers by Cloning the Transmitter

We mentioned earlier that mpsc was an acronym for multiple producers, single consumer. Let's use mpsc and expand the previous code to create multiple threads that send values to the same receiver. We can accomplish this by cloning the channel's transmitting half:

Filename: src/themain.rs

```rust
let (tx, rx) = mpsc::channel();

let tx1 = tx.clone();
thread::spawn(move || {
    let vals = vec![
        String::from("hello"),
        String::from("everyone"),
        String::from("from"),
        String::from("thread"),
    ];

    for val in vals {
        tx1.send(val).unwrap();
        thread::sleep(Duration::from_secs(1));
    }
});

thread::spawn(move || {
    let vals = vec![
        String::from("many"),
        String::from("messages"),
        String::from("from"),
        String::from("us"),
```

```
    ];

    for val in vals {
        tx.send(val).unwrap();
        thread::sleep(Duration::from_secs(1));
    }
});

for receive in rx {
    println!("Got: {}", receive);
}
```

Before we create the first spawned thread this time, we call clone on the transmitter. This will give us a new sending handle that we can pass to the first thread that is spawned. We pass the original sending end of the channel to a second thread spawned. This results in two threads, each sending a different message to the channel's receiving end.

SHARED-STATE CONCURRENCY

Message passing is an excellent method for dealing with concurrency, but it is not the only one. Consider the following phrase from the Go language documentation: "Do not communicate by sharing memory."

What would it look like to communicate by sharing memory? Furthermore, why would message-passing enthusiasts not use it and instead do the opposite?

Channels are similar to single ownership in that once a value is transferred down a channel, it should no longer be used. With shared-memory concurrency, multiple threads can access the same memory location at the same time, similar to multiple ownership. Rust's type system and ownership rules are extremely helpful in getting this management right. Consider mutexes, which are one of the most commonly used concurrency primitives for shared memory.

Using Mutexes to Allow Data Access from Only One Thread at a Time

Mutex is an abbreviation for mutual exclusion, as a mutex only allows one thread to access some data at a time. A thread must first signal its intent to access the data in a mutex by requesting the mutex's lock. The lock is a mutex data structure that keeps track of who has exclusive access to the data at any given time. As a result, the mutex is described as protecting the data it holds using the locking system.

Mutexes have a bad reputation for being difficult to use because of the two rules that need to be observed:

1. Before we can use the data, we must first try to obtain the lock.

2. When we're finished with the data that the mutex is protecting, we must unlock it so that other threads can acquire the lock.

Consider a panel discussion at a conference with only one microphone as a real-world metaphor for a mutex. Before a panelist can speak, they must request or indicate that they wish to use the microphone. When they get the microphone, they can speak for as long as they want before passing it to the next panelist who requests to speak. No one else can speak if a panelist forgets to turn off the microphone when they're finished. If the shared microphone is not managed correctly, the panel will not function as intended.

Mutex management can be challenging to master, which is why so many people are enthusiastic about channels. However, because of Rust's type system and ownership rules, we can't go wrong with locking and unlocking.

API of Mutex<T>

Let's start with a mutex in a single-threaded context as an example of how to use one:

Filename: src/themain.rs

```
use std::sync::Mutex;

fn main() {
    let mt = Mutex::new(5);

    {
        let mut numb = mt.lock().unwrap();
        *numb = 6;
    }

    println!("mt = {:?}", mt);
}
```

We create Mutex<T> using the associated function new, as we do with many other types. We use the lock method to acquire the lock to access the data inside the mutex. This call will block the current thread, preventing it from doing anything until it is our turn to have the lock.

If another thread holding the lock panicked, the call to lock would fail. No one would ever be able to get the lock in that case, so we've decided to unwrap and have this thread panic if we find ourselves in that situation.

After we've obtained the lock, we can treat the return value, in this case num, as a mutable reference to the data contained within. Before we use the value in m, the type system ensures that we obtain a lock: Mutex<i32> is not an i32, so we must obtain the lock before using the i32 value. We must not forget; otherwise, the type system will not allow us to access the inner i32.

Mutex<T>, as you might expect, is a smart pointer. More specifically, the call to lock returns a MutexGuard smart pointer wrapped in a LockResult, which we handled with the unwrap call.

Deref is used by the MutexGuard smart pointer to point to our internal data, the smart pointer also has a Drop implementation that automatically releases the lock when a MutexGuard exits scope, which occurs at the end of the inner scope. As a result, we don't have to worry about forgetting to release the lock and preventing other threads from using the mutex because the lock release is automatic.

We can print the mutex value after dropping the lock and see that we could change the inner i32 to 6.

Sharing Mutex<T> Between Multiple Threads

Now, let's see if we can use Mutex<T> to share a value between multiple threads. We'll start ten threads, each of which will increment a counter value by 1, bringing the total up to ten. The following example will contain a compiler error, which we will use to learn more about Mutex<T> and how Rust can help us use it correctly.

Filename: src/themain.rs

```
use std::sync::Mutex;
use std::thread;

fn main() {
    let counter = Mutex::new(0);
```

```
    let mut handles = vec![];

    for _ in 0..11 {
        let handle = thread::spawn(move || {
            let mut numb = counter.lock().unwrap();
            *numb += 1;
        });
        handles.push(handle);
    }

    for handle in handles {
        handle.join().unwrap();
    }

    println!("Results: {}", *counter.lock().unwrap());
}
```

As before, we create a counter variable to hold an i32 inside a Mutex. Then, we generate ten threads by iterating over a range of numbers. We use thread::spawn and assign the same closure to all threads, one that moves the counter into the thread, acquires a lock on the Mutex by calling the lock method, and then adds 1 to the mutex value. When a thread completes its closure, num exits scope and releases the lock, allowing another thread to acquire it.

We collect all of the join handles in the main thread. Then, as before, we call join on each handle to ensure that all of the threads are finished. The main thread will acquire lock and print the program's output at that point.

We alluded to the fact that this example would not compile. Let us now investigate why!

```
$ cargo run
   Compiling shared-state v0.1.0 (file:///projects/
shared-state)
error[E0382]: use of moved value: `counter`
  --> src/themain.rs:9:36
   |
5  |     let counter = Mutex::new(0);
   |         ------- move occurs because `counter` has
                     the type `Mutex<i32>`, which does
                     not implement the `Copy` trait
...
```

```
9  |                let handle = thread::spawn(move || {
   |                                          ^^^^^^^ value
moved into closure here, in previous iteration of loop
10 |              let mut numb = counter.lock().unwrap();
   |                             --------- use occurs due
                                     to use in closure
```

The error message indicates that the counter value was moved during the previous loop iteration. So Rust is telling us that we can't move the ownership of the lock counter across multiple threads.

EXTENSIBLE CONCURRENCY WITH SYNC AND SEND TRAITS

Surprisingly, the Rust programming language has very few concurrency features. Almost every concurrency feature we've discussed in this chapter has been part of the standard library rather than the language. We are not limited to the language or the standard library for handling concurrency; you can write your own concurrency features or use those written by others.

However, the language includes two concurrency concepts: the std::marker traits Sync and Send.

Allowing Transference of the Ownership between Threads with Send

The Send marker trait indicates that values of the type implementing Send can be transferred between threads. Almost every Rust type is Send, but there are a few exceptions, including Rc<T>: This cannot be sent because if we cloned a Rc<T> value and tried to transfer ownership to another thread, both threads may update the reference count at the same time. As a result, Rc<T> is designed for use in single-threaded situations where we don't want to pay the thread-safe performance penalty.

As a result, Rust's type system and trait bounds ensure that we never send an Rc<T> value across threads in an unsafe manner. When we attempted this in our example, we received the error Rc<<Mutexi32>> trait Send is not implemented. The code compiled when we switched to Arc<T>, which is Send.

Any type that is entirely made up of Send types is automatically marked as Send. Except for raw pointers, almost all primitive types are Send.

Allowing Access from the Multiple Threads with Sync

The Sync marker trait indicates that the type implementing Sync can safely reference from the multiple threads. In other words, any type T is Sync if

&T is Send, indicating that the reference can safely be passed to another thread. Primitive types, like Send, are Sync, and types composed entirely of Sync types are also Sync.

For the same reasons that it is not Send, the smart pointer Rc<T> is not Sync. The RefCell<T> type and its related Cell<T> types are not Sync. RefCell<T> implementation of borrow checking is not thread-safe. The smart pointer Mutex<T> is Sync and can be used to share the access with multiple threads, as demonstrated in the section "Sharing Mutex<T> Between Multiple Threads."

Implementing the Send and Sync Manually Is Unsafe

We don't have to manually implement Send and Sync traits because types made up of those traits are automatically Send and Sync. They don't even have methods to implement as marker traits. They are only useful for enforcing concurrency invariants.

Manually implementing these traits necessitates the use of unsafe Rust code. The important thing to remember is that creating new concurrent types that aren't made up of Send and Sync components necessitates careful consideration to maintain the safety guarantees.

We discussed run code simultaneously using threads, using message passing to transfer data between threads, shared-state concurrency, and extensible concurrency with the Sync and Send traits in this chapter.

CHAPTER 12

Object-oriented Programming in Rust

IN THIS CHAPTER

➤ Implementing an object-oriented design pattern

➤ Macros

In the previous chapter, we covered how to use threads to run code and message passing to transfer data. We also learned shared-state concurrency and extensible concurrency with the Sync and Send traits. This chapter will discuss implementing an object-oriented design pattern and macros.

IMPLEMENTING AN OBJECT-ORIENTED DESIGN PATTERN

State pattern is a design pattern that is used in object-oriented programming. The pattern's crux is that a value has an internal state represented by a set of state objects, and the value's behavior changes depending on the internal state. The functionality of the state objects is shared: in Rust, we use structs and traits rather than objects and inheritance. Each state object is responsible for its behavior and deciding when to change states. The value that holds a state object is unaware of the various behaviors of the states or when to transition between them.

Using the state pattern means that if the program's business requirements change, we won't have to change the code of the value that holds the state or the code that uses the value. To change the rules of one of the

DOI: 10.1201/9781003311966-12

state objects or possibly add more state objects, we'll only need to update the code inside one of the state objects. Let's look at a state design pattern example and how to use it in Rust.

We'll implement a blog post workflow step-by-step. The final functionality of the blog will look like this:

- An empty draft is the starting point for a blog post.

- When the draft is finished, the post is reviewed.

- The post is published once it has been approved.

- Unapproved posts cannot accidentally publish because only published blog posts return content to print.

Any additional changes made to a post should have no effect. For example, if we attempt to approve a draft blog post before requesting a review, the post should remain unpublished.

This workflow is illustrated in the code below:

This is an example of how one can use the API in a library crate called blog. This will not compile because we have not yet implemented the blog crate.

Filename: src/themain.rs

```
use blog::Post;

fn main() {
    let mut post = Post::new();

    post.add_text("We ate a salad for dinner today");
    assert_eq!("", post.content());

    post.request_review();
    assert_eq!("", post.content());

    post.approve();
    assert_eq!("we ate a salad for dinner today",
               post.content());
}
```

With Post::new, we want to allow the user to create a new draft blog post. Then, while the blog post is still in draft mode, we want to allow text to be added to it. Nothing should happen if we try to get the post's content right away, before approval, because the post is still a draft. For demonstration purposes, we've added assert eq! to the code. An excellent unit test would assert that a draft blog post returns an empty string from the content method, but we won't write tests for this example.

Next, we'd like to enable a request for a post review, and we'd like content to return an empty string while we wait for the review. When the post is approved, it should be published, which means that the post's text will be returned when the content is called.

It's worth noting that the Post type is the only one we're interacting with from the crate. This type will employ the state pattern and contain a value that will be one of three state objects representing the various states in which a post can be found draft, waiting for review, or published. The Post type will handle the transition from one state to another internally. The states tend to change in response to our library users' methods on the Post instance, but they are not required to manage the state changes directly. Furthermore, users cannot make mistakes with the states, such as publishing a post before being reviewed.

Defining Post and Creating New Instance in the Draft State

Let's get started on the library's implementation. We need a public Post struct with some content, so we'll start with the struct definition and an associated public new function to create a Post instance. We'll also create a personal State trait. Then, in a private field named state, Post will store a trait object of Box<dyn State> inside an Option<T>. In a moment, we'll understand why Option<T> is required.

Filename: src/thelib.rs

```
pub struct Post {
    state: Option<Box<dyn State>>,
    content: String,
}

impl Post {
    pub fn new() -> Post {
        Post {
            state: Some(Box::new(Draft {})),
            content: String::new(),
        }
```

```
        }
}

trait State {}

struct Draft {}

impl State for Draft {}
```

The State trait defines the shared behavior of different post states, and it will be implemented by the Draft, PendingReview, and Published states. For the time being, the trait does not have any methods, and we will begin by defining only the Draft state because that is the state in which we want a post to begin.

When we make a new Post, we set its state field to Some, which includes a Box. This Box points to a new Draft struct instance. This guarantees that whenever we create a new instance of Post, it will begin as a draft. There is no way to create Post in other state because the state field of Post is private! We set the content field to new, empty String in the Post::new function.

Storing the Text of the Post Content

The preceding example demonstrated that we want to call a method named add_text and pass it a &str, which is then added to the blog post's text content. Rather than exposing the content field as pub, we implement it as a method. This means that we can later implement a method to control how the data in the content field is read. The method of add_text is pretty straightforward, so let's add the implementation to the impl Post block:

Filename: src/thelib.rs

```
impl Post {
    // ---snip---
    pub fn add_text(&mut self, text: &str) {
        self.content.push_str(text);
    }
}
```

As we're changing the Post instance that we're calling add_text on, the add_text method requires a mutable reference to self. Then, we call push_str and pass the text argument to add to the saved content on the String in content. Because this behavior is independent of the post's state, it is not part of the state pattern. Although the add_text method has no interaction with the state field, it is part of the behavior we want to support.

Ensuring Content of a Draft Post Is Empty

Because the post is still in the draft state, we want the content method to return an empty string slice even after we've used add_text and added some content to it. For the time being, let's implement the content method with the most essential thing to satisfy this requirement: always returning an empty string slice. Later, when we can change the state of a post so that it can be published, we'll change this. Posts can only be in the draft state for the time being, so the post content should always be empty. This is a placeholder implementation, as shown in the code below.

Filename: src/thelib.rs

```
impl Post {
    // ---snip---
    pub fn content(&self) -> &str {
        ""
    }
}
```

Requesting a Review Changes the State of the Post

Following that, we must add functionality to request a review of a post, which should change its state from Draft to PendingReview.

Filename: src/thelib.rs

```
impl Post {
    // ---snip---
    pub fn request_review(&mut self) {
        if let Some(sm) = self.state.take() {
            self.state = Some(sm.request_review())
        }
    }
}

trait State {
    fn request_review(self: Box<Self>) -> Box<dyn State>;
}
```

```
struct Draft {}

impl State for Draft {
    fn request_review(self: Box<Self>) ->Box<dyn State>{
        Box::new(PendingReview {})
    }
}

struct PendingReview {}

impl State for PendingReview {
    fn request_review(self: Box<Self>) ->Box<dyn State>{
        self
    }
}
```

We provide Post with a public request review method, which accepts a mutable reference to self. Then, on the current state of Post, we call an internal request_review method, and this second request_review method consumes the current state and returns a new state.

The request_review method has been added to the State trait; all types that implement the trait must now implement the request_review method. Instead of self, &self, or &mut self as the method's first parameter, we have self: Box<Self>. This syntax indicates that the method is only valid when called on a Box that contains the type. This syntax takes Box<Self> ownership, invalidating the old state and allowing the Post's state value to transform into a new state.

The request_review method must take ownership of the state value to consume the old state. This is where the Option in Post's state field comes in: we use the take method to remove the Some value from the state field and replace it with a None, because Rust does not allow us to have unpopulated fields in structs. This allows us to remove the state value from Post rather than borrow it. The post's state value will then be set to the result of this operation.

To gain ownership of the state value, we must temporarily set state to None rather than directly setting it with code like self.state = self.state .request review(). This prevents Post from reusing the old state value after being transformed into a new state.

The request_review method on Draft must return a new, boxed instance of a new PendingReview struct, which represents the state of a post while it is awaiting review. The PendingReview struct implements the request_review method as well, but it does not perform any transformations. Instead, it returns to itself because when we request a review on a post that is already in the PendingReview state, it should remain in that state.

Now we can see the benefits of the state pattern: the request_review method on Post is the same regardless of its state value. Each state is responsible for its own set of rules.

We'll leave the Post content method on its own, returning an empty string slice. We can now have a Post in both the Draft and PendingReview states, but we want the same behavior in the PendingReview state.

The approve method will function similarly to the request review method in that it will set state to the value that the current state indicates it should have when that state is approved, as shown below:

Filename: src/thelib.rs

```rust
impl Post {
    // --snip--
    pub fn approve(&mut self) {
        if let Some(sm) = self.state.take() {
            self.state = Some(sm.approve())
        }
    }
}

trait State {
    fn request_review(self: Box<Self>) ->Box<dyn State>;
    fn approve(self: Box<Self>) ->Box<dyn State>;
}

struct Draft {}

impl State for Draft {
    // --snip--
    fn approve(self: Box<Self>) ->Box<dyn State>{
        self
    }
}

struct PendingReview {}

impl State for PendingReview {
    // ---snip---
```

```
    fn approve(self: Box<Self>) ->Box<dyn State>{
        Box::new(Published {})
    }
}
```

```
struct Published {}
```

```
impl State for Published {
    fn request_review(self: Box<Self>) ->Box<dyn State>{
        self
    }

    fn approve(self: Box<Self>) ->Box<dyn State>{
        self
    }
}
```

We then add the approve method to the State trait and a new struct, the Published state, that implements State.

Similar to request_review, calling the approve method on a Draft has no effect because it returns self. When we use the approve method on PendingReview, we get a new, boxed instance of the Published struct. The Published struct in the statement implements the State trait, and it returns itself for both the request_review and approve methods, because the post should remain in the Published state in the cases.

The next step is to update the content method on Post so that if the state is Published, we return the value in the post's content field; otherwise, we return an empty string slice, as shown below:

Filename: src/thelib.rs

```
impl Post {
    // ---snip---
    pub fn content(&self) ->&str {
        self.state.as_ref().unwrap().content(self)
    }
    // ---snip---
}
```

Because the idea is to maintain all of these rules inside the structs that implement State, we call a content method on the value in state and send the post instance (that is, self) as an argument. Then we return the result of calling the content method on the state value.

We invoke the as_ref method on the Option because we want a reference to the value contained within the Option rather than ownership of the value. This is because the state is an Option<Box<dyn State>>, when we call as_ref, we get an Option<&Box<dyn State>> back. We'd get an error if we didn't call as_ref as we cannot move the state out of the borrowed &self of the function parameter.

Further, we call the unwrap method, which we know will never panic because the methods on Post guarantee that state will always contain a Some value when those methods are completed. This is one of the cases discussed in "Cases in Which We Have More Information than the Compiler" section in Chapter 7, where we know that a None value is never possible, despite the compiler's inability to understand it.

When we call content on the &Box<dyn State> at this point, deref coercion will affect the & and the Box, causing the content method to be called on the type that implements the State trait. That means we'll need to add content to the State trait definition, and that's where we'll put the logic for what content to return based on the state we're in, as shown below:

Filename: src/thelib.rs

```rust
trait State {
    // ---snip---
    fn content<'a>(&self, post: &'a Post) ->&'a str {
        ""
    }
}

// ---snip---
struct Published {}

impl State for Published {
    // ---snip---
    fn content<'a>(&self, post: &'a Post) ->&'a str {
        &post.content
    }
}
```

The content method now has a default implementation that returns an empty string slice. This means we don't need to add content to the Draft and PendingReview structs. The content method will be overridden by the Published struct, and the value in post.content will be returned.

This method requires lifetime annotations, as discussed in Chapter 8. We take a post reference as an argument and return a reference to a portion of that post, so that the lifetime of the returned reference is related to the lifetime of the post argument.

Trade-offs of the State Pattern

We've demonstrated that Rust can implement the object-oriented state pattern to encapsulate the various types of behavior that a post should have in each state. Post's methods have no knowledge of the various behaviors. Because of how we organized the code, we only need to look in one place to learn about the various ways a published post can behave: the implementation of the State trait on the Published struct.

If we didn't use the state pattern, we could instead use match expressions in the methods on Post or even in the main code that checks the state of the post and changes behavior in those places. That means we'd have to look in several places to understand all of the implications of a post being published! As we added more states, this would only worsen: each of those match expressions would require another arm.

The state pattern eliminates the need for match expressions in Post methods and places where we use Post, and to add a new state, we only need to add a new struct and implement the trait methods on that one struct.

The state pattern implementation is simple to extend to add more functionality. Try considering these suggestions to see how easy it is to maintain code that uses the state pattern:

- Add a reject method that returns the post from PendingReview to Draft.

- Two calls must be approved before the state can change to Published.

- Allow users to add text content to a post only when it is in the Draft state. *Hint:* Make the state object responsible for any changes to the content but not for modifying the Post.

One disadvantage of the state pattern is that some of the states are coupled to each other because the states implement the transitions between states. If we add a new state between PendingReview and Published, such as Scheduled, to convert from PendingReview to Scheduled we'll need to alter the code in PendingReview. The work will be minimized if PendingReview didn't have to change with the addition of a new state, but that would necessitate switching to a different design pattern.

Another disadvantage is that we have duplicated some logic. To reduce duplication, we could create default implementations for the State trait's request_review and approve methods that return self; however, this would violate object safety because the trait doesn't know what the concrete self will be. Because we want to use State as a trait object, its methods must be object safe.

Other instances of duplication include Post's similar implementations of the request_review and approve methods. Both methods delegate to the same method the implementation of the value in Option's state field and set the new value of the state field to the result. If we had multiple methods on Post following this pattern, we could define a macro to eliminate the repetition.

There's a disadvantage as we here are not taking full advantage of Rust's strengths by implementing the state pattern exactly as it's defined for object-oriented languages. Let's have a deep insight into some changes we can make to the blog crate that will result in invalid states and transitions, resulting in compile-time errors.

MACROS

Throughout this book, we've used macros like println!, but we haven't fully explored what a macro is and how it works. The term macro refers to a Rust feature family: declarative macros with macro_rules! as well as three types of procedural macros:

- Custom #[derive] macros for structs and enums that specify code added with the derive attribute.

- Attribute-like macros that define custom attributes that can be applied to any item.

- Function-like macros that look like function calls but perform operations on the tokens passed to them as arguments.

We'll go over each of these in turn, but first, consider why we need macros at all when we already have functions.

Difference between Macros and Functions

Macros are fundamentally a method of writing code that writes other code, a technique known as metaprogramming. We discuss the derive attribute in Appendix C, which generates an implementation of various traits for us. Throughout this book, we've also used the println! and vec! macros. All of these macros expand to produce more code than we wrote manually.

Metaprogramming is a useful programming tool for reducing the amount of code that must be written and maintained, which is also one of the roles of functions. On the other hand, Macros have some additional capabilities that functions do not.

The number and type of parameters must declare in the function signature. On the other hand, Macros can take an unlimited number of parameters: we can call println!("hello") with one argument or println!("hello {}", name) with two. Furthermore, macros are expanded before the compiler interprets the meaning of the code so that a macro can implement a trait on a given type, for example. A function cannot do so because it is called runtime, whereas a trait must be implemented at compile time.

The disadvantage of using a macro rather than a function is that macro definitions are more complex than function definitions because we're writing Rust code that writes Rust code. Because of this obfuscation, macro definitions are more difficult to read, understand, and maintain than function definitions.

Another significant distinction between macros and functions is that macros must be defined or brought into scope before being called in a file, whereas functions can be defined and called anywhere.

Declarative Macros with macro_rules! for General Metaprogramming

Declarative macros are the most common type of macro in Rust. These are also known as "macros by example," "macro_rules! macros," or simply "macros." Declarative macros, at their core, allow us to write something similar to a Rust match expression. As discussed in Chapter 5, match expressions are control structures that take an expression, compare its resulting value to patterns, and then run the code associated with the matching pattern.

Macros can also compare a value to patterns associated with specific code: in this case, the value is the literal Rust source code passed to the macro; the patterns are compared to the structure of that source code; and the code associated with each pattern, if matched, replaces the code passed to the macro. This all happens during the compilation process.

The macro_rules! construct is used to define a macro. Let's look at how the vec! macro is defined to see how we can use macro rules! For instance, the following macro generates a new vector with three integers:

```
let vs: Vec<u32> = vec![1, 2, 3];
```

The vec! macro could also create a vector of two integers or a vector of five string slices. We couldn't use a function to accomplish the same thing because we wouldn't know the number or type of values ahead of time.

The following is a slightly simplified definition of the vec! macro:

Filename: src/thelib.rs

```
#[macro_export]
macro_rules! vec {
    ($($c:expr),*) => {
        {
            let mut temp_vec = Vec::new();
            $(
                temp_vec.push($c);
            )*
            temp_vec
        }
    };
}
```

The #[macro_export] annotation indicates that this macro should be made available whenever the crate in which it is defined enters scope. The macro cannot bring into scope unless this annotation is present.

The macro definition then begins with macro_rules! and the name of the macro we're defining without the exclamation mark. The name, in this case vec, is followed by curly brackets, which represent the body of the macro definition.

The structure of the vec! body resembles that of a match expression. One arm has the pattern ($($x:expr),*), followed by => and the code block associated with this pattern. If the pattern is found, the associated block of code is executed. Because this is the only pattern in this macro, there is only one way to match; any other pattern will result in an error. More complex macros will have multiple arms.

Because macro patterns are matched against Rust code structure rather than values, valid pattern syntax in macro definitions differs from pattern syntax. Let's go over the pattern pieces; see the reference for the complete macro pattern syntax.

First, a set of parentheses surrounds the entire pattern. Following that is a dollar sign ($), followed by a set of parentheses that capture values that match the pattern within the parentheses for use in the replacement code. $c:expr is a function within $() that matches any Rust expression and gives it the name $c.

The comma after $() denotes that a literal comma separator character may appear after the code that matches the code in $(). The * indicates that the pattern must match zero or more of whatever comes before the *.

When we use vec![1, 2, 3]; to invoke this macro, the $c pattern matches three times with the three expressions 1, 2, and 3.

Let's take a look at the pattern in the code associated with this arm: temp_vec.push() within $()* is generated zero or more times for each part that matches $() in the pattern, depending on how many times the pattern matches. Each matched expression replaces the $c. When we call this macro with vec![1, 2, 3];, the code that is generated to replace this macro call is as follows:

```
{
    let mut temp_vect = Vec::new();
    temp_vec.push(1);
    temp_vec.push(2);
    temp_vec.push(3);
    temp_vec
}
```

We've created a macro that can take any number of arguments of any type and generate code to create a vector with the specified elements.

With macro_rules, there are some strange edge cases! In coming years, Rust will have a second type of declarative macro that will function similarly but will address some of these edge cases. The macro_rules! will be effectively deprecated after that update. Given this, the fact that most Rust programmers will use macros rather than write macros, we won't go into detail about macro_rules! any further.

Procedural Macros for Generating Code from the Attributes

Procedural macros, which behave more like functions, are the second type of macro (and are a type of procedure). Procedural macros accept some code as input, operate on that code, and produce some code as output, as opposed to declarative macros, which match against patterns and replace the code with other code.

The three types of procedural macros (custom derive, attribute-like, and function-like) all function in the same way.

The definitions must be kept in their own crate with a unique crate type when creating procedural macros. This is due to various technical issues that we hope to resolve in the future. The code for using procedural macros looks like this, where some_attribute is a placeholder for using a specific macro.

Filename: src/thelib.rs

The function that defines a procedural macro accepts a TokenStream as input and outputs a TokenStream. The proc_macro crate, included with Rust, defines the TokenStream type, representing a sequence of tokens. This is the heart of the macro: the source code on which the macro operates is the input TokenStream, and the code produced by the macro is the output TokenStream. The function also has an attribute that specifies the type of procedural macro we're creating. In the same crate, we can have different types of procedural macros.

Let's dig deep into the various types of procedural macros. We'll begin with a custom derive macro and then explain the minor differences between the other forms.

How to Write a Custom derive Macro

Let's make a crate called hello_macro that defines a trait called HelloMacro and one function called hello_macro. Instead of requiring our crate users to implement the HelloMacro trait for each of their types, we'll provide a procedural macro that allows users to annotate their type with #[derive(HelloMacro)] to get a default implementation of the hello_macro function. By default, this will be printed: "Hello, Macro! My name is TypeName," and TypeName is the name of the type on which this trait has been defined. In other words, we'll create a crate that allows another programmer to use our crate to write code.

Filename: src/themain.rs

```
use hello_macro::HelloMacro;
use hello_macro_derive::HelloMacro;

#[derive(HelloMacro)]
```

```
struct Pancake;

fn main() {
    Pancake::hello_macro();
}
```

This code will generate a printout. Hello, Macro! My name is Pancake! when we're finished, The first step is to create a new library crate, as shown below:

```
$ cargo new hello_macro --lib
```

Attribute-like Macros

Attribute-like macros are similar to custom derive macros in that they generate code for the derive attribute instead of allowing us to create new attributes. They're also more versatile: derive only works on structs and enums, whereas attributes can apply to other types of objects, such as functions. Here's an example of an attribute-like macro in action: assume we have a route attribute that annotates functions in a web application framework:

```
#[route(GET, "/")]
fn index() {
```

The framework would define this #[route] attribute as a procedural macro. The macro definition function's signature would be as follows:

```
#[proc_macro_attribute]
pub fn route(attr: TokenStream, item: TokenStream)
            ->TokenStream {
```

We have two TokenStream parameters here. The first is for the attribute's contents: the GET, "/" part. The second component is the item's body to which the attribute is attached: in this case, fn index() and the remainder of the function's body.

Aside from that, attribute-like macros function in the same way as custom derive macros: we create a crate with the proc-macro crate type and implement a function that generates the desired code.

Function-like Macros

Function-like macros define macros that have the appearance of function calls. They are more flexible than functions, similar to macro_rules!

macros; for example, they can take an unknown number of arguments. Macro_rules! On the other hand, macros can only be defined using the match-like syntax described earlier in the section "Declarative Macros with macro_rules! for General Metaprogramming." Function-like macros take a TokenStream parameter and, like the other two types of procedural macros, manipulate that TokenStream using Rust code. An sql! macro is an example of a function-like macro, which could be named as follows:

```
let sql = sql!(SELECT * FROM posts WHERE id=2);
```

This macro would parse the SQL statement contained within it and ensure that it is syntactically correct, which is far more complex processing than a macro_rules! macro can perform. The sql! macro would be defined as follows:

```
#[proc_macro]
pub fn sql(input: TokenStream) -> TokenStream {
```

This definition is similar to the signature of the custom derive macro: we receive the tokens inside the parentheses and return the code we wanted to generate.

In this chapter, we covered implementing an object-oriented design pattern and macros.

Appendix A: Keywords

THE KEYWORDS LISTED BELOW are reserved for current or future use by the Rust language. As a result, names of functions, variables, parameters, struct fields, modules, crates, constants, macros, static values, attributes, types, traits, or lifetimes cannot be used as identifiers (except as raw identifiers, as discussed in the "Raw Identifiers" section).

Keywords in Use

The functionality described below is currently attached to the following keywords:

- **as:** perform primitive casting, disambiguate specific trait containing an item, or rename items in use and extern crate statements

- **async:** return Future instead of blocking current thread

- **Await:** suspend execution until result of a Future is ready

- **break:** exit the loop immediately

- **const:** define constant items or constant raw pointers

- **continue:** continue to next loop iteration

- **crate:** link an external crate or macro variable representing the crate in which macro is defined

- **dyn:** dynamic dispatch to trait object

- **else:** The fallback for if and if let control the flow constructs

- **enum:** define enumeration

- **extern:** link external crate, function, or a variable
- **false:** Boolean false literal
- **fn:** define function or function pointer type
- **for:** loop over items from an iterator, implement trait, or specify a higher ranked lifetime
- **if:** branch based on result of conditional expression
- **impl:** implement the inherent or trait functionality
- **in:** part of for loop syntax
- **let:** bind variable
- **loop:** loop unconditionally
- **match:** match value to patterns
- **mod:** module define
- **move:** make closure take ownership of all its captures
- **mut:** denote mutability in the references, raw pointers, or pattern bindings
- **pub:** denote public visibility in the struct fields, impl blocks, or modules
- **ref:** bind by reference
- **return:** return from the function
- **Self:** a type alias for type we are defining or implementing
- **self:** current module or method subject
- **static:** the global variable or lifetime lasting entire program execution
- **struct:** define a structure
- **super:** parent module of current module
- **trait:** trait define
- **true:** Boolean true literal
- **type:** define type alias or associated type

- **union:** define union and is only a keyword when used in a union declaration
- **unsafe:** denote the unsafe code, functions, traits, or implementations
- **use:** bring symbols into the scope
- **where:** denotes clauses that constrain type
- **while:** loop conditionally based on result of an expression

Keywords Reserved for the Future Use

The following keywords have no functionality but have been reserved by Rust for possible future use:

- abstract
- become
- box
- do
- final
- macro
- override
- priv
- try
- typeof
- unsized
- virtual
- yield

Raw Identifiers

Raw identifiers are the syntax that allows us to use keywords in places where they would usually be forbidden. A raw identifier is created by pre-fixing a keyword with r#.

Match, for example, is a keyword. If we try to compile the following function, which has the name match:

Filename: src/themain.rs

```
fn match(needles: &str, haystack: &str) ->bool {
    haystack.contains(needles)
}
```

we'll get this error:

```
error: expected identifier, found keyword `match`
 --> src/themain.rs:4:4
  |
4 | fn match(needles: &str, haystack: &str) ->bool {
  | ^^^^^ expected identifier, found keyword
```

The error indicates that the keyword match cannot be used as the function identifier. To use match as a function name, use the raw identifier syntax, which looks like this:

Filename: src/themain.rs

```
fn r#match(needle: &str, haystack: &str) ->bool {
    haystack.contains(needle)
}

fn main() {
    assert!(r#match("foo", "foobar"));
}
```

This code will compile without issue. Take note of the r# prefix on the function name in its definition and the location of the function in main.

Raw identifiers allow us to use any word we want as an identifier, even if it is a reserved keyword. Furthermore, raw identifiers enable us to use libraries written in a different Rust edition than the one used by our crate.

Appendix B: Operators and Symbols

This appendix includes a glossary of Rust syntax, which provides operators and other symbols that appear alone or in the context of paths, generics, trait bounds, macros, attributes, comments, tuples, and brackets.

TABLE B.1

Operator	Examples	Explanations	Overloadable?
!	ident!(...), ident!{...}, ident![...]	Macro-expansion	
!	!expr	Bitwise or the logical complement	Not
!=	var != expr	Nonequality comparison	PartialEq
%	expr % expr	Arithmetic remainder	Rem
%=	var %= expr	Arithmetic remainder and assignment	RemAssign
&	&expr, &mut expr	Borrow	
&	&type, &mut type, &'a type, &'a mut type	Borrowed pointer type	
&	expr & expr	Bitwise AND	BitAnd
&=	var &= expr	Bitwise AND assignment	BitAndAssign
&&	expr && expr	Short-circuiting logical AND	
*	expr * expr	Arithmetic multiplication	Mul
*=	var *= expr	Arithmetic multiplication and assignment	MulAssign
*	*expr	Dereference	Deref
*	*const type, *mut type	Raw pointer	
+	trait + trait, 'a + trait	Compound type constraint	
+	expr + expr	Arithmetic addition	Add
+=	var += expr	Arithmetic addition and assignment	AddAssign
,	expr, expr	Argument and element separator	

(Continued)

Operator	Examples	Explanations	Overloadable?
-	- expr	Arithmetic negation	Neg
-	expr - expr	Arithmetic subtraction	Sub
-=	var -= expr	Arithmetic subtraction and assignment	SubAssign
->	fn(...) -> type, |...| -> type	Function and closure return type	
.	expr.ident	Member access	
..	.., expr.., ..expr, expr..expr	Right-exclusive range literal	PartialOrd
..=	..=expr, expr..=expr	Right-inclusive range literal	PartialOrd
..	..expr	Struct literal update syntax	
..	variant(x,..), struct_type {x,..}	"And the rest" pattern binding	
...	expr...expr	(Deprecated, use ..= instead) In a pattern: inclusive range pattern	
/	expr / expr	Arithmetic division	Div
/=	var /= expr	Arithmetic division and assignment	DivAssign
:	pat: type, ident: type	Constraints	
:	ident: expr	Struct field initializer	
:	'a: loop {...}	Loop label	
;	expr;	Statement and item terminator	
;	[...; len]	Part of fixed-size array syntax	
<<	expr << expr	Left-shift	Shl
<<=	var <<= expr	Left-shift and assignment	ShlAssign
<	expr < expr	Less than comparison	PartialOrd
<=	expr <= expr	Less than or equal to comparison	PartialOrd
=	var = expr, ident = type	Assignment/equivalence	
==	expr == expr	Equality comparison	PartialEq
=>	pat => expr	Part of match arm syntax	
>	expr > expr	Greater than comparison	PartialOrd
>=	expr >= expr	Greater than or equal to comparison	PartialOrd
>>	expr >> expr	Right-shift	Shr
>>=	var >>= expr	Right-shift and assignment	ShrAssign
@	ident @ pat	Pattern binding	
^	expr ^ expr	Bitwise exclusive OR	BitXor
^=	var ^= expr	Bitwise exclusive OR and assignment	BitXorAssign
|	pat | pat	Pattern alternatives	
|	expr | expr	Bitwise OR	BitOr
|=	var |= expr	Bitwise OR and assignment	BitOrAssign
||	expr || expr	Short-circuiting logical OR	
?	expr?	Error propagation	

Operators

Table B.1 includes Rust operators, an example of how the operator would appear in context, a short explanation, and whether the operator is over-loadable. If an operator can be overloaded, the relevant trait for overloading that operator is listed.

Non-Operator Symbols

The list below includes all non-letters that do not function as operators; they do not behave like a function or method call.

The symbols in Table B.2 appear on their own and are valid in various contexts.

The symbols in Table B.3 appear in the context of a path through the module hierarchy to an item.

Table B.4 displays symbols that appear when using generic type parameters.

Table B.5 depicts the symbols that appear when constraining generic type parameters with trait bounds.

Table B.6 displays the symbols that appear when calling or defining macros and specifying attributes on an item.

Table B.7 displays the symbols that generate comments.

Table B.8 displays symbols that appear when tuples are used.

Curly braces are used in the following contexts, as shown in Table B.9.

The contexts in which the square brackets are used are shown in Table B.10.

TABLE B.2

Symbol	Explanation
'ident	Named lifetime or loop label
...u8, ...i32, ...f64, ...usize, etc.	Numeric literal of specific type
"..."	String literal
r"...", r#"..."#, r##"..."##, etc.	Raw string-literal, escape characters not processed
b"..."	Byte string-literal; constructs a [u8] instead of a string
br"...", br#"..."#, br##"..."##, etc.	Raw byte string-literal, the combination of a raw and byte string literal
'...'	Character-literal
b'...'	ASCII byte-literal
|...| expr	Closure
!	Always empty bottom type for the diverging functions
_	"Ignored" pattern binding; also used to make the integer literals readable

TABLE B.3

Symbol	Explanation
ident::ident	Namespace path
::path	Path relative to crate root (i.e., an explicitly absolute-path)
self::path	Path relative to current module (i.e., an explicitly relative-path).
super::path	Path relative to the parent of the current-module
type::ident, <type as trait>::ident	Associated constants, functions, and types
<type>::...	Associated item for a type that cannot directly name (e.g., <&T>::..., <[T]>::..., etc.)
trait::method(...)	Disambiguating method call by naming the trait that defines it
type::method(...)	Disambiguating method call by naming the type for which it is defined
<type as trait>::method(...)	Disambiguating method call by naming the trait and type

TABLE B.4

Symbol	Explanation
path<...>	Specifies parameters to the generic type in a type (e.g., Vec<u8>)
path::<...>, method::<...>	Specifies parameters to the generic type, function, or method in an expression; often referred to as turbofish (e.g., "42".parse::<i32>())
fn ident<...> ...	Define generic-function
struct ident<...> ...	Define generic-structure
enum ident<...> ...	Define generic-enumeration
impl<...> ...	Define generic-implementation
for<...> type	Higher-ranked lifetime-bounds
type<ident=type>	Generic type where one or more associated types have the specific assignments (e.g., Iterator<Item=T>)

TABLE B.5

Symbol	Explanation
T: U	Generic parameter T constrained to the types that implement U
T: 'a	Generic type T must outlive lifetime 'a
T: 'static	Generic type T contains no borrowed references other than 'static ones
'b: 'a	Generic lifetime 'b must outlive lifetime 'a
T: ?Sized	Allow generic type parameter to be dynamically sized type
'a + trait, trait + trait	Compound-type constraint

TABLE B.6

Symbol	Explanation
#[meta]	Outer attribute
#![meta]	Inner attribute
$ident	Macro substitution
$ident:kind	Macro capture
$(...)...	Macro repetition
ident!(...), ident!{...}, ident![...]	Macro invocation

TABLE B.7

Symbol	Explanation
//	Line comment
//!	Inner line doc comment
///	Outer line doc comment
/*...*/	Block comment
/*!...*/	Inner block doc comment
/**...*/	Outer block doc comment

TABLE B.8

Symbol	Explanation
()	Empty tuple, both literal and type
(expr)	Parenthesized expression
(expr,)	Single-element tuple expression
(type,)	Single-element tuple type
(expr,...)	Tuple expression
(type,...)	Tuple type
expr(expr,...)	Function call expression; also used to initialize the tuple structs and tuple enum variants
expr.0, expr.1, etc.	Tuple indexing

TABLE B.9

Context	Explanation
{...}	Block expression
Type {...}	struct literal

TABLE B.10

Context	Explanation
[...]	Array literal
[expr; len]	Array literal containing len-copies of expr
[type; len]	Array type containing len-instances of type
expr[expr]	Collection indexing. Overloadable (Index, IndexMut)
expr[..], expr[a..], expr [..b], expr[a..b]	Collection indexing pretending to be a collection slicing, using the Range, RangeFrom, RangeTo, or RangeFull as the "index"

Appendix C: Derivable Traits

THROUGHOUT THIS BOOK, WE'VE discussed the derive attribute, which can be applied to a struct or enum definition. The derive attribute generates code that will implement a trait on the type we've annotated with the derive syntax with its own default implementation.

This contains a list of all the standard library traits that can be used with derive. Each section discusses:

- What this trait will enable operators and methods.

- What the trait implementations provided by derive does.

- What the trait's implementation means about the type.

- The circumstances under which you are or are not permitted to use the trait.

- Exemplifications of operations that necessitate the trait.

If we want to override the behavior provided by the derive attribute, consult the standard library documentation for each trait for details on how to do so.

The rest of the standard library traits cannot be implemented on your types using derive. Because these traits have no sensible default behavior, it is up to us to implement them in a way that makes sense for what you're trying to accomplish.

Display, which handles formatting for end-users, is an example of a trait that cannot be derived. We should always think about the best way to display a type to a user. What parts of the type should a user be able to see? What parts would they find interesting? What would data format be most beneficial to them? Because the Rust compiler lacks this knowledge, it cannot provide appropriate default behavior for us.

This appendix's list of derivable traits is not exhaustive: libraries can implement derive for their own traits, leaving the list of traits we can use derive with truly open-ended.

Debug for Programmer Output

The Debug trait allows for debug formatting in format strings, which is indicated by inserting:? within {} placeholders.

The Debug trait enables you to print instances of a type for debugging purposes, allowing us and other programmers who use our type to inspect an instance at a specific point in the program's execution.

The Debug trait is required when using the assert_eq! macro, for example. If the equality assertion fails, this macro prints the values of the instances passed as arguments so that programmers can see why the two instances were not equal.

Equality Comparisons with PartialEq and Eq

The PartialEq trait compares instances of a type to check for equality and supports the == and != operators.

The eq method is implemented in Deriving PartialEq. When PartialEq is applied to structs, two instances are equal only if all of their fields are equal, and they are not equal if any of their fields are not equal. When derived from enums, each variant is equal to itself but not to the others.

The PartialEq trait, for example, is required when using the assert_eq! macro, which requires comparing two instances of a type for equality.

There are no methods for the Eq trait. Its purpose is to indicate that the value is equal to itself for every value of the annotated type. The Eq trait is only applicable to types that also implement PartialEq, and not all types that implement PartialEq can also implement Eq. Floating point number types are an example: the implementation of floating point numbers states that two instances of the not-a-number (NaN) value are not equal to each other.

For keys in a HashMap<K, V>, Eq is required so that the HashMap<K, V> can determine whether two keys are the same.

PartialOrd and Ord for Ordering Comparisons

The PartialOrd trait compares instances of the same type for sorting purposes. A type that implements PartialOrd can be used with the operators <, >,< =, and >=. The PartialOrd trait can only apply to types that also implement PartialEq.

Deriving PartialOrd uses the partial_cmp method, which returns an OptionOrdering> that is None if the given values do not produce an ordering. The not-a-number (NaN) floating point value is an example of a value that does not produce an ordering, despite the fact that most values of that type can compare. When called with any floating point number and the NaN floating point value, partial_cmp returns None.

PartialOrd compares two instances by comparing the values in each field in the order in which the fields appear in the struct definition when derived on structs. Variants of enum declared earlier in the enum definition are considered less than variants listed later when derived on enums.

The PartialOrd trait is required, for example, by the rand crate's gen_range method, which generates a random value within the range specified by a range expression.

The Ord trait indicates that a valid ordering exists for any two values of the annotated type. Because a valid ordering is always possible, the Ord trait implements the cmp method, which returns an Ordering rather than an Option<Ordering>. The Ord trait can only apply to the types that also implement PartialOrd and Eq. cmp behaves the same way when derived on structs and enums as the derived implementation for partial cmp does with PartialOrd.

When storing the values in a BTreeSet<T>, a data structure that stores the data based on the sort order of the values, Ord is required.

Clone and Copy for the Duplicating Values

The Clone trait allows us to create an explicit deep copy of a value, and the duplication process may include running arbitrary code and copying heap data. For more information on Clone, see the "Variables and Data Interactions: Clone" section in Chapter 3.

Deriving Clone implements the clone method, which calls clone on each of the type's parts when implemented for the entire type. This means that in order to derive Clone, all of the fields or values in the type must also implement Clone.

For example, when calling the to_vec method on a slice, Clone is required. The slice does not own the type instances it contains, but the vector returned by to_vec does, so to_vec calls clone on each item. As a result, the type stored in the slice must support Clone.

The Copy trait allows us to duplicate a value by simply copying bits from the stack; no arbitrary code is required. For more information on Copy, see the "Stack-Only Data: Copy" section in Chapter 3.

Copy trait does not define methods to prevent programmers from overloading those methods and violating the assumption that no arbitrary code is being run.

Copy can be deduced from any type whose parts all implement Copy. Because type that implements Copy has a trivial implementation of Clone that performs same task as Copy, a type that implements Copy must also implement Clone.

Copy trait is rarely required; types that implement the Copy have optimizations available, which means we don't have to call clone, making the code shorter.

Everything that Copy can do, Clone can also do, but the code may be slower or require the use of clone in some places.

Hash for Mapping a Value to a Fixed Size Value

The Hash trait allows you to use a hash function to map an instance of a type of arbitrary size to a fixed size value. Deriving Hash is a class that implements hash method. The derived implementation of hash method combines the results of calling hash on each of the type's parts, which means that all fields or values must also implement Hash in order to derive Hash.

An example of when the Hash is required is when storing keys in a HashMap<K, V> to store data efficiently.

Default for Default Values

The Default trait allows us to define a type's default value. Deriving Default is a function that implements the default function. To derive Default, the derived implementation of the default function calls the default function on each part of the type, which means that all fields or values in the type must also implement Default.

The Default::default function is frequently used in conjunction with the struct update syntax discussed in "Creating Instances from Other Instances with Struct Update Syntax" in Chapter 4.

By using Default::default(), we can customize a few fields of a struct and then set and use a default value for the remaining fields.

When using the method unwrap_or_default on Option<T> instances, for example, the Default trait is required. If Option<T> is None, the method unwrap_or_default returns the Default::default result for the type T stored in the Option<T>.

Appraisal

R UST IS A MULTI-PARADIGM, elevated, statically typed scripting language. With a primary emphasis on safety and performance, this language assists developers in developing strong and secure apps. Compared to C/C++, which struggles with memory errors and concurrent programming, Rust has already overcome these issues.

Rust language was initially designed to tackle C/C++ difficulties. However, it has proven so successful that it is now used by many top firms, including Dropbox, Firefox, and Cloudflare, both startups and large corporations.

Hundreds of businesses throughout the world use Rust because of its tremendous advantages. It is quick and low on memory. The language can provide many performance functions, interface with other languages, and run on embedded devices while requiring no runtime or garbage collector.

Rust's robust type system and ownership concept enable it to eliminate many errors at build time. It has integrated package management, multi-editor support with type analyses, and auto-completion.

RUST'S BACKGROUND

Graydon Hoare at Mozilla Research created Rust with the assistance of a team of collaborators. The Mozilla Foundation is behind it.

Rust is a community-driven open-source language. Many prominent corporations, like Amazon, Google, and Microsoft, use it. Rust is a concurrent and safe language appropriate for programming codes.

WHY IS BORROW CHECKER IMPORTANT IN RUST?

The borrow checker is an essential element of the Rust programming language and one feature that distinguishes Rust. It aids in the management of ownership. Another distinguishing element of Rust is ownership. It allows the language to offer memory safety without requiring the use of a garbage collector.

To begin, what does the borrow checker accomplish for us, and how does it connect to other memory management strategies like garbage collectors and ownership? Let's keep things simple because there's a lot going on.

So, what exactly is the borrow checker? Most scripting languages don't need us to consider where your variables are kept because the garbage collector does it for us. However, with the Rust code, the borrow checker handles everything. Although there is no stated memory model in Rust, applications can store data in two types of memory: the stack and the heap. Data saved on the stack must specify size, but data saved on the heap can be of any size.

Data access is straightforward and rapid, but the data must match certain criteria. Because there are no stringent data requirements, the heap approach is slower but more configurable. It is useful when the stack is unavailable.

We don't have to worry about where the data goes in a garbage-collected language: the stack or the heap. Memory must explicitly be allocated to the heap in C languages. Remember that memory must be removed once we've avoided memory leaks, but only once.

WHAT IS THE PURPOSE OF RUST?

It's time to see what the Rust software program can do. It can, however, be utilized in programming. The language is excellent for developing operating systems and micro-controller applications. Rust has already been used to build several powerful operating systems, including QuiltOS, Rux, Redox, and intermezzOS. Mozilla also employs the language in its web engine. In general, the Rust programming language may use to create the following software:

SPECIAL CHARACTERISTICS OF THE RUST LANGUAGE

The greatest advantage of Rust over other scripting languages is its privacy. This is accomplished in part through error management. If a mistake occurs during compilation that cannot be corrected, the "panic!" macro is used. This terminates the application and an error message is displayed, ensuring that no damage occurs.

Rust's memory management is also safe. The benefit is that Rust ensures memory safety without the use of a garbage collector. Memory has been a frequent target for hackers in various computer languages.

When memory runs out, it might cause faults in the system and, as a result, a vulnerability that can exploit. A "garbage collector" guarantees that unneeded things are removed from memory. This, however, decreases the code's execution speed. The "trash collector" is rendered obsolete by the Rust compiler. Alternatively, it checks for any memory errors during compilation.

However, the enhanced security protections do not come at the expense of performance. Rust is a system software application that runs at the same speed as C/C++. On the one hand, this relates to rejecting a "trash collector." Fast runtime is also assured by "zero cost abstraction," which implies that you may write in a language with high degrees of abstraction without experiencing performance degradation.

As a result, Rust is a hybrid of high-level and low-level computer languages. Rust, like C/C++, is near to the hardware, ensuring fast performance while being as simple to develop as high-level languages.

Rust is easy to learn for both novice and professional programmers. The language is similar to known alternatives in its usage. On the other hand, the amount of work that went into the design of the error alerts is a significant advantage. Whereas other scripting languages display mistakes confusingly, Rust gives practical and valuable information about how to solve them.

BENEFITS OF THE RUST PROGRAMMING LANGUAGE

Rust began as a Mozilla research project, with the goal of re-implementing essential components of the Firefox browser. That choice was motivated by a few significant factors: Firefox deserves to make greater use of current multicore CPUs, and the sheer prevalence of web browsers necessitates their safety.

However, those benefits are required by all software, not only browsers, which is why Rust grew from a browser component effort to a full-fledged language project. Rust achieves its safety, speed, and usability through the following features:

- **Rust provides memory safety:** Rust will not build programs that attempt to use unsafe memory. The majority of memory problems are found when a program is executing. Rust's syntax and linguistic metaphors ensure that common memory-related issues in other languages—null or dangling pointers, data races, and so on—are never implemented. The compiler detects these problems and compels them to be resolved before the execution of the program.

- **Rust is adaptable:** Rust allows us to live recklessly if necessary. Rust's safeties can be partially suspended when we need to directly modify memory, such as dereferencing a raw reference in C/C++. Because Rust's memory safety actions can never totally deactivate, the essential term is "partially." Even said, for most common use situations, we virtually never have to remove the seatbelts, so the end result is software that is safer by default.

- **Rust is cross-platform:** It runs on all three major operating systems: Linux, Windows, and MacOS. Others are supported in addition to these three. Cross-compiling or producing binaries for a different architecture or platform than the one we're presently running requires minimal more work, but one of Rust's overall aims is to reduce the amount of heavy lifting required for such tasks. Furthermore, while Rust works on the majority of available systems, it is not the intention of its authors to have Rust compile completely everywhere but only on popular platforms where they do not have to make excessive sacrifices to the language.

- **Rust comes with a handy standard library:** Rust's bigger objective includes encouraging C and C++ developers to choose Rust instead of those languages wherever possible. However, C and C++ users demand a good standard library – they want to be able to utilize containers, collections, and iterators; manipulate strings; manage processes and threads; do network and file I/O; and so on. Rust's standard library performs all of this and more. Rust's standard library can only contain features that can be safely transferred across platforms since it is meant to be cross-platform. Platform-specific functions, such as Linux's epoll, must be provided by third-party libraries.

- **Rust has a strong language:** Few developers like to begin working in a new language if it offers fewer, or weaker, capabilities than the ones they are accustomed to. Rust's native language characteristics are comparable to those of languages such as C++: Rust treats macros, generics, pattern matching, and composition (through "traits") as first-class citizens. Some capabilities prevalent in other languages, such as inline assembler, are also accessible in Rust, albeit with the "unsafe" mark.

- **Rust is simple to set up:** If Rust's safety and integrity features aren't employed, they don't mean anything. That is why Rust's programmers and community have worked hard to make the language as helpful and friendly to novices as possible.

Everything required to build Rust binaries is included in the same package. External compilers, such as GCC, are required only when building components outside of the Rust ecosystem (for instance, a C library compiled from a source). Microsoft Windows users are not treated as second-class citizens; the Rust tool chain is just as powerful on Windows as it is on Linux and MacOS.

WHY DO COMPANIES USE RUST?

If we are concerned about memory security, Rust is a fantastic solution. Nonetheless, many individuals began to use it after growing unhappy with the limitations of the C and C++ programming languages. When designing the Rust computer language, engineers focused on building an environment with an efficient workflow.

The primary reasons why corporations prefer Rust over other scripting languages are as follows:

1. A thriving and engaged community

2. Assurance of steady software performance

3. Memory safety with superior efficiency

4. Allowing simultaneous programming

5. The ever-increasing amount of Rust documentation

Bibliography

Abiodun, A. D. (2020, June 24). *A Practical Guide to Testing React Applications with Jest — Smashing Magazine.* Smashing Magazine. https://www.smashingmagazine.com/2020/06/practical-guide-testing-react-applications-jest/

Akintayo, S. (2020, May 14). *Styling Components in React — Smashing Magazine.* Smashing Magazine. https://www.smashingmagazine.com/2020/05/styling-components-react/

Atto, E. (2020, April 20). *Understanding the Fundamentals of Routing in React.* The Andela Way | Medium. https://medium.com/the-andela-way/understanding-the-fundamentals-of-routing-in-react-b29f806b157e

Avinash, A. (n.d.). *Lazy Loading in React.* LoginRadius Blog. Retrieved July 9, 2022, from https://www.loginradius.com/blog/engineering/lazy-loading-in-react/

Banks, A., & Porcello, E. (n.d.). *Learning React: Functional Web Development with React and Redux [1ed.] 1491954620, 9781491954621.* Dokumen.Pub. Retrieved July 9, 2022, from https://dokumen.pub/learning-react-functional-web-development-with-react-and-redux-1nbsped-1491954620-9781491954621.html

baoipc. (2022, January 20). *GitHub - baoipc/JS-HTML-DOM_Basic.* GitHub. https://github.com/baoipc/JS-HTML-DOM_Basic

Borges, R. (n.d.). *(JAVASCRIPT) - Learning React Functional Web Development with React and Redux - Algoritmo e Programação - 38.* Passei Direto. Retrieved July 9, 2022, from https://www.passeidireto.com/arquivo/107550538/javascript-learning-react-functional-web-development-with-react-and-redux/38

Catal, M. (2019, October 13). *How to Set Up Lazy Loading Components in React.* Medium. https://muratcatal.medium.com/lazy-loading-in-react-2a43ea2b2dd1

Complex State Management with Redux - Pro React. (n.d.). Docobook.Com. Retrieved July 9, 2022, from https://docobook.com/complex-state-management-with-redux-pro-react.html

Conditional Rendering. (n.d.). React. Retrieved July 9, 2022, from https://reactjs.org/docs/conditional-rendering.html

Context API in React.js. (n.d.). tutorialspoint. Retrieved July 9, 2022, from https://www.tutorialspoint.com/context-api-in-react-js

Dashora, S. (2022, March 24). *How to Use React Context with Class Component?* ProgressiveWebNinja. https://progressivewebninja.com/how-to-use-react-context-with-class-components/

Egwuenu, G. (2021, January 12). *Programmatically Navigate with React Router.* Telerik Blogs. https://www.telerik.com/blogs/programmatically-navigate-with-react-router

Entering Multiple Voices with Layers. (n.d.). usermanuals.finalemusic.com. Retrieved July 9, 2022, from https://usermanuals.finalemusic.com/FinaleWin/Content/Finale/Tut2EnteringNotes4.htm

Event Bubbling and Capturing in JavaScript. (n.d.). Javatpoint. Retrieved July 9, 2022, from https://www.javatpoint.com/event-bubbling-and-capturing-in-javascript

Explore Microsoft Dynamics 365 Finance and Operations Together – Microsoft Dynamics 365. (2022, June 30). Microsoft Dynamics 365. https://exploredynamics365.home.blog/

Facebook. (2022, July 8). *GitHub - Facebook/Flipper: A Desktop Debugging Platform for Mobile Developers.* GitHub. https://github.com/facebook/flipper

fdecampredon. (n.d.). *React-typescript/react.d.ts at master · fdecampredon/react-typescript.* GitHub. Retrieved July 9, 2022, from https://github.com/fdecampredon/react-typescript/blob/master/declarations/react.d.ts

Form Validation in Java Servlet. (2021, May 12). Know Program. https://www.knowprogram.com/servlet/form-validation-in-java-servlet/

Form Validation. (2016, July 4). Gist. https://gist.github.com/ABKC/bafd9c461d671e966552a13a7ce7bdae

Fraser, D. (2018, July 17). *Mocking HTTP Requests with Nock. This is a "How To" Article on Using.* Medium. https://codeburst.io/testing-mocking-http-requests-with-nock-480e3f164851?gi=5da14792fe1d

Ghodekar, Y. (2021, February 13). *What is DOM Manipulation?. In this Blog, We Will Learn What is DOM.* The Startup | Medium. https://medium.com/swlh/what-is-dom-manipulation-dd1f701723e3

How to Pass Parameters to a Destination URL through Tracking Links. (2022, March 11). ClickMeter Blog. https://blog.clickmeter.com/passing-parameters-through-tracking-link/

How to Select All Checkboxes Using JavaScript. (n.d.). JavaScript Tutorial In 2021 - W3cschoool.COM. Retrieved July 9, 2022, from https://w3cschoool.com/tutorial/how-to-select-all-checkboxes-using-javascript

https://vanvelzermath.weebly.com/uploads/2/3/5/2/23525212/3.4_equivalent_linear_relations.pdf *(It is a document randomly uploaded on google).*

Introduction to Redux Saga. (n.d.). LoginRadius Blog. Retrieved July 9, 2022, from https://www.loginradius.com/blog/engineering/introduction-to-redux-saga/

Javascript - How to Resume Script When New Window Loads. (2011, June 17). Stack Overflow. https://stackoverflow.com/questions/6386995/how-to-resume-script-when-new-window-loads

Javascript - TypeError: Super Expression Must Be Null or a Function, not Undefined with Babeljs. (2016, March 3). Stack Overflow. https://stackoverflow.com/questions/35777991/typeerror-super-expression-must-be-null-or-a-function-not-undefined-with-babel

JavaScript DOM EventListener. (n.d.). W3Schools. Retrieved July 9, 2022, from https://www.w3schools.com/JS/js_htmldom_eventlistener.asp

JavaScript Form. (n.d.). Javatpoint. Retrieved July 9, 2022, from https://www.javatpoint.com/javascript-form

JavaScript Form Validation. (n.d.). Javatpoint. Retrieved July 9, 2022, from https://www.javatpoint.com/javascript-form-validation

JavaScript Form Validation. (n.d.). W3Schools. Retrieved July 9, 2022, from https://www.w3schools.com/JS/js_validation.asp

Jesus Becker Becker. (n.d.). Art Might - Just Art. Retrieved July 9, 2022, from https://artmight.com/user/profile/518482

Kumar, P. (2021, August 11). *Start Working with React Context API.* DEV Community. https://dev.to/pankajkumar/start-working-with-react-context-api-38h

Kumar, R. (2022, March 17). *What is Reactjs and How it Works? An Overview and Its Use Cases.* DevOpsSchool. https://www.devopsschool.com/blog/what-is-reactjs-and-how-it-works-an-overview-and-its-use-cases/

Laichenkov, Y. (2022, April 11). *API Testing with Playwright & odottaa.* Medium. https://elaichenkov.medium.com/api-testing-with-playwright-odottaa-77451917342f

Maurya, P. (2019, December 14). *How to Import or Use Images in ReactJS.* TutorialsWebsite. https://www.tutorialswebsite.com/how-to-import-or-use-images-in-reactjs/

MFC - Getting Started. (n.d.). tutorialspoint. Retrieved July 9, 2022, from https://www.tutorialspoint.com/mfc/mfc_getting_started.htm

Moreno, L. (2022, July 7). *5 Health Benefits of Chicken Wings.* TheSite.Org. https://www.thesite.org/health-benefits-of-chicken-wings/

Myntra PPMP. (2021, August 3). Vinculum Knowledge Central. https://vinculumhelpdesk.freshdesk.com/support/solutions/articles/9000198514-myntra-ppmp

Omondi, E. (2021, July 27). *Working with Styled-Components in React.* Engineering Education (EngEd) Program | Section. https://www.section.io/engineering-education/working-with-styled-components-in-react/

The Power of UserDefaults in Swift. (2019, March 3). Swift by Sundell. https://www.swiftbysundell.com/articles/the-power-of-userdefaults-in-swift/

Programmatic Navigation. (n.d.). Frontend Armory. Retrieved July 9, 2022, from https://frontarm.com/navi/en/guides/programmatic-navigation/

Pros and Cons of ReactJS. (n.d.). Javatpoint. Retrieved July 9, 2022, from https://www.javatpoint.com/pros-and-cons-of-react

React Book - Router and Query Params. (n.d.). softchris.github. Retrieved July 9, 2022, from https://softchris.github.io/books/react/router-parameters/

React Form Validation. (n.d.). Educative: Interactive Courses for Software Developers. Retrieved July 9, 2022, from https://www.educative.io/answers /react-form-validation

React Introduction, Why Learn ReactJS? (n.d.). W3cschoool.COM. Retrieved July 9, 2022, from https://w3cschoool.com/react-introduction

React Render Props解释_culiu9261的博客-CSDN博客. (2001, June 11). blog .csdn.net. https://blog.csdn.net/culiu9261/article/details/107539020

React Router. (n.d.). Javatpoint. Retrieved July 9, 2022, from https://www.javat-point.com/react-router

React.Component. (n.d.). React. Retrieved July 9, 2022, from https://reactjs.org/ docs/react-component.html

React.js Render Props. (2021, March 15). GeeksforGeeks. https://www.geeksfor-geeks.org/react-js-render-props/

ReactEnlightenment.com. (n.d.). *3.1 Using react.js & react-dom.j.* React Enlightenment. Retrieved July 9, 2022, from https://reactenlightenment .com/react-basic-setup/3.1.html

ReactEnlightenment.com. (n.d.). *3.2 Using JSX via Babel.* React Enlightenment. Retrieved July 9, 2022, from https://reactenlightenment.com/react-basic -setup/3.2.html

ReactEnlightenment.com. (n.d.). *7.1 What Are Component Props?* React Enlightenment. Retrieved July 9, 2022, from https://www.reactenlighten-ment.com/react-props/7.1.html

ReactEnlightenment.com. (n.d.). *8.2 Working with Component State.* React Enlightenment. Retrieved July 9, 2022, from https://reactenlightenment .com/react-state/8.2.html

ReactEnlightenment.com. (n.d.). *8.3 State vs. Props.* React Enlightenment. Retrieved July 9, 2022, from https://reactenlightenment.com/react-state/8 .3.html

ReactJS - Why is Lazy Loading not the Default for React? (2019, November 5). Stack Overflow. https://stackoverflow.com/questions/58710241/why-is-lazy -loading-not-the-default-for-react

Redux-Saga. (2022, June 28). *redux-saga/BeginnerTutorial.md at master.* GitHub. https://github.com/redux-saga/redux-saga/blob/master/docs/introduction/ BeginnerTutorial.md

Render Props. (n.d.). React. Retrieved July 9, 2022, from https://reactjs.org/docs/ render-props.html

risalat. (2020, August 3). *How to Get Rid of Hair Algae in a Reef Tank: Complete Guide.* Reef Craze. https://reefcraze.com/hair-algae-in-a-reef-tank/

rocLv. (n.d.). *Extracting Container Components Visibletodolist Addtodo | Redux Getting Started.* GitBooks. Retrieved July 9, 2022, from https://roclv.git-books.io/redux-getting-started/content/23.redux-extracting-container -components-visibletodolist-addtodo.html

S.M., it19214580 B. (2021, May 31). *React js. What is React JS?* Medium. https:// maleeshabulner.medium.com/react-js-5c6420883b6a

Saraf, P. (2020, October 12). *The React Context API. Hello Everyone! Today We are Going To...* Medium. https://medium.com/cleverprogrammer/the-react -context-api-364da590aa73

Sebhastian, N. (2021, March 7). *React Testing Library – Tutorial with JavaScript Code Examples.* freeCodeCamp.Org. https://www.freecodecamp.org/news/ react-testing-library-tutorial-javascript-example-code/

Sharma, V. (2019, June 28). *Posting Profiles.* Microsoft Dynamics AX. https:// dynamicsaxsharma.blogspot.com/2019/06/posting-profiles.html

Singh, M. (2021, June 15). *Top 5 React JS Training Institutes in Chandigarh.* Training Institute Mohali. https://traininginmohali.com/chandigarh/top-5 -react-js-training-institutes-in-chandigarh/

Sketch Me! (2021, March 19). App Store. https://apps.apple.com/gb/app/sketch -me/id364365478

softchris. (2021, January 18). *React-book/lazy-loading.md at master.* GitHub. https://github.com/softchris/react-book/blob/master/4-routing/lazy-load- ing.md

Taming the React Setup. (2016, May 25). Telerik Blogs. https://www.telerik.com/ blogs/taming-react-setup

There's Never Been a Better Time to Study Agriculture. (2022, June 20). The University of Sydney. https://www.sydney.edu.au/science/news-and-events /2022/06/20/there-s-never-been-a-better-time-to-study-agriculture.html

Top 65 React Interview Questions (2022). (n.d.). Javatpoint. Retrieved July 9, 2022, from https://www.javatpoint.com/react-interview-questions

Vorontsova, M. (2019, March 15). *20 JavaScript Interview Questions - Part 2 | Theory and Practice.* Soshace. https://soshace.com/30-javascript-interview -questions-part-2/

WTF is JSX? (n.d.). Egghead. Retrieved July 9, 2022, from https://egghead.io/ learn/react/beginners/wtf-is-jsx

面试哥. (2020, March 28). *8.2 Working with Component State-[英文]React Enlightenment-面试哥* . 面试哥. https://www.mianshigee.com/tutorial/ ReactEnlightenment/react-state-8.2.md

Index

Printed in the United States
by Baker & Taylor Publisher Services